SEASONAL GUIDE TO THE NATURAL YEAR

A Month by Month Guide to Natural Events

Southern California and Baja

Judy Wade

Fulcrum Publishing
Golden, Colorado

For my parents, who taught me to appreciate the difference between a meadowlark's trill and the inventive song of a mockingbird, and for my sister, with whom I hiked forest trails and paddled leaky canoes as we learned that nature was indeed more entertaining than television.

Wade, Judy.
    Seasonal guide to the natural year : a month by month guide to
natural events : southern California and Baja California / Judy Wade.
        p.   cm. — (The Seasonal guide to the natural year series)
    Includes bibliographical references and index.
    ISBN 1-55591-368-7 (prepack). — ISBN 1-55591-271-0 (pbk.)
    1. Natural history—California, Southern—Guidebooks. 2. Natural
history—Mexico—Baja California—Guidebooks. 3. Seasons—
California, Southern—Guidebooks. 4. Seasons—Mexico—Baja
California—Guidebooks. 5. California, Southern—Guidebooks.
6. Baja California (Mexico)—Guidebooks. I. Title. II. Series.
QH105.C2W32   1997
508.794'9—dc21   96-37240
                                                                                               CIP

Printed in the United States of America

0 9 8 7 6 5 4 3 2 1

Fulcrum Publishing
350 Indiana Street, Suite 350
Golden, Colorado 80401-5093
(800) 992-2908 • (303) 277-1623

The Seasonal Guide to the Natural Year Series

Pennsylvania, New Jersey, Maryland, Delaware, Virginia, West Virginia and Washington, D.C., Scott Weidensaul

New England and New York, Scott Weidensaul

Illinois, Missouri and Arkansas, Barbara Perry Lawton

Colorado, New Mexico, Arizona and Utah, Ben Guterson

Northern California, Bill McMillon

Oregon, Washington and British Columbia, James Luther Davis

Texas, Steve Price

North Carolina, South Carolina and Tennessee, John Rucker

Florida with Georgia and Alabama Coasts, M. Timothy O'Keefe

Minnesota, Michigan and Wisconsin, John Bates

Contents

CONTENTS

Acknowledgments

It seems axiomatic that people involved with nature and the environment have helpful dispositions. At least that was my experience in gathering information for this book. Time after time busy people set aside the tasks they were tackling to spend time answering my questions.

Many times people offered to send brochures, pamphlets and books that helped me pinpoint details and get spellings correct. Others offered phone numbers for further sources. Still others, when I told them what I was writing, made suggestions about places and topics to include. Without their input this book wouldn't have been nearly so complete.

Managers at the various Nature Conservancy Preserves and at the Catalina Island Conservancy were always ready with an answer. People at the Department of Fish and Game came through with facts and statistics I could have obtained no other way. Managers at the national, state and county parks were always forthcoming. It was a pleasure to work with all of them.

But besides their helpfulness, the most significant thing that remains with me is that all of these people have such a keen and knowledgeable appreciation of the natural world. Through them, I developed a much more directed point of view concerning the world in which we live. To them, and to the dozens of others who had a hand in bringing this book into being, I extend my most heartfelt thanks.

Introduction

Nature is filled with wonderful surprises. Nowhere is this more evident than in Southern California. The state's biodiversity, the variety of living organisms that live here, is extraordinary. Its varied terrains and myriad microclimates include temperatures kept moderate by the Pacific Ocean along the south and central coast as well as intense inland extremes of heat and cold. This diversity makes it a habitat for more species of plants and animals than any other state.

Unfortunately, the Golden State also is home to a greater number of imperiled species than any other state, with more than 220 wildlife species and 600 types of plants in danger. One of the organizations that monitors this region and its inhabitants is the Nature Conservancy, a nonprofit organization whose mission is to preserve the plants, animals and natural communities that represent the diversity of life on earth by protecting the lands and waters they need to survive. In some places, entire habitats may soon be wiped out.

These creatures and their habitats make up ecosystems, complex communities of organisms that interact with their environment. Ecosystems are unruled by boundaries of towns, states and counties. California is divided into ten such regions, with Southern California encompassing all of the South Coast and Colorado Desert systems, parts of the South Central Coast, San Joaquin Valley and Mojave systems and just the very tip of the Sierra system where it touches the Mojave Desert. These are the regional guidelines by which California's biological diversity now is viewed when it comes to conservation and preservation. In the Mojave ecosystem, at 282 feet below sea level, Death Valley is the lowest point in California and North America. Mount Whitney, at 14,495 feet above sea level, is the highest point in the state and in the contiguous United States. Of the 563 bird species identified statewide, more than 475 species live or pass through Southern California.

The same diversity of amiable weather and variety of climates that support wildlife have attracted increasing numbers of people as well. The state has about 32 million residents, more than 20 million of whom live in Southern California. The Los Angeles metropolitan area alone is home to more than 15 million people. The San Diego–Orange County–Los Angeles corridor is fast becoming a cement throughway. With each passing day the state assimilates more people and retains less wildlife. With each new housing development and strip mall, habitat is lost. Development has wiped out 90 percent of coastal wetlands. The plants and animals that called it home must find other means of survival.

This fragmentation of habitat affects migration patterns. River flows are seasonal because water is directed for other uses. However, the water irrigation and storage systems that the state must have to produce its vast agricultural crops also provide habitat for many species of birds and mammals. Migratory birds, especially, depend on the man-made lakes, reservoirs and even golf courses that dot Southern California.

Before they reach California, however, migratory birds may pass through a number of countries where pollution laws are lax or nonexistent. Thousands of birds may perish in a single migration period. Recently, an estimated 40,000 birds died at a polluted reservoir in Mexico. More than 20 species, including ruddy ducks, green-winged teal and white-faced ibises, were killed. The National Audubon Society requested an investigation under the environmental side accord of the North American Free Trade Agreement (NAFTA).

If Southern California is famous for its variety of wildlife, it is no less noted for its variety of environmentalists, who operate on various levels of righteousness. The endangered California condor was the subject of much controversy several years ago as environmentalists quibbled over how best to keep the enormous bird from complete extinction. In Northern California, the spotted owl is the center of another such debate, with loggers wanting to make a living on one team and bird lovers reluctant to lose another species on the other.

Considering California's vast population, it's amazing that any habitat at all survives to support nature's creatures. But Californians as a lot seem to try to be sensitive to their environment and do their best to set aside areas that can remain wild and natural. Consider Malibu, just north of Los Angeles along the coast, where nine city parks join two additional parks at its borders to form a wilderness area within a half-hour drive of America's second-largest metropolitan area. In increasingly populous Orange County, the communities being developed by The Irvine Company have been prevented from swallowing up all habitat by the creation of The Irvine Company Open Space Reserve, which permanently set aside 17,000 acres as wilderness.

The California Desert Protection Act, which was passed by Congress on October 8, 1994, created a patchwork of protected desert in the Mojave, including Nevada and Arizona, the San Gabriel Mountains, the Mexican border and the Sierra Nevada. Already it is under assault by those who think it went too far too fast.

Naturalist research management teams, forest rangers and wildlife preserve managers have found they must be a bit cagey when divulging information about California's wildlife. When asked for information about desert bighorn sheep for inclusion in this book, a tactful but cautious ranger declined to pinpoint a herd's location within a reserve, noting that not every reader may have the sensibilities to view the sheep in a responsible manner. The same thing happened when I sought information on the desert tortoise. Wildlife officials have learned the hard way that in a state as populous as California, some residents will never understand the reasons for protecting our remaining plants and animals and will therefore never respect them. This book is intended as a framework for enjoying to the fullest the riches of California's natural world. I hope that through its revelations it helps each reader assign a personal value to the plants, animals, sunsets and rainbows that enrich our lives simply by virtue of their existence. Disregarding our natural resources becomes impossible, once we come to know what we are destroying.

Most Nature Conservancy Preserves are open to the public. Many have limited hours or restricted access. Check with individual preserves or the Nature Conservancy office in San Francisco at (909) 659-2607 before setting out.

Because a book must be written months and sometimes years ahead of its publication date, it is impossible for every bit of information to be completely up to date. Tidepools are destroyed, roads closed, phone numbers change and other situations develop that can create inaccuracies. If in reading this book you find things that need updating, or if some spectacular natural event in Southern or Baja California has been omitted, please notify the author, Judy Wade, c/o Fulcrum Publishing, 350 Indiana Street, Suite 350, Golden, CO 80401.

January

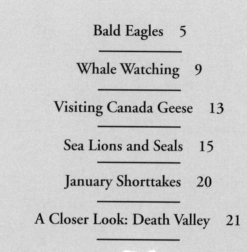

JANUARY HOTSPOTS

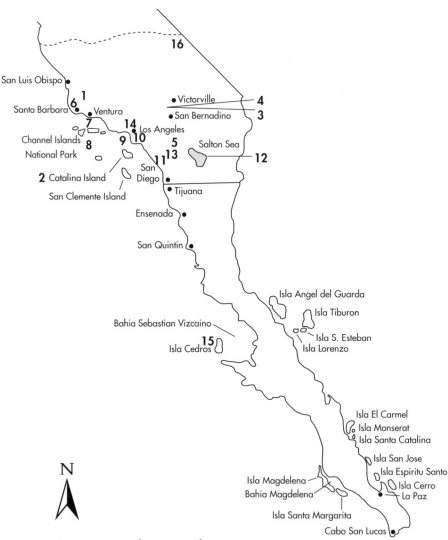

San Luis Obispo •

1

6 Santa Barbara •

7 Ventura •

Channel Islands **8**

National Park

2 Catalina Island

San Clemente Island

14 Los Angeles

9 **10**

5

11 **13**

San
Diego •

• Tijuana

Ensenada •

San Quintin •

• Victorville   **4**

• San Bernadino   **3**

Salton Sea

12

Isla Angel del Guarda

Isla Tiburon

Bahia Sebastian Vizcaino

15

Isla Cedros

Isla S. Esteban

Isla Lorenzo

Isla El Carmel

Isla Monserat

Isla Santa Catalina

Isla San Jose

Isla Espiritu Santo

Isla Magdelena

Bahia Magdelena

Isla Santa Margarita

Cabo San Lucas

Isla Cerro

La Paz

16

N

Seasonal Guide to
the Natural Year

SITE LOCATOR MAP

LIST OF SITES
January

1. Lake Cachuma
2. Catalina Island
3. Big Bear Valley Preserve
4. Silverwood Lake State Recreation Area
5. Lake Hemet
6. Santa Barbara (Shoreline Park, Goleta Point, Devereux Point, El Capitan, Point Conception, Stearns Wharf)
7. Point Mugu State Park
8. Channel Islands National Park
9. Point Vicente Interpretive Center
10. Point Fermin Lighthouse, Cabrillo Marine Museum
11. Point Loma, Cabrillo National Monument
12. Salton Sea National Wildlife Refuge
13. Santa Rosa Plateau Preserve
14. San Fernando Valley
15. Islas San Benito and Isla Cedros
16. Death Valley National Park

Notes

1

Bald Eagles

The white head and substantial body are unmistakable. Poised among the gray branches of a winter-nude oak, its imposing silhouette is breathtaking. It adorns our money. Its carved marble form decorates impressive buildings. It has given its name to aircraft and automobiles. Its mystique has made it a legend.

The American bald eagle seems to know that it is a symbol of a nation. It is a survivor, and the poster bird for endangered species. Once almost wiped out because of indiscriminate hunting and destruction of habitat, the great bird gained a reprieve from a federal law passed in 1940. Still, its population declined to as few as 417 nesting pairs in the continental United States in the 1960s. Then, DDT and other chemicals introduced as means to destroy mosquitoes and unwanted forest insects posed a new threat. Besides contaminating the food supply, the toxic substances prevented eagles from producing eggshells that were sturdy enough to support their young for the entire period of development.

By the early 1970s an awareness of DDT's deadly threat to birds and other creatures forced limits on its use. The regal raptor was given another stay of execution and a foothold in the future with the passing of the Endangered Species Act in 1973. Today it is recovering in full force, numbering more than 3,000 breeding pairs. Although that figure is significantly fewer than the 25,000 pairs that once were believed to dot the skies, it is far more encouraging than the diminished numbers that naturalists counted just a decade ago.

Not all species, however, hold the eagle in such high regard. If the big bird's hunting forays have not met with success, it doesn't hesitate to purloin tasty provisions from other birds. It even has been observed snatching fish from sea otters as they loll on their backs, preparing to eat the catch that they've draped on their chests. If a tug of war ensues, observers report that the eagle usually wins.

A pontoon boat takes guests on an eagle-watch cruise at Lake Cachuma.

With a body length of 30 to 40 inches, and a 78- to 98-inch wingspan, the American bald eagle is one of California' largest raptors. The female is larger than the male. The adult eagle is brownish black with a white head and tail, a large yellow hooked bill, and mighty talons. Immature bald eagles, as large as their parents at 12 weeks, are entirely brownish black with gray wing linings. As a young eagle approaches adulthood, it often displays large patches of white body feathers during molting. It doesn't acquire the white head and tail until it is four or five years old.

Besides their coloration, bald eagles are distinguishable from the more common golden eagle because their legs are not feathered, or "booted" to the feet. This is why they are called a "bald" eagle, not because their white head appears bald.

Eagles maintain their pair-bond for many years, often returning to the same huge sticks-and-twigs nest year after year. Both assume the duties of feeding their chicks, typically a brood of two.

The bald eagle is a "fish eagle" whose feet have specially adapted rough bumps on the toes so it can snatch and grasp surface-swimming fish. Often sharing a habitat with vultures, bald eagles are distinguishable by their larger head that appears to protrude from the wings when the bird is in flight. Eagles soar with flattened wings, while vultures often wobble with their wings in a V-shape.

In winter months hundreds of the splendid creatures migrate from Northern California, Oregon, Western Canada and Alaska, seeking the warmer climates and more abundant food sources of the southern part of the state. They often follow migrations of waterfowl to inland lakes where food is plentiful and the impact of human development is minimal.

Hot Spots

Oftentimes, when humans alter nature, disaster results. But when the Bradbury Dam was built to corral the Santa Ynez River in 1953, 20 miles north of Santa Barbara, the creation of **Lake Cachuma** became an enrichment beyond expectations. The dam created a 7-mile-square reservoir that attracts rich wildlife, including more than a hundred bald eagles. They come for the same reason as anglers, to snare the trout that are part of an active weekly trout-stock program. The eagles are in residence from late November through mid-March.

An easy way to see them is to take a two-hour eagle-watch cruise aboard a pontoon boat with a resident naturalist as guide. The trips run morning and afternoon, Wednesday through Sunday, November through February. A similar cruise is available the rest of the year, guaranteeing sightings of great blue herons, ospreys, loons, red-tailed hawks, acorn woodpeckers, mallard and ruddy ducks, a variety of grebes and California quail. More than 275 bird species have been identified at the lake. Landlubbers can hike the Sweetwater Trail, which meanders along the lake through a thick oak woodland. The highlight of the 5-mile trail is an overlook with an impressive view of Cachuma.

To reach Lake Cachuma, take Hwy 101 north out of Los Angeles to Hwy 154 and follow the signs to Lake Cachuma Recreation Area. For more information and eagle-watch cruise reservations, contact Lake Cachuma Recreation Area, Star Route, Santa Barbara, CA 93150; (805) 568-2460.

Bald eagles have been reintroduced to **Catalina Island**, just off the Southern California coast. Second generation eagles now help make up a total adult population of 10 birds that soar above Seal Rocks, Twin Rocks, the West End and China Point. Catalina Express (see Appendix) offers frequent one-hour shuttles from San Pedro and Long Beach on the California coast to Catalina. Island Express (see Appendix) offers 15-minute helicopter rides to Catalina from the San Pedro area.

Bald eagles often winter at **Big Bear** in the **Big Bear Valley Preserve** and **Baldwin Lakes** in the **San Bernardino Mountains**. They dive, talons extended, from the pines that surround the lakes to the shimmery blue surfaces below. From I-10 east out of Los Angeles take Hwy 38 to Big Bear. Check with the local chamber of commerce in Big Bear, (909) 866-7000, for best viewing areas.

Silverwood Lake State Recreation Area hosts overwintering bald eagles from December through March and offers boat trips by reservation. Located on the Rim of the World Scenic Byway in the northern Mojave, the lake is part of the aqueduct system that brings water from Northern to Southern California. For eagle trip information, call (619) 389-2303.

Other places likely to produce bald eagle sightings are **Lake Hemet** in the **San Jacinto Mountains** east of Los Angeles, and **Stallion Springs** near Tehachapi.

2

Whale Watching

California, and indeed the world in general, has a great deal of affection for the gray whale. It is the state marine mammal and the darling of nature lovers as the ocean's "Comeback Kid." It recently was removed from the federal list of endangered species.

The first views of gray whales migrating south along the California coastline usually are reported in late December, though sightings are most numerous in January. By mid-February most of the grays are calving and mating in warm Baja California waters (see chapter 13) as the quickening life the females carry instinctively draws them southward. They're followed by younger females and ardent male admirers, and lastly by immature males who simply follow the behavior of adults. They can cover 60 to 80 miles per day. They begin their northbound passage in late February and usually can be seen on the Pacific Coast until April.

Calves weigh 1,500 to 3,000 pounds at birth and are about 15 feet long. When they are about eight months old they are weaned at the northern feeding grounds. At this point they have doubled in length and weight. A fully mature gray whale can be 45 feet long and weigh as much as 30 tons, yet they are reliably gentle leviathans. It is common for them to curiously approach within touching distance of small rubber rafts as well as medium-sized ships. However, some whales can be extremely aggressive, especially a mother separated from her calf. The older a whale, the more likely it is to be covered with scratches, lice, barnacles and other parasites that give it a mottled color. These marks allow whales to be identified and their movements to be tracked and even let watchers "adopt" a whale as their own, eagerly watching for it on its annual migration.

Whales have been following this route for centuries, finding their way not by the sophisticated sonar adaptations used by toothed whales and dolphins, as some scientists have thought, but rather by following depth contours from memory. The skill apparently is passed down

Interpretive Center

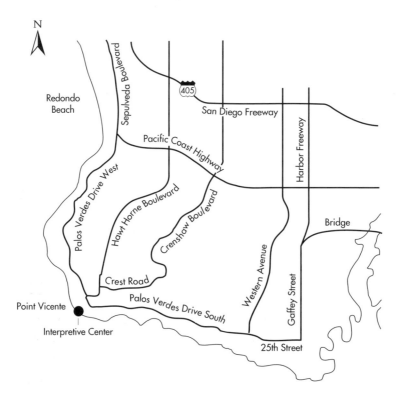

the generations; whale skeletons more than 200,000 years old have been found off San Pedro. On the northbound migration the whales hug the coastline much more closely than when they're going south. It is thought to be an evasive tactic to avoid the orcas, or killer whales, that can make easy prey of a newborn gray. The whales also stay close to shore to feed. The Santa Barbara newspaper reported recently that a young gray whale paused for lunch off the city's yacht club, rooting around for sand crabs in the breaker line.

Whales often are spotted by their "blows," a watery plume that on still days may be heard as far away as half a mile. Other spotting techniques include scanning the water (the calmer the water, the easier it is) for a telltale spout. Although a gray whale has two blowholes, the water is exhaled in a single vaporized stream that reaches as high as 12 feet in the air. Where there is one whale there usually are more, so once you see a blow, stick with it.

When you locate a whale, there are several types of behavior to watch for. Breaching is probably the most spectacular. The enormous creature propels more than half of its body into the air in a great leap, sometimes doing a midair rotation, then dashes itself back into the water. It is thought that whales breach to let their companions know where they are. The glassy, slightly rippled patch on the surface created by this huge splash is called the whale's "footprint." A footprint also can form when a whale swimming just below the surface disturbs the water with vertical tail thrusts.

"Spy hopping" is another interesting behavior in which the whale noses out of the water, seemingly trying to stand on its tale, apparently just for a look around. Another theory is that the vertical position allows whales to eat more efficiently, letting debris filter out of their mouths.

Hot Spots

You can glimpse a California gray whale from shore, from a boat or even a helicopter almost anywhere along the coast. Commercial whale-watching boats sometimes will have a naturalist aboard, which can greatly enrich the experience. During whale migrations, you can catch one out of any sizable harbor anywhere on the coast (see Appendix). **San Diego**, **San Pedro** and **Marina del Rey**, **Ventura** and **Santa Barbara** all have numerous whale tour operators.

If you simply hop in a boat with a friend, keep in mind you must stay at least a hundred yards from whales. Observers say no one has told the whales about that rule because the big guys often approach a boat very closely. But it is strictly forbidden to chase a whale down in order to get closer to it. Whales are protected by the Marine Mammals Act, and if you are seen frightening or interrupting the whales' activities or approaching too closely, you may well be picked up and fined by park services representatives or U.S. Fish and Wildlife service officers. Boaters may unthinkingly separate mothers and calves, interrupt feedings and drive whales from areas that they rely on for food. After enough harassment, whales have been known to breach on a boat. If whales seem disturbed, leave them immediately.

Watching whales from shore is best done early in the morning from a peninsula or raised bank with a good pair of binoculars. When the ocean's surface is calm, before waves develop whitecaps, it is easiest to see and hear blows. Because whales often swim in shallow waters quite close to shore, sightings from land are often as rewarding as those from boats.

Shoreline Park, Goleta Point, Devereux Point, El Capitan and **Point Conception** north of Santa Barbara are promising places.

Point Mugu along Hwy 1 south of Oxnard offers likely spotting. Visitors are welcomed to Santa Barbara's **Stearns Wharf,** the oldest working West Coast pier, by a water-spouting fountain of dolphins. Benches at the end provide a comfortable place to wait for whales swimming through the Santa Barbara Channel.

The **Channel Islands National Park Visitors' Center** in Ventura Harbor has a tower with telescopes that can be used for whale watching.

At the **Point Vicente Interpretive Center** on the Palos Verdes Peninsula you can learn about whales through videos and displays and check the daily and seasonal tally of whale sightings on a chalkboard at the entrance. Then enjoy a picnic lunch outdoors at the tables that overlook the ocean while you try to spot whales yourself.

The **Point Fermin Lighthouse** in San Pedro, built in the 1800s and now open to the public, is a great vantage point from which to catch a spout. Nearby, the **Cabrillo Marine Museum** has instructional materials that help identify whales. Stop by the visitor center at **Cabrillo National Monument** in San Diego to catch a film or lecture on migrating grays, then drive on over to **Point Loma** with a pair of binoculars for a look at the real thing.

3

Visiting Canada Geese

Birders and nonbirders alike agree that an overhead sound, like that of yapping pups, brings a thrill as you scan the skies and spot the perfect V-shape formation that means Canada geese are on their long twice-yearly journey. If you watch carefully you may see the lead goose, the one at the point of the wedge, drop back and let another take his place. These remarkable creatures know that by cleaving the air for the others in their flock they make the long, arduous journey easier for everyone. Then, when they spot an appropriate place to feed, drink and feel safe, the wedge drops and the geese settle in for the night.

These large, elegant birds have a long black neck, black head and bill and distinctive white cheek patches. The body is a fashionable taupe. The yapping honk that is so characteristic of the birds in flight is a "contact call," used to keep in touch with others in the flock or to find the flock if separated. Males can weigh as much as 12 pounds, which makes them a sought-after game bird in many areas. They are not endangered and are widely hunted.

From mid-October through mid-March many Canada geese make Southern California their winter home, dotting farmers' fields, grasslands and even school campuses. If there is a food source and water, the geese may land there. In spring they return to their original breeding grounds. The remarkable ability to return to the same place year after year is thought to be passed on from parent to offspring on an immature goose's first migration and is never forgotten.

Hot Spots The **Salton Sea National Wildlife Refuge** teems with mixed flocks of Canada, snow and Ross's geese, as well as an occasional blue goose and white-fronted goose. It's difficult to get very close to most of them because of the marshy land, so bring your binoculars, or better yet, a telescope. From Hwy 86/78 take Forrster (Gentry Road) north to Sinclair and the refuge entrance.

Migrating Canada Geese begin to form a V as they fly overhead.

An easy trail starts at the refuge's observation platform and heads west along a dike, turning north as it reaches the sea shoreline. At the top of a little volcanic rise called Rock Hill you can get a panoramic view of the Salton Sea.

The Nature Conservancy's **Santa Rosa Plateau Preserve** provides a resting and feeding stop for the geese along vernal pools, which are reliably full during winter months. Self-guided nature trails lead you to the geese. The reserve is located in Riverside County, approximately 40 miles south of the city of Riverside, along I-15 southwest of the town of Murietta.

A traditional resting spot for Canada geese is the **Silverwood Lake State Recreation Area** on the Rim of the World Scenic Byway. If you're a hiker, you'll want to take the Pacific Crest Trail that runs along the slopes above the lake for magnificent views of the landscape below. Then head to the lake, to the relatively quiet area between the boat launch facilities and the ski area. From the city of San Bernardino take I-15 to Hwy 138, turn left and proceed to the recreation area.

In the **San Fernando Valley,** the open fields and meadows at Pierce College in Woodland Hills north of Los Angeles have for decades hosted hundreds of thousands of Canada geese. Families consider it an annual event to watch the graceful creatures feed, then rise into the air to form the perfect V so characteristic of their symmetrical flight.

4

Sea Lions and Seals

From the deck of our small ship cruising the coast of Baja California, we hear a chorus of what we're told are California sea lions. Although they are still out of sight, their characteristic "bark" is unmistakable. We're approaching Los Islotes, a group of rocks north of La Paz in the Sea of Cortez that are home to a colony of the sleek creatures.

We shimmy into wet suits (braver souls rely on swimsuits and T-shirts), grab snorkelling gear and clamber into rubber boats to anchor just off the rocks. The sea lions regard us with languid curiosity, except for the large males (who can be aggressively territorial). We're advised simply to swim away if they display belligerence. Occasionally an inquisitive pinniped, especially a younger one, approaches a snorkeler. Curiosity satisfied, it retreats to the rocks it shares with blue-footed boobies and double-crested cormorants. At least 15 of the mammals, hauled out on the rocks to dry in the sun, have their ears tagged with little yellow radios, antennas extending a couple of inches beyond their heads. They aren't tuned into hard rock. The radios are part of a conservation tracking program to learn more about their diving depths and feeding habits.

California sea lions (*Zalophus californianus*) resemble Pacific harbor seals, except that sea lions have an external ear. They seldom grow longer than 7 feet and are the "seals" usually seen as performers in aquatic shows and at marine life parks. Their long, tapering bodies help these streamlined marine mammals to swim at speeds up to 25 miles per hour. They have flippers larger than those of true seals. They use the front ones to propel themselves through the water, and the hind ones, which they are able to turn forward beneath their bodies, enable them to walk on land with a great deal of efficiency. Their tail is used as a rudder.

Favorite foods for sea lions are fish, squid and crustaceans, which is one reason the mammals are plentiful on the Channel Islands (see chapter 60) off the coast of Santa Barbara. The surrounding waters are a Marine Sanctuary, which allows the foods that the sea lions love best to abound. They can dive as deep as 900 feet to snag a particular delicacy. Pleasure-boaters report seeing the sea lions in the "jug handle" position, floating on the surface with flippers in the air, apparently resting or snoozing.

California sea lions have highly developed social systems, with males protecting their harems with fierce roars and displays of powerful teeth. A very successful male may have more than a dozen lovely lady lions in his care. On some shores it is not unusual to see hundreds of sea lions hauled out, snoozing in the sun, digesting a meal, drying their short, coarse coats that appear to become lighter as moisture disappears. California sea lions breed from May through August in the Channel Islands off California's southern coast and are easy to see from any small boat. A large colony exists on East Anacapa Island near Arch Rock.

The characteristic sea lion bark sounds like a cross between a hoarse puppy's bark and the cough of someone with a serious respiratory disorder. The sound is so distinctive that an acceptable medical term to describe a deep, chronic cough is seal-bark cough.

Although they are part of the same family, the enormous steller sea lions *(Eumetopias jubatus)* make California sea lions look like toys, outweighing them by about 1,700 pounds. An adult male steller can weigh in at well over a ton. Now listed as federally threatened, they once were widely hunted for their blubber, a source of high-quality commercial oil at the time. As late as the 1920s, they were shot as they hauled out in their rookeries because they gave commercial fishermen a bit of competition for the same aquatic prey. In California their numbers now total fewer than a thousand, mainly because the large marine mammals react poorly to human intrusion. And with California's coastline becoming ever more developed, it is unlikely that the creatures will survive without well-enforced protection. Presently they are established in rookeries in Northern California at Año Nuevo Island and in the Farallon Islands and all the way to Alaska. Steller sea lions once inhabited San Miguel Island, but there have been no recently reported sightings. It is theorized that commercial

Sea lions relax on the rocks of San Isolotes in the Sea of Cortez, Baja California.

fishing has disturbed the way that the sea lions' main food, the sablefish, gather in schools, making it difficult for the stellers to feed.

Seals (family Phocidae) are similar to sea lions except for their lack of ears and long front flippers. They especially like cold waters, which makes them plentiful at the North and South Poles. They are fast and graceful swimmers, with hind flippers that provide powerful thrust. Unlike sea lions, they cannot pivot their flippers forward under their body to walk on land. But their hind flippers do allow them to rise straight up out of the water and sink back down out of sight, whereas sea lions must dive forward to submerge. Both sea lions and seals are pinnipeds.

Seals are insulated with a thick layer of blubber but must feed on vast amounts of fish, squid and crustaceans to maintain their body temperature and energy. They have been known to dive beyond 300 feet for almost half an hour. Although it is unproven, some scientists believe that seals have an echolocation system similar to that of dolphins and bats that allows them to feed and locate breathing holes during periods of polar darkness.

Harbor seals, the most common of the seals along the California coast, often sun themselves on large buoys, apparently unperturbed by the bell's loud clanging. They like kelp forests, and sometimes will playfully thunk divers on the head as they swim through their territory. Seals can reach six feet in length and weigh more than 200 pounds. Identifying spots on their coats disappear as they dry. They haul out and breed on the isolated shores of San Miguel and Santa Barbara Islands as well as Anacapa Island, although you won't see the seals actually breeding because they accomplish the act in the water where buoyancy makes it easier. Before mating, females deliver a pup that was conceived the previous year. As soon as the pup is weaned, the female is ready and willing to mate again.

Until 1938, harbor seals were hunted commercially, and their population dwindled to just a few hundred. But with state and federal laws now in place to protect them, the Department of Fish and Game estimates that 30,000 harbor seals are alive and well along the California coast. When humans have invaded their favorite haul-out areas during the day, in some places the seals simply wait until the intruders leave and then haul out at night. Particular importance is attached to their movements and abundance because they are at the top of the food chain. A change in habits can reflect changes in the environment as a whole.

The largest of the seals is the gargantuan southern elephant seal, which can weigh up to four tons and dive to more than 3,000 feet. It spends almost 90 percent of its time underwater. These snout-nosed behemoths can travel as much as 12,000 miles a year between the Channel Islands and other feeding grounds in the Pacific. The largest rookery is at the Ano Nuevo State Preserve in Northern California, but there is a substantial winter breeding colony on Santa Barbara Island in the Channel Islands. There also are colonies off the coast of Baja on tiny Islas San Benito and Isla Cedros. To observe these colonies you either have to have your own boat and a good sense of direction, or you can hire a fishing boat in the little abalone town of Bahia Tortugas on the Viscaíno Peninsula in Baja.

The elephant seal was at one time nearly extinct. Because it is a fierce and fearless fighter, it bravely stood up to nineteenth-century sealers who prized it for its oil. But it was no match for guns and harpoons. At one time only a hundred were left, secluded on

Guadalupe Island 150 miles off the coast of Baja California. Thanks to protection from both the Mexican and U.S. governments, the island is now a biosphere reserve and the seal population has rebounded to an estimated 200,000 individuals. Part of the blimp-shaped mammal's fascination comes from its large, conical snout that gives the seal its name and that the animal inflates to produce a frightening roar. Huge bulls dominate harems of as many as 50 cows, mating with them in a noisy, flamboyant and altogether spectacular display and driving off rival bulls with vicious roars and bites.

The Guadalupe fur seal, on state and federal lists of threatened species, apparently is making a comeback on San Miguel and San Nicholas Islands. Although fewer than a dozen have been reported, there is hope that they will once again populate these islands in large numbers. Along with the elephant seal, fur seals have a flourishing breeding colony on Guadalupe Island, where they once were thought to be extinct.

Because of their history of being hunted excessively for oil and for their fur, a permit is now required to hunt pinnipeds of any sort.

Hot Spots

Seals and sea lions are observable almost anywhere along the Southern California coast. They are particularly plentiful in the **Channel Islands.** There is a large colony of sea lions on **East Anacapa Island** near Arch Rock, mixed with a few harbor seals. **San Miguel** and **Santa Barbara Islands** have breeding colonies of harbor seals. The elephant seal has a winter breeding colony on Santa Barbara Island. The elephant seal also breeds off the coast of Baja on **Islas San Benito** and **Isla Cedros.** The Guadalupe fur seal is reestablishing on San Miguel Island.

5

January Shorttakes

Sanderlings

These small, scurrying sandpipers are the clowns of the coast. In groups of up to a dozen, they scamper like windup toys at the water's edge, their movements orchestrated by the surge of the surf. They are quite tame, and will allow you to approach within two or three feet as they scamper at the waterline. They're looking for a meal, which could be a small invertebrate that the waves have brought ashore. Or, it could be an elusive crustacean buried in the damp sand, trying to hide from the sanderling's long, probing bill. After breeding north of the Arctic Circle along the fringes of the Arctic Ocean, they migrate south to warm up and winter along the **coast of Baja and Southern California.** Sanderlings are easy to observe along the water's edge during any winter month, providing endless chuckles to observers as they are chased by the waves.

6

A Closer Look: Death Valley

In the early days of television a program called *Death Valley Days* was sponsored by the makers of 20 Mule Team Borax, a then-popular laundry product. The connection between the two was that in 1873 borax, a water-soluble crystal used as a cleansing agent, was discovered in Death Valley. It was brought out by mule team because the hardy animals were among the few creatures that could withstand what is the hottest region in North America. Visitors today can see slag piles in Borax Canyon leftover from mining days. Nearby, the Borax Museum traces the era's history with old mining tools and artifacts from the Harmony Borax Works where the borax was refined.

Why would anyone want to visit a place whose claim to fame is having the highest air temperature ever recorded in the United States (134 degrees Fahrenheit), where salt flats prevent almost everything from growing and which claimed the lives of dozens of gold-seekers who tried to cross the arid expanse during California's 1849 Gold Rush?

Because it is far more than a stark, arid desert.

Death Valley National Park in the Mojave Desert was established in 1933, when naturalists and conservationists recognized its astonishing variety of resources and terrain. Within its boundaries are areas of parched desert as well as snowcapped peaks. Area names—Furnace Creek, Coffin Peak, Last Chance Range—help promote its image as an unwelcoming place. Badwater, the lowest point in the Western Hemisphere, is 282 feet below sea level. The inch and a half of rain that nature accords this area every year is hardly noticeable.

But when you're high above Badwater, at Dante's View at the crest of the Black Mountains, your perspective changes. From this vantage point you get a panoramic vista of Death Valley and the surrounding Panamint and Amargosas Mountains. The desert basin stretches 140 miles before you, varying from 5 to 15 miles in width, extending partly into Nevada. Its vast, rambling nothingness is in itself impressive. Prehistoric lakes have left their history as great white salt flats, and patches of green mark struggling oases.

Death Valley is far from barren. Using Furnace Creek Inn (closed from May through October) or Furnace Creek Ranch as base camp, you can explore the variety of grasses, cactus, wildflowers and small mammals that live here (see chapter 22). Birders can have a good time near the city of Tecopa, where resident winter birds include the phainopepla with its jaunty black crest, little yellow-capped verdin, Gambel's quail and Lucy's warbler. Almost 300 bird species either live here or pass through the area. They are generally easy to spot because of sparse vegetation. At Saratoga Springs, where pupfish spawn, wading birds, shorebirds and waterfowl are common. Furnace Creek hosts white-throated swifts and velvety great-tailed grackles.

The area near Stovepipe Wells is blanketed with shifting, shimmery sand dunes that provide habitat for the little desert kit fox, which is most active at dawn and dusk. The dunes also provide a template for the S-shaped tracks of sidewinders, two-foot-long rattlesnakes that move by looping their bodies forward in the shape of an S. Their sandy color with brown or gray blotches can make them hard to spot, but if you startle them so that they move, their unusual method of locomotion will immediately identify them. Like the kit fox, they are most active during cooler hours when they hunt the lizards and rodents that are their main food supply.

If you want to see three species of flowers that occur nowhere else, head for Eureka Dunes between the Owens Valley and Death Valley in the newest northern addition to Death Valley National Park. On enormous white sand dunes you'll find Eureka Dunes milk vetch, Eureka dune grass and large, pretty, white Eureka Dunes evening primrose. January and February are the months to catch the primrose in bloom.

Winter is the most comfortable time to visit Death Valley, but summer is not impossible if you plan properly. At any time it is essential to take plenty of water. It's easy to become dehydrated within just an hour without realizing that your headache is the first sign of heatstroke.

To get to Death Valley take I-15 to Hwy 127 and travel north to Hwy 178. Turn west to the entrance.

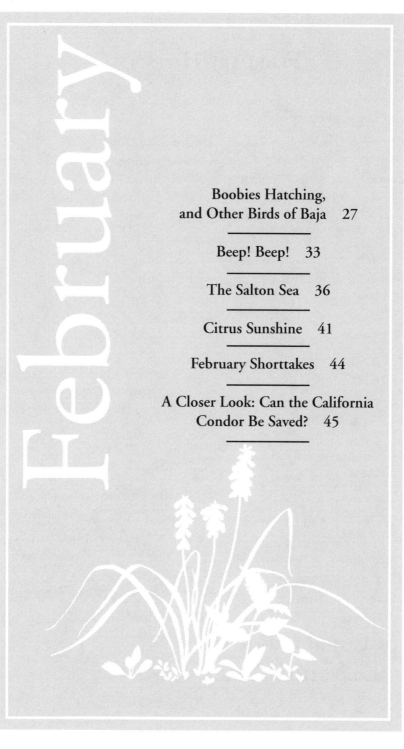

February

February Hotspots

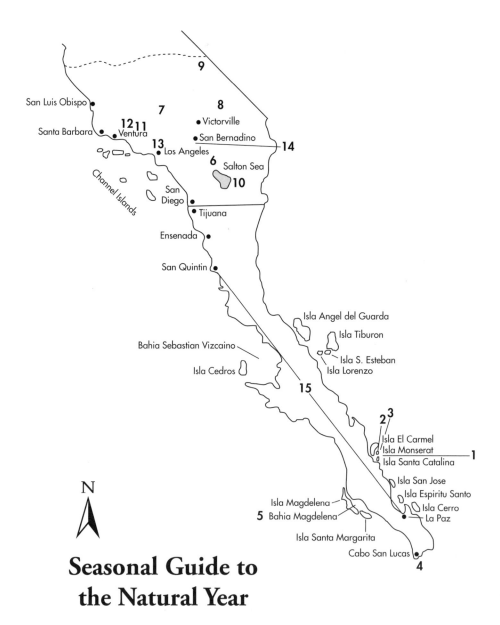

San Luis Obispo •

7

Santa Barbara • **12 11**
• Ventura

13
• Los Angeles

Channel Islands

San
Diego •
• Tijuana

Ensenada •

San Quintin •

Bahia Sebastian Vizcaino

Isla Cedros

8
• Victorville

• San Bernadino

14

6
Salton Sea

10

9

Isla Angel del Guarda

Isla Tiburon

Isla S. Esteban
Isla Lorenzo

15

2 3
Isla El Carmel
Isla Monserat
Isla Santa Catalina **1**

Isla San Jose
Isla Espiritu Santo

Isla Magdelena
5 Bahia Magdelena

Isla Santa Margarita

Cabo San Lucas
4

Isla Cerro
La Paz

N

Seasonal Guide to
the Natural Year

Site Locator Map

LIST OF SITES
February

1. Isla Santa Catalina
2. Puerto Gato
3. Los Islotes
4. Cabo San Lucas
5. Magdalena Bay (Bahia Magdalena)
6. Living Desert
7. Desert Tortoise Natural Area
8. Providence Mountains State Recreation Area
9. Death Valley National Park
10. Salton Sea National Wildlife Refuge
11. Piru, Fillmore and Santa Paula
12. Ojai
13. Northridge
14. Redlands
15. Boojum Tree Area

Notes

Boobies Hatching,
and Other Birds of Baja

The fascinating sliver of land called Baja California extends like a pointing finger south from the state of California. The 800-mile-long strip of desert is bounded by the Pacific Ocean on the west and the Gulf of California, also called the Sea of Cortez, on the east, which separates it from mainland Mexico.

Except for a small northwest corner that is in the Mojave Desert and a tiny bit at its tip that is part of the Chihuahuan Desert, it is entirely within the Sonoran Desert, one of the largest intact arid eco-systems in the world. Lowest and hottest of North America's four deserts, the Sonoran Desert's winter and summer rains make it the richest biologically. It shelters a glorious diversity of bird life that in-cludes desert species, shorebirds, waterbirds, migratory species and pelagics. Winters are warm and sunny and particularly good for sight-ing winged creatures.

The peninsula's human population totals just under 3 million, with most people concentrated in the north in Mexicali, Tijuana and Ensenada. The resort cities of Cabo San Lucas and Los Cabos have been developed in the south. In between are vast, lovely, lonely stretches, especially in the coastal islands where footprints are those of feral cats and resident coyotes, and sounds are bird chirps and gentle waves. It can be rugged, empty and enchanting.

The abundance of bird life in Baja is immediately apparent. In the Sea of Cortez, any given day brings spectacular sightings. A mile-long horizontal column of double-crested cormorants define what one observer dubbed "the sea's rush hour." A white royal tern diving for a fish dinner, magnificent frigate birds (looking like ancient ptero-dactyls) stealing the catches of others, graceful great white egrets and snowy egrets with golden slippers are common. On the Pacific side, great blue herons wade stiltlike along the edges of the mangroves, and long-billed curlews probe for dinner beside the similar, straight-billed godwits. The curlews and godwits are here from early November until March. A clutch of brants, small geese that have winged in from the Canadian Arctic for the winter, display their white rumps as they up-end to dive. Phalanxes of pelicans regularly fly in formations against the crisp blue sky.

One of the avian characters of the Sea of Cortez is the blue-footed booby, a tropical seabird about the size of a chubby goose that really does have big, blue clown-like feet. They form a dramatic contrast with its brown and white plumage and gray bill. But nobody laughs when it executes one of its spectacular dives. Gliding deliberately over the water, scanning for signs of fish, it streaks suddenly downward, sometimes from as high as 80 feet, to enter the water in an almost splashless dive. More often than not it emerges with a slippery, wiggling fish clasped firmly within the serrated edges of its tapering bill.

The name *booby* comes from the Spanish word *bobo,* which means dunce or fool. A buffoonlike clumsiness on land and lack of fear convinced early Spaniards that the creatures were slow-witted. But its sharp instincts have helped it survive, although there are fewer than 40,000 breeding pairs in its distribution range, which extends from Baja California south along the coast of Ecuador and northern Peru. Twenty thousand breeding pairs live in colonies in the Galapagos Islands, where the species is legally protected. Elsewhere, unprotected, its biggest enemy is man, who collects the big bird's eggs. The brown booby and the masked booby also are Baja residents.

Besides keeping him upright, the booby's big blue feet are used in courtship. He gambols around his nesting territory, executing a high-stepping walk to attract a mate. If that doesn't work, he appeals to her interior-decorating instinct by offering her bits of nesting material. After mating, the female deposits two or three eggs in a shallow depression, and both parents take turns incubating them. The feet once again play an important role in the booby's existence. Most birds have "brooding patches," areas of bald skin through which heat is transmitted. Lacking such a refinement, the booby uses its broad, webbed feet, which have a higher-than-usual blood supply that provides heat at a constant 103-degree temperature, ideal for incubating. Once the fledgling family has arrived, the chicks continue to sit on the parents' feet for about a month, at which time they begin to control their own body temperature.

The chicks, who require a constant food supply, are fed regurgitated fish by both parents. When fishing is good, all chicks will be fed. But if fish are in short supply, only the strongest chick will be nourished, thereby assuring that at least one of the brood will survive.

Magnificent frigate birds live in the same habitat as boobies. They are beautiful to watch because their enormous wingspan, greater in

The tiny verdin's cocoon-like nest made of dried vegetation has a side entrance hole.

relation to weight than that of any other bird, allows them to execute dramatic swoops and soars with ease. But they are a decided annoyance to the boobies. The booby generally feeds in the early morning and late afternoon, possibly to avoid the frigate bird, which is a kleptoparasite, chasing other birds for their food.

Almost everywhere in Baja the tiny verdin is in residence, flitting among mesquite and paloverde, identifiable even before it's seen by its rapid, chipping call. At first it may look like a small, hyperactive sparrow, but on closer inspection its yellow head will be apparent. Verdin nests are particularly interesting because they are not the traditional cup shape of other birds. Rather, they are a ball-like cocoon of dried vegetation with an entrance hole in the side. They are easy to spot in low bushes because they form an obvious mass among slight vegetation.

Along the volcanic cliffs on many of the isolated islands in the Sea of Cortez, a kettle (a group of birds on an updraft) of common ravens can put on a marvelous show, silhouetted against a seamless blue sky as they catch zephyrs and perform barrel rolls. On any particular day they may be spotted harassing a lone red-tailed hawk, taunting it with aerobatic maneuvers. Their purpose may be to force the hawk to drop its prey so the ravens can feast, or they may simply be having fun. This could explain why the collective noun for the birds is an "unkindness" of ravens. When they tire of aerial tricks, they form a long line to return to their communal roost. Unlike Edgar Allan Poe's raven, these glossy purple-black birds emit sharp, croaking calls that couldn't possibly be mistaken for "Nevermore."

Hot Spots

The islands in the Sea of Cortez north of La Paz are wonderfully rich in birds and wildlife. Two reliable companies, Special Expeditions and Baja Expeditions (see Appendix) offer seasonal cruises to some of the islands, with naturalists and ornithologists aboard.

The shadowy canyons of **Isla Santa Catalina** are lined with dozens of cardon, chain-link cholla and giant barrel cactus intermingled with desert scrub that provides habitat for dozens of birds. Dingies and skiffs that nudge up to the deserted beach are met by chattering gulls, annoyed at having their solitude disrupted. In the glassy bay a row of pelicans skims the water like a string of odd-shaped beads. During a walk back into a cool canyon you can spot red-headed turkey vultures, red-tailed hawks, ospreys and ravens circling overhead. Flitting among the scrub are verdin, gnatcatchers, loggerhead shrikes, red-headed house finches, mockingbirds and black-throated sparrows. An occasional red flash in the underbrush may be a cardinal. Costa's hummingbirds hover over the blossoms of purple nightshade, the little red flowers of desert mistletoe, crimson blossoms of palo adan and arroyo lupine. This is an island of great serenity where human footprints are decidedly out of sync with nature. It provides a unique opportunity to tune into the sounds, smells and rhythm of the surrounding land and sea.

Puerto Gato, a small bay on the peninsula, is ringed with spectacular fossilized sand from 55 million years ago, rusted red by the iron in the rock and now towering in layered cliffs that bear the striations of sedimentary cross-bedding. Turkey vultures swirl gracefully on thermals from the cliffs, and ravens share the air currents. Bird life is similar to that of Isla Santa Catalina, but in a slightly different setting.

On the island of **Los Islotes,** which is really more of a large rocky outcropping than a genuine island, the lusty barking of a large sea lion colony announces the island's presence even before it comes into view. Upthrusting rock, eroded by ocean waves, provides nesting places for blue-footed boobies that scrape out nests on level rock shelves. Scores of yellow-footed gulls mingle with sea lions lazing on the rocks. Double-crested cormorants roost on the craggy outcroppings, wings spread to the breezes to help them dry. Don't try to identify these cormorants by their crest, which is seldom observable despite their name. Rather, look for their orange-yellow throat pouch and a kink in their necks when in flight.

Leaving the port of **Cabo San Lucas** at sunset, you will encounter what is perhaps one of the most spectacular displays of bird life in Baja. This onetime commercial fishing port, now a sport-fishing mecca and resort destination at the very tip of Baja California, is marked by spectacular granite rock formations called Land's End. A flurry of magnificent frigate birds riding the thermals and hovering over the cliffs, ospreys, great blue herons and brown pelicans are silhouetted against the jewel tones of sunset. A chorus of California sea lions barks farewell.

On the Pacific side of Baja, **Magdalena Bay** is a rich habitat for diverse birdlife. White royal tern dive for fish and Heermann's gulls follow brown pelicans, hoping something choice will fall from a carelessly closed pouch. Graceful great egrets and snowy egrets mingle with herons along a fringe of mangroves. Marbled godwits, white ibis and long-billed curlews hunt the shallows for crustaceans, fish and other small aquatic life. A large shorebird called a willet pays an annual winter visit to Baja's salt marsh. An occasional sharp-shinned hawk, another winter visitor, strays from its accustomed woodland hunting grounds to coastal areas to try its luck. Pink-legged western gulls are observable everywhere.

An amazing number of colorful bird species breed, winter or live permanently in Baja California. In a single day it is not only possible, but likely, to see several dozen.

8

Beep! Beep!

It's the roadrunner! For decades he's been outsmarting Wyle E. Coyote in colorful cartoons, scampering away to seemingly disappear into thin air. In real life the greater roadrunner uses the trick of remaining motionless after his frantic dash, snugging against a piece of brush, a rock, whatever cover is at hand.

These amusing birds inhabit Southern California's chaparral, desert scrub and other arid brush the year around. February is a good time to watch them simply because the desert has cooled off a bit and birding is more comfortable. And in chillier weather the birds sometimes are easier to spot as they linger in sunny patches, allowing their dark-colored feathers to absorb the warmth.

If this behavior seems a little cuckoo, it's because roadrunners (*Geococcyx californianus*) belong to the cuckoo family. They are between 20 and 24 inches long, much of it tail, with a proud, bushy crest and streaky brown plumage that provides protective coloration. If you get close enough, or if your binoculars are good, you can see iridescence on their tails and backs. Sometimes you'll hear their melancholy series of descending "coo-coo-coos," clucks and whines before you see them.

You'll most often spot them sprinting across a road in front of you at speeds that have been documented at up to 12 miles an hour, hence the name roadrunner. They are not doing it for sport. You've simply startled the secretive bird, and it is trying to get out of your way. Its amazing ground speed allows it to handily nab the little lizards that are a staple of its diet. It also enjoys small snakes and has been known to entice a predatory rattler to strike. At the last moment the bird hops out of harm's way, returning to grab the hapless snake by its head and fling it into the air. As it lies stunned, the bird grabs it again, securing its grip, and beats the dazed reptile to death.

Roadrunners are devoted mates. During courtship, the male often brings the female a gift of a lizard, caterpillar, small snake or insect. If she accepts it, she is willing to mate. Observers say they've watched a female accommodate a male without first accepting the gift, in which case the male downs the proffered treat. They both gather sticks and brush to create a nest lined with feathers and soft grasses about a foot across, usually concealed in a palm tree, mesquite bush or large shrub. The female lays three to six eggs that hatch at intervals. As with many birds, not all will survive, because stronger hatchlings grab food from their weaker siblings until the weaker ones starve. Both parents forage for food, mincing lizards and small prey with their long bills before stuffing the morsels into the chicks' hungry mouths.

When you watch for roadrunners, remember their hiding habits and be alert for the tiniest movement. They can flatten themselves against the ground, scuttling like a rat or mouse. Look for their tracks, easily identifiable because two toes point forward and two point backward. Although sightings will be brief, they are reliably rewarding and seldom fail to make the sternest individual break into a smile.

Hot Spots

Roadrunners live almost anywhere on the desert floor from California's central valleys south. They love desert scrub and often are seen on the outskirts of golf courses where they'll sprint onto a green or fairway in pursuit of a lizard lunch. They are particularly common in the Palm Springs and Palm Desert area. All you have to do is get off the highway and onto little-traveled back roads, and you're almost assured of a sighting.

The **Living Desert** west of the city of Palm Desert, a desert botanical garden and wildlife park, showcases the roadrunner among creosote bushes and cacti. This is a guaranteed sighting because the bird is protected in this area, lingering because he knows when he's well off. The Living Desert is 2 miles from Palm Desert, 1.5 miles south of Hwy 111 on Portola Avenue.

In the **Desert Tortoise Natural Area** north of California City, watch for roadrunners darting among the yellow-flowered creosote bushes. The scenery of the eastern Mojave Desert surrounds the **Providence Mountains State Recreation Area,** an extremely remote place where the roadrunner finds plenty of banded and green-collared lizards to provide well-balanced meals. From I-40 about 100 miles east of Barstow, exit on Essex Road and proceed north 16 miles to the visitors' center. Roadrunners also love the dry desert heat of **Death Valley National Park** and can be seen just about everywhere (see chapter 6). To get to Death Valley, take I-15 to Hwy 127 and travel north to Hwy 178. Turn west to the entrance.

9

The Salton Sea

One of nature's anomalies in Southern California is a body of water that's 10 percent saltier than the Pacific Ocean, is 227 feet below sea level and represents one of the most unusual ecosystems anywhere. The Salton Sea National Wildlife Refuge (NWR) has the greatest diversity of bird species found on any of the country's more than 400 refuges. The best time for rewarding feathered sightings is between November and May.

The Salton Sea is California's largest lake. It covers 380 square miles, is 35 miles long and has about 115 miles of shoreline. In prehistoric times the Gulf of California reached into what are now the deserts of the Coachella and Imperial Valleys. Silt deposits formed by the Colorado River created a natural dam that blocked off the Gulf and resulted in the formation of an ancient sea. Over time, the sea evaporated and became a barren, dusty alkaline basin. At the turn of the century the area was covered with dry desert shrub.

And then, one of those glitches that so often occurs when humans attempt to change the course of nature altered the terrain dramatically. In 1901, Colorado River waters were diverted from Yuma, Arizona, into Mexico and back into the Salton Sea basin for agricultural development. The project made this region, where the Coachella and Imperial Valleys join, one of the lushest growing areas in the world. But in 1905, failure of a diversion structure caused the Colorado to flow into the Imperial Valley. For two years it gushed unchecked, creating what is now the Salton Sea.

Almost a century later the sea is sustained by agricultural drainage and runoff from the surrounding mountains. Because water is removed only by evaporation, the level of salinity is continually increasing, standing presently at about 40,000 parts per million. The Pacific Ocean has a salinity of 35,000 parts per million. In recent years the sea level has risen dramatically, preempting much of what is now the Salton

The Salton Sea

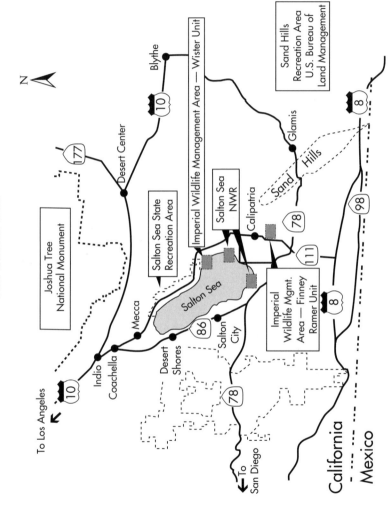

Sea National Wildlife Refuge. But as the southernmost refuge on the Pacific flyway, it still has sufficient habitat to support amazing numbers of migratory birds.

During the 1920s, increasing amounts of water were diverted to the area from the Colorado River to grow crops of citrus fruits and dates. The marshlands created by this water soon attracted waterfowl from their former winter home in the drying Colorado River delta. In the 1940s farming surged, shrinking marshlands along with the birds' food supplies. Today, the refuge has land dedicated to growing food for the wintering waterfowl, which keeps them from eating farmers' crops and in turn keeps the farmers friendly.

The refuge was formed in 1930 when it became apparent that great numbers of birds were breeding and nesting in and migrating through the area. Avian winter visitors number in the thousands. The refuge's primary purpose is to provide protected habitat for migrating and wintering waterfowl and endangered species. The endangered Yuma clapper rail breeds successfully in the marsh habitat around the southeastern portion of the sea. Other endangered and threatened species that occasionally visit the refuge are the bald eagle, California brown pelican and peregrine falcon.

Hot Spots

To get to the **Salton Sea NWR** from Hwy 86/78, take Forrester (Gentry Road) north to Sinclair, which will bring you to the refuge entrance. At the end of Garst Road, across a narrow causeway, a small island called Red Hill Marina County Park is a good place to see dozens of eared grebes, common goldeneyes, and lots of little ground doves. Right at the end of Sinclair Road, where it deadends into marshland and the lake, look for the topknotted Gambel's quail, little yellow-headed verdin and, with luck, green-tailed towhees and white-faced ibis.

Along the lakeshore, **Obsidian Butte** is a good observation point from which, with binoculars, many species are easily spotted. American avocets, black-necked stilts, pintails, green-winged teal and dozens of other species are commonly seen during the winter. Canada geese, snow geese and the smaller Ross's geese often are present in huge flocks.

Close-Up of the Salton Sea National Wildlife Refuge

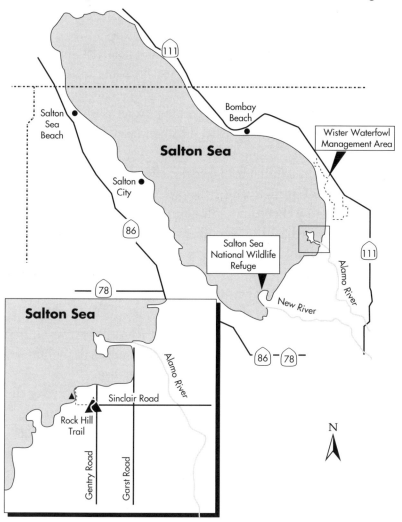

Oftentimes during winter months a ranger is available at Refuge Headquarters to tell about recently sighted birds and to hand out a list of birds currently in residence.

Go to the marshland and alkali flats at the south end of the sea at the end of Vendel Road to look for stilt sandpipers, an occasional ferruginous hawk and mountain plover, Wilson's phalaropes (best in April and May), horned larks and Say's phoebes, which are common during the winter. Orange-crowned and yellow-rumped warblers also are common, as are elegant great blue herons that roost in large trees along the shore.

A word of caution: waterfowl hunting is permitted at certain times of the year under California state and federal regulations on lands adjacent to the refuge, so occasionally some areas are closed to the birding public. In October through January you are likely to hear twelve-gauge shotguns blasting away. Within the refuge there is a goose and duck season during those same months, with hunting by assigned blind only. Areas open only to hunters are posted, and the wildlife manager can advise visitors where to go.

Because of its high salinity (some swimmers enjoy the buoyancy created by the water's salt content, and others aren't comfortable with what they describe as a "muddy" feeling), many people don't think of the Salton Sea as having much fish life. But aquatic "transplants" have flourished and only in recent years has increased salinity threatened them. The orange-mouth corvina, sargo and gulf croaker, all transplanted from the Gulf of California, thrive in the sea. The tilapia, an African species, was introduced with good results and now is well established. Only time, and salinity, will tell what will become of the fish.

So far as the area is concerned, its beauty is in the eye of the beholder. Some parts of the sea are fringed with date palms, with citrus orchards extending further beyond. Others are crusty alkali flats, salt marshes and scrubby desert that perhaps are an acquired taste. But to wildlife lovers the sea and the refuge are rich repositories of some of the best that nature has to offer.

10

Citrus Sunshine

This is the month that a California tradition comes to fruition in the Golden State. Navel oranges are ripe.

Although oranges are in evidence pretty much throughout the year—sweet-scented blossoming trees in the spring, ripening Valencias in June and almost always an abundance of the golden orbs in supermarket produce departments—February signals the first of the new crops.

Oranges were growing in California by the early 1860s, but it wasn't until the navel orange was imported from Brazil in 1873 that citrus crops as an industry truly took hold. Sweet, seedless and succulent, navel (named for their "belly-buttons") oranges were an instant hit. The easy-to-peel navels are ideal for eating out of hand although they also produce considerable juice.

The Riverside and Redlands area proved to have ideal soil and climatic conditions. Around this same time the Valencia orange, the quintessential juice orange, was developed in Orange County and met with similar success. Citrus co-ops marketed the fruit in the East, depending on colorful fruit crate labels to help in the selling process.

The Sunkist orange, familiar to generations, first appeared in 1907 when the California Fruit Growers Exchange decided to identify its top-grade fruit with a seal—an orange inside a sunburst. It was used until 1917, when it was replaced by a seal with an orange wrapped in tissue. Eventually the tissue was discontinued, and a naked orange with the familiar Sunkist label became the identifier.

All this success seemed almost too good to be true, and it was. Less than a century later the great groves of Riverside and Redlands have toppled under developers' bulldozers and smog. Row upon row of citrus trees, their trunks traditionally whitewashed to ward off sunburn, became parking lots and shopping centers. In a few of the better-planned subdivisions some trees were left standing, everbearing reminders of the land's history.

Southern California's famous navel oranges.

Some growers moved north to the state's Central Valley. Others simply sold out, enjoying the enormous financial profits that land can bring when it is used to live on, rather than live off of.

For those who want to stroll within sniffing distance of fragrant citrus blossoms, where orange trees help purify smog-darkened air, a few places remain. The seemingly endless rows of succulent fruit as depicted on early citrus crates and in brochures that enticed Easterners to the West Coast are gone, but for a mini-experience, try the places that follow.

Hot Spots

In Ventura County's Santa Clara Valley along Hwy 126 between I-5 and Hwy 101 you'll find the greatest concentration of groves in Southern California. From **Piru, to Fillmore and on to Santa Paula** you'll find wonderfully fragrant rows of Valencias as well as lemons. You can purchase oranges by the box, crate or

Old fruit crate labels, such as this 1890s version, tout California's golden sunshine.

pound and refresh yourself with a freshly squeezed glass of orange juice while you choose. An interesting way to see the groves is to hop aboard the "Orange Festival Flyer" for a ride through the groves. Full-sized passenger trains—an old-time steam train and a 1940s streamliner—clackety-clack over a rail line built in 1877 as part of the Southern Pacific Los Angeles–to–San Francisco Coast Route. The trains chug through acres of citrus groves, giving riders a glimpse of what the state's citrus industry was like 75 years ago. Call (805) 524-2546 for information on train schedules and prices.

To get to the Ojai Valley near the town of **Ojai,** take Hwy 101 north along the coast from Los Angeles, and head inland on Hwy 33 about 15 minutes to the valley. You'll see neatly placed rows of orange trees nestled up against sloping hills.

In the San Fernando Valley north of Los Angeles, once a prime agricultural and citrus-growing area, small groves still stand in **Northridge** along Nordhoff west of Reseda Boulevard. In **Redlands,** along California Street, glossy-leafed trees burgeon with navels.

11

February Shorttakes

The Boojum

It's found only in a narrow belt across Baja California, and nowhere else, and because of its odd shape is named for the mysterious monster in Lewis Carroll's narrative nonsense poem, "Hunting of the Snark." Although it can be seen at any time, February is a particularly pleasant month in Baja and therefore a good time to pursue the wily boojum.

The boojum (*Idria* or *Fouquieria columnaris*) is a thorny deciduous tree that belongs to the Candlewood family. It looks like a throwback to some primitive age. The tree can grow to more than 60 feet and often flourishes in remote places. One of the best areas to search is between San Quintin on the north and La Paz on the south, where this woody shrub finds the altitude and climate it likes best. Some of the unusual trees look like lone, misshapen flagpoles, while others grow arching branches from a soft, sometimes hollow trunk that can take root where they touch the ground. Leaves are small and oval, wider at the end. When spring rains cooperate, the boojum produces greenish yellow flowers at its very top. If you spot a forest of cardon, Baja's saguaro cactus lookalike, be alert for boojums. They often grow in the same area.

12

A Closer Look: Can the California Condor Be Saved?

Curiosity killed the cat, so they say, and it certainly isn't doing much for the California condor.

On the brink of extinction in 1986 with only 21 birds left, they are still endangered. Fewer than 100 birds survive, most of them in captivity. Efforts to reintroduce them to the areas where they once soared naturally have been thwarted by the birds' innate curiosity.

These gigantic grayish brown creatures are the largest land birds in North America, having a wingspan of more than 9 feet and body weight of 17 to 24 pounds. They probably were never abundant. Fossils indicate, however, that during the Pleistocene epoch 11,000 years ago the California condor once had an extensive range, from British Columbia to Baja California. The La Brea Tar Pits in Los Angeles are full of its bones.

The birds do not fit the romantic notion of endangered species, like the enormous gray whale, elegant peregrine falcon or diminutive spotted owl. The huge red-headed vulture is ugly, it feasts on carrion and so far efforts to reintroduce it to the wild have consumed more than $20 million in federal, state and local funding. Animal lovers maintain, however, that there is much romanticism in the great bird's soaring, graceful flight and its inquisitive, gregarious nature. Its feathers and bones have been part of the legend and ceremony of California Indian mythology for generations. In addition, scientists point out that there is still so much we don't know about the world's creatures that it is foolish to think that any of them are disposable.

Those who remember seeing condors in the wild attest to the fact that they rely on soaring, rather than flapping, flight. A condor roosts in a spot where it can launch itself easily with just a few wingbeats, using uplifting winds along mountain ridges to stay aloft. Its graceful spiraling means that the bird is using a warm thermal updraft to gain altitude, after which it can glide for long distances before seeking another uplifting thermal.

The condor is close kin to the smaller turkey vulture and the black vulture. The only bird larger than the California condor is the male Andean condor, which weighs up to 33 pounds and has a wingspan of up to 10 feet. As recently as the 1970s the condor population was sustaining itself in the mountain wilds along the California coast from Monterey south to Los Angeles, as well as in the southern parts of the San Joaquin Valley, where it foraged in the grasslands. The last known nesting population was in the mountains in Los Padres National Forest, west of Gorman. In 1987 a consortium of federal, state and private organizations initiated a rescue program. With a total population of just 27, the last wild California condors were captured and brought to the San Diego Wild Animal Park and the Los Angeles Zoo in an effort to keep the species from dying out completely. The remaining condors were split between two sites because small populations are subject to "crashes" due to epidemic diseases and natural disasters.

Encroaching development that invaded nesting territories and loss of foraging habitat helped thin condor ranks to their current periously low numbers. Other hazards have been indiscriminate shooting, pesticide residues that have caused eggshell thinning, poisoning by lead bullets eaten while feeding on the remains of hunters' unrecovered prey that is part of their carrion diet, and ingesting poisoned carcasses of wolves and coyotes set out by farmers.

Condors raise only one young every other year from a single, pale aqua-colored egg placed in a remote cave, sheltered outcrop or crevice on a cliff. No nesting material is added. Young condors develop slowly, not perfecting flying skills until they're almost a year old. Parents may continue to feed a chick for more than a year. Condors do not breed until age five or six.

Captive breeding programs are being carried out at the Los Angeles Zoo, the San Diego Wild Animal Park and the World Center for Birds of Prey near Boise, Idaho. Successful egg hatching is not the problem. In fact, scientists say that early in the program, captive condors couldn't hatch without human assistance in pulling back their shells. Now, 90 percent hatch on their own. The problem comes when it's time to release the birds into the wild. Because they never have lived in the wild, they lack many of the survival skills that would allow them to flourish. Their innate curiosity also works against them. Since 1992, 13 birds have been released in the Los Padres National Forest. Four birds died after they collided with power lines. The remaining birds were removed to a more remote area.

It was apparent to naturalists that some sort of behavior modification was in order. Los Angeles Zoo biologists even tried shock therapy to keep the terminally curious creatures from flying near power poles and power lines in the Santa Barbara County area, where birds bred in captivity have been released. A life-size replica of a power pole was erected inside the birds' habitat at the zoo. Whenever a bird lands on its crossbar it receives a mild shock. Through this aversion therapy it is hoped the condors will learn to avoid power poles in the wild.

Within their aviary are plenty of alternative natural branches and perches on which they can roost that will not shock them. The minor jolt administered to the birds is similar to the electric fence wire used to keep cattle corralled and is safe for humans and other wildlife. It is not enough to do any damage but is sufficiently unnerving to encourage them to look elsewhere for a perch. This technique worked well on Andean condors. In earlier attempts, the birds were taken to the release area and kept there in flight pens for up to two months before they were set free. Using the new shock therapy technique, they remain at the zoo until about two weeks before their release.

Condors are released when they are six to eight months old. To reinforce the jolts they received in captivity, additional fake power poles are placed in their release area. Three of the solar-powered poles stand within 300 feet of the release site, and others are placed near feeding sites.

In another aversion technique designed to create a fear and dislike of humans, scientists rush into condor cages and hold the birds upside down. This, too, seems to work as scientists say the birds have grown so fearful of their keepers that they will actually regurgitate at the sight of them. The aversion technique has come under fire by some environmental groups because it seeks to force restrictions on the birds' natural curiosity. Program proponents point out, however, that teaching the condors to avoid people and the hazards of civilization may be the only way to ensure their survival in natural habitat.

Some biologists question whether even this sort of conditioning can save the condor, because Southern California has become so urbanized and is crammed with manmade structures that are a potential danger to the birds. In fact, program officials admit that they will never be able to eliminate all the deaths that released birds meet in the wild. They hope to control the mortality rate so that the condor population recovers sufficiently to make it economically feasible to continue the program. Transferring the release program to more remote areas in Arizona and New Mexico also is being considered.

The long-term goal of the California Condor Recovery Program (under the auspices of the California Fish and Game Commission and the U.S. Fish and Wildlife Service) is to establish three separate, self-sustaining populations of 100 or more birds each. The captivity program would be divided among three institutions, augmented by two populations in the wild. If the program is successful, the California condor's status may be upgraded from endangered to threatened.

Some naturalists theorize that condor extinction is part of a natural progression. The birds' prey base is diminishing as civilization moves in, climatic changes have altered habitat and the gene pool is shrinking. Fossil records show that the condor population had been diminishing over many hundreds of years. These scientists feel that to preserve a species, habitat must first be preserved, and there is very little condor habitat left. Reintroducing condors now means drawing from an inferior gene pool that never was meant to sustain the once-lusty species.

As of this writing, a dozen condors have been released in Arizona in the Vermilion Cliffs area of the Grand Canyon, where young condors can find the good thermals critical for their flight development. Also, the Vermilion Cliffs are pockmarked with caves and ledges for roosting and nesting. Although condors were last sighted in Arizona in 1924, condor bones that date back 11,000 years have been found in the Vermilion Cliffs area. It seems a natural site in which to release condors today.

Presently there are 93 California condors, so the great bird seems destined to endure, if only in captivity. Whether its great, soaring 6-foot wingspan ever will ride the thermals of the wild again is another question.

There is currently no place where you can see condors in captivity. Call the San Diego Zoo at (619) 234-3153 to check on the condor's current status.

March

MARCH HOTSPOTS

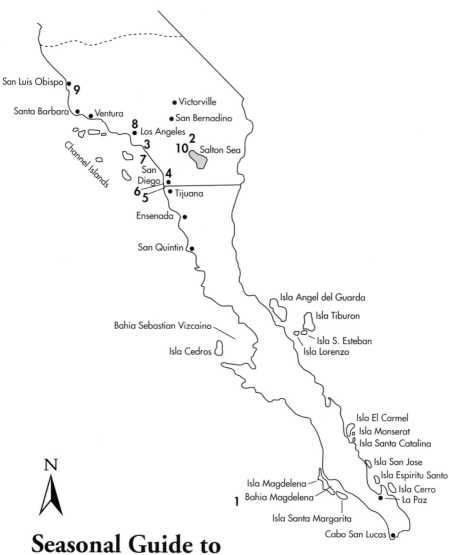

San Luis Obispo • 9
Santa Barbara • • Ventura
• Victorville
• San Bernadino
8
• Los Angeles 2
3 10 • Salton Sea
Channel Islands
7
San 4
Diego •
6 5 • Tijuana
Ensenada •
San Quintin •

Isla Angel del Guarda
Isla Tiburon
Bahia Sebastian Vizcaino
Isla S. Esteban
Isla Cedros Isla Lorenzo

Isla El Carmel
Isla Monserat
Isla Santa Catalina

N

Isla San Jose
Isla Espiritu Santo
Isla Magdelena Isla Cerro
1 Bahia Magdelena La Paz
Isla Santa Margarita
Cabo San Lucas •

Seasonal Guide to
the Natural Year

SITE LOCATOR MAP

LIST OF SITES
March

Notes

13

Where the Whales Go

In any success story about the value of environmental efforts to restore diminishing species, the California gray whale is the star. There now are about 21,000 in the Pacific, where at one time there were fewer than 1,000. Gray whales recently were removed from the list of endangered species.

The California gray whales leave the Arctic waters of Siberia and Alaska in December, cruising at 5 to 6 miles per hour in a 5,000-mile journey that ends in the welcoming warmth of the waters surrounding Mexico's Baja California. The best of this 800-mile-long dangling peninsula that points south from California's border into the blue Pacific is contained in its natural side. The gray whales and the marine life they depend on are an integral part of its nature.

On a still March morning I poke my head out of my cabin aboard the M/V *Sea Lion* and sniff the fresh salt air. We're cruising off the west coast of Isla Santa Margarita, one of the barrier islands that forms and protects Magdalena Bay. This sheltered area of tangled mangrove channels on the Pacific side of Baja is a favored breeding and calving area for gray whales.

As I'm deciding whether to shuffle below for coffee or linger in the warmth of the morning sun, I hear a shout: "Just off the starboard quarter." I grab my binoculars and race to the aft deck where a dozen of my shipmates are glassing the horizon in the direction of the pointing finger of Jim, our expedition leader.

"There's another! At about two o'clock," he cries. All lenses swing to port. Just 300 yards from the ship a whoosh of vapor dulls the shiny stainless steel sea, and a sleek gray wedge of dorsal fin verifies that we've spotted an enormous gray whale. The captain immediately cuts the engines and the ship bobs quietly. Then, as if on cue, the magnificent mammal surfaces just yards from our bow. It is so close we can count the white, crusty barnacles on its mammoth head. Yet as it submerges it raises barely a ripple. The friendly, curious whale has given us all an experience we'll never forget.

In previous days a single blow had been enough to cause a massive rush to the foredeck. Now we have half a dozen blowing grays around us at any given time. Jim says it is not unusual to see a gray whale rolling on its side so its newborn calf can nurse. For more than two hours we sit at the hub of this group of magnificent, gentle creatures. We move slowly through the protected waters of the bay, passing sand dunes and stands of mangroves drooping over the water's edge. As the sky turns a gray flannel and the sea a white-flecked tweed, the whales disappear.

If it had been 400 years earlier, our experience would have been quite different. In the 1500s the gray whale was hunted to near-extinction. Records show that more than 50 whaling vessels once pursued the huge mammals in Magdalena Bay. Currently they are protected under a number of national and international agreements and have recovered almost to pre-whaling numbers.

The female gray whale migrates from the plankton-rich waters of the north to calve. Males follow the females, so that they can mate. Females produce a one-ton calf every two years. Almost as soon as the marine biologist on board explains these processes, we're summoned on deck to see the mating game in progress. Singles and groups of gray whales come together, then move apart. They roll over one another, spinning in the water before going in search of other whales. That such bulk can move so gracefully is a marvel to us all.

"Mag Bay," as the *Sea Lion*'s crew calls it, is really a channel rather than a bay. It extends more than 50 miles, fringed with sand dunes that would be appropriate as a setting for *Lawrence of Arabia*. Its mangroves are the nurseries of fisheries. Young fry thrive here, luring birds, sea lions and other creatures. Jumbo shrimp, clams, scallops and spiny lobsters draw local fishermen, who pursue their trade from brightly colored orange and turquoise *pangas*.

In recent years the locals have learned that during whale season it is more profitable to use their pangas for whisking tourists around the channel in search of whales than it is to fish. To help explain the whales' role in the economic as well as the ecological picture here,

Passengers on the Sea Lion *scout for whales in Baja California.*

Special Expeditions, the sponsor of the trip that I'm on, employs local fishermen as guides to ride in the rubber boats it uses to bring passengers closer to the whales. The company hopes that by promoting responsible, restrained whale watching, it will discourage the local populace from charging at the whales with motors chugging. The lesson is, if the whales are pursued to the point that they leave for other, quieter waters, the tourist dollars will leave with them.

On one particular day we're treated to a look at sperm whales, the largest of the toothed whales, a family that also includes common and bottlenose dolphins. A sperm whale can make prolonged deep dives for over an hour. Studies have confirmed that its dive cycles agree with the old-time whalers' rule, that for every foot of a sperm whale's length, it breathes once at the surface to stay submerged one minute. This means that a 50-foot whale blows about 50 times, then goes down for 50 minutes. We learn that just like scuba divers, whales need surface time. Divers surface to get rid of nitrogen, whereas whales have to become reoxygenated. Fortunately, the ones we're watching stay down only about 12 minutes, then surface for three or four, spewing vapor from S-shaped blowholes on the left side of their heads.

Sperm whales are endangered, and marine biologists say it is unlikely they will recover unless a complete ban can be placed on hunting for at least the next 50 years. Even if that can be accomplished among nations that are members of the International Whaling Commission, there is little chance that nations outside the commission will comply.

During our days on the *Sea Lion* we also spot Bryde's, humpback and fin whales. We learn that the easiest way to identify the various species is by the differences in dorsal fins. Along with the gray, those three whales are in the baleen whale category, which means they feed by filtering nutrients through a fringe that hangs like a horse's mane from the upper jaw.

The humpback population is estimated at about 5,000 individuals and inhabit all oceans of the world. The 40-tonners are famous for the squeaks, grunts and moans that constitute their song. Several times we see dolphins surfacing at the bow of the ship, visible as light gray torpedoes under the water. They emerge in great arching leaps, apparently having fun keeping pace with their motorized counterpart.

On this trip many of us see for the first time the "green flash," an intense emerald aura that momentarily appears around the sun at the instant it rises or falls beneath the horizon. In the remote Sea of Cortez, far from city smog and pollution, the atmosphere is clear enough to see the refraction that creates the flash, if the observer is attentive. Jim instructs us not to confuse the green flash with the green flush, which is what we see in our toilets. The seawater that is used in the ship's sewage system is rich with phytoplankton, which glows with an eerie bioluminescence when agitated.

It's all part of the remarkable marine ecosystem that has for centuries ensured the return of the California gray whale to Baja California's Magdalena Bay.

14

Trees Shaped Like Joshua

The Joshua tree is one of many plants and animals with a Biblical connection. It was named by Mormon pioneers following the call of Brigham Young to go to Salt Lake City. They thought the tree branches resembled the arms of Joshua motioning them onward in their quest for the Promised Land. A fertile imagination and inventive eye surely can discern "arms," wispy "hair" and perhaps a scraggly beard in a Joshua tree when silhouetted against a red desert sunset.

Home for the Joshua tree is one of the state's most unusual wild areas. It received a major and most welcome shot in the arm in 1994 when President Clinton signed the California Desert Protection Act. Joshua Tree National Monument was elevated to national park status, thereby adding another level of protection to one of the country's last remaining wildernesses.

Along with its upgraded status, Joshua Tree National Park also gained about 234,000 acres, expanding its total area to 792,000 acres. Now more than 80 percent of the park is designated wilderness. With unobstructed views that in some places exceed 50 miles, it is a place of unusual beauty and stillness. Its main attraction is the Joshua tree, which some say is a fascinating example of nature's sense of humor. After viewing a Joshua tree, it is impossible to remain neutral about its attractiveness or lack of same. Its contorted branches are considered grotesque by some and eerily beautiful by others.

Found in the desert from California to Utah and in parts of Arizona and Nevada at elevations between 2,000 and 6,000 feet, the Joshua tree bristles with dagger-shaped, spine-tipped leaves and greenish-white flowers in long clusters that bloom from February to late April, and generally are at their best in March. Blossoms open quite unspectacularly for just one night, then close to remain on the tree for two to three weeks. The tree can reach a height of 40 feet, but most specimens here are in the 20- to 30-foot range. The Joshua tree belongs

Joshua Tree National Monument

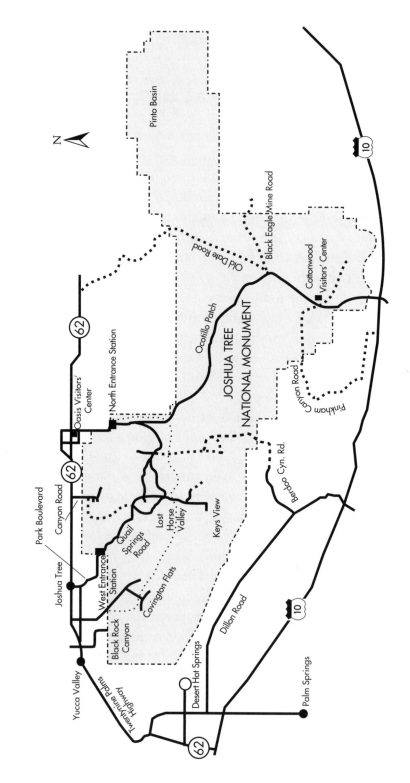

to the Agavaceae family that also includes the century plant *(Yucca brevifolia),* so it has many family members among the agave and yuccas with which it shares the desert.

Without a tiny creature called the yucca moth to pollinate its blossoms, the Joshua tree wouldn't be able to flower. One cannot exist without the other. The female moth collects the tree's pollen in a ball and carefully spreads it within the flower, thus fertilizing the tree. She's not an altruistic conservationist. She's just assuring her offspring a food source when they hatch from her eggs. The hungry larvae eat only a few seeds, however, leaving more than enough to be scattered by the wind across the desert. Although the tree may propagate via its root system, it must have the seeds it produces in pollinated flowers to establish itself in new areas.

The Joshua tree's shallow root system and top-heavy growth pattern cause it to cling tenaciously to the sandy desert soil. It may not bloom every year, choosing to display its blossoms based on nature's distribution of rainfall and warm weather. It grows slowly, taking its time in developing new branches and blooms, adding just a third to a half-inch each year. Because it doesn't have rings like a conventional tree, it is difficult to determine the age of a Joshua tree. But if the harsh desert environment allows, the many-armed elders can survive for several hundred years.

The largest trees, some believed to be as tall as 60 feet, succumbed to the saws and axes of early settlers who saw them as a ready source of firewood and fencing material. Because of their protected status today, the trees are once again rebuilding into a forest, attracting the wildlife that depend on it for survival.

Within the park are two distinct desert regions: the Mojave, or high desert, and the Colorado, or low desert. The trees grow in California's Mojave Desert at an elevation of about 3,000 feet. Besides their interesting architectural appearance, the Joshua trees provide focal points for a complex wildlife community. Oftentimes a graceful red-tailed hawk or canny sparrow hawk uses the tree's topmost reaches as a lookout point to find its next meal. Noisy cactus wrens flit and chatter among its branches as they nibble away at insects. A sacklike hanging nest indicates that a lemon-yellow Scott's

Joshua Tree National Park is 80 percent wilderness.

oriole has chosen it for a home. Red-capped ladder-backed wood-peckers sometimes work their rapid-fire techniques on the fibrous trunk in a search for bugs.

Creamy, waxy, podlike Joshua tree flowers supply food for more than two dozen bird species as well as Beechey ground squirrels and even an occasional deer. The fleshy fruits and, later, the dry seeds are an important food source for antelope ground squirrels.

The shaggy trunks are a source of fibers that augment the nest-building materials of desert birds. Fallen trees provide a safe haven for the seldom-seen desert night lizard. Termites find protection from heat and cold in the decaying fiber and convert plant energy to animal energy. Stink bugs munch on the tree's fibrous trunk, helping transform its nutrients into another living form. So even as it dies the Joshua gives life.

Other desert plants in the park that are especially lovely this time of year include the crimson-shafted ocotillo and the fuzzy teddy bear or Bigelow cholla. Despite its fluffy appearance, don't touch the cholla. Its penetrating spines are vicious. The pale puff of the smoke tree, the creamy white yucca and tiny yellow-flowered creosote also add to the desert's appeal.

Sharp-eyed visitors occasionally may spot a desert bighorn sheep at one of the five lovely fan palm oases in the park. The water supply also attracts coyotes, kit foxes, an occasional bobcat and bouncy little desert cottontails. A visitor willing to sit quietly in the shade at dawn or sunset has the best chance of being rewarded by a glimpse of these elusive creatures.

The park's jumbles of huge granite boulders make it a mecca for rock climbers. The arches and hollows that are a pleasing artistic complement to the Joshua trees help to distinguish the high desert from the mountains above and the low desert below. More than 3,000 established climbing sites help account for the 1.3 million visitors that enjoy the park each year. Campgrounds with facilities and desert hiking trails make it a year-round destination for many outdoor activities.

Hot Spots

Joshua Tree National Park is about an hour's drive from Palm Springs. To get to the Mojave where the Joshua trees are, take I-10 north to Hwy 62 to the town of Joshua Tree. Turn south on Park Boulevard to the Oasis Visitors' Center. By taking I-10 south you can reach the Cottonwood Visitors' Center for access to the park.

Guided jeep tours may be arranged through Golden Eagle Tours, P. O. Box 356, Twentynine Palms, CA 92277; (800) 428-1833.

You can drive through the park in a single day, stopping for photos of the Joshua trees and fan palms. However, true desert discoverers opt for the interpreted nature foot trails that range from 0.75 to 1.75 miles and cover only gentle, mellow terrain. Trail maps are available at the visitors' centers.

For a close-up view of the Joshua trees, try the Skull Rock 1.75-mile trail that begins at Jumbo Rocks Campground. The walk is a Whitman's Sampler of the best the desert has to offer. It winds through a forest of Joshua trees, then across a moonlike sandscape studded with the Joshua's relative, Mojave yucca. Imagination comes into play here again as the weathered quartz monzonite rocks emerge as shapes and forms. The "skull" for which the trail is named and other creatures and beings appear as works of art sculpted by erosion.

For a look at Joshua trees as well as the rock formations so sought by climbers, take the Barker Dam 1.25-mile loop that begins in the Barker Dam parking area. It gives a glimpse of the 12-square-mile Wonderland of Rocks that appears to have been disordered by a giant's hand. In and among the rocky labyrinth are more Joshua trees, half-hidden as though they play some arboreal game of hide and seek. The path's first part focuses on botanical highlights; Native American petroglyphs are found near the end.

15

Grunion Run

Southern California beaches come alive with small, silvery fish this month. From March through September, hundreds of thousands of grunion will flop onto beaches from Santa Barbara to Baja. They'll fling themselves from nighttime coastal waters onto the sand in a bizarre ritual that has held observers (and anglers) in thrall for years.

The California grunion, a small 5- to 7-inch metallic greenish blue fish *(Leuresthen tenuis)* is a member of the Silversides family, related to the jacksmelt and topsmelt but not a true smelt. Early Spanish settlers named it *grunion,* which means "grunter," because of the feeble sounds it emits while spawning.

Grunion spawn at night on sandy beaches at high tide, two to six nights after full and new moons. With faint squeaking noises they perform their unusual ceremony, then disappear back into the retreating surf.

All the stories you've heard about midnight grunion grabbers, flashlight in hand, stuffing grunion into plastic bags and gunny sacks are true. For some it's an annual party. Toting coolers and picnic baskets and sporting fishing licenses, groups of cheerful anglers in pursuit of the elusive grunion settle on blankets on the sand, dashing toward the silvery slivers to grab them with bare hands and stuff them in sacks.

The almost ceremonial rite that the grunion go through has been compared to a dance. The female swims against the drag of a retreating wave onto the beach and bores herself into the wet sand, tail first. With powerful thrusting and squirming movements she arches from side to side until she is half buried. In this damp nest of sand she deposits a ball of more than 3,000 eggs. Two weeks later the eggs hatch out as they are agitated from the sand by the next series of spring tides. Incoming waves disperse the egg clusters and the watersoaked eggs are washed out to sea where, within two to three minutes, baby grunion emerge to swim freely.

Within a year the tiny specks are 5 inches long, spawning and eating size, and can top out at 7 inches. If not grabbed by grunion hunters, they have a life span of about three years, which they spend in shallow coastal waters rarely deeper than 60 feet.

The reproductive cycle of the grunion is so predictable it can be charted a year in advance. Spawning occurs on two to four nights after the new moon and after the full moon, a short time after the turn of the high tide. California Department of Fish and Game marine biologists actually produce a table of expected grunion runs that pinpoints the fishes' activity so precisely that runs can be forecast for four-day time cycles in two-hour time slots. Along Los Angeles beaches, the probable two-hour interval during which a spawning run may occur begins at the approximate time of the nightly high tide at the Los Angeles Harbor entrance. Times vary along the coast, with San Diego's spawning spurts occurring about five minutes earlier and Santa Barbara's about 25 minutes later.

Fish and Game Department officials say that more grunion do their thing during the second hour than the first, with best runs normally happening on the second and third nights of the four-night cycle.

If you are 16 years old or older, you must obtain a California fishing license from a bait and tackle shop or from the Department of Fish and Game that must be worn in plain sight. It allows you to take grunion with your bare hands only. It's against the law to dig holes in the sand to trap the wiggly creatures or to scoop them up with a net, pan lid, bucket or any other utensil. It also is unlawful to take more than you can use. Leave the rest to spawn again another day. Fish and Game Department officials recommend adhering to the rules, because wardens often work late on grunion run nights to check for violations.

The Fish and Game Department offers tips for getting a good grasp on grunion. Resist the urge to grab early-arrival "scout" fish, they advise. Let the first-act grunion return to the ocean, and you could be rewarded with a cast of thousands. Try to position yourself on the ends of beaches, away from crowds. Keep lights to a minimum. Fires and flashlights often will chase grunion out of a beach area. Once a wave has subsided, use a flashlight to briefly illuminate the surf to spot early arrivals. Take along an old pillowcase for a creel. Expect to get wet and cold, and plan to stay up late, because grunion often wait until the very last minute to make an appearance. Those who leave too early can miss all the fun.

If it sounds like the poor grunion don't have a chance, rest assured that they'll be OK. During April and May fishing is prohibited, so the fish can spawn undisturbed. During March, June, July and August, however, it's every grunion for itself.

Grunion are particularly good eating. To prepare, just clean, scale and coat with a mixture of beaten egg and cornmeal or cracker crumbs, then pan fry or deep fry. Their delicate flavor is complemented by a tossed green salad, boiled potatoes and a light white wine.

Hot Spots

Grunion spawn on Southern California and Baja California beaches. Among the strips of sand that often play host to the befuddled fish are **Cabrillo Beach, Long Beach, Belmont Shore** and **Seal Beach** in Los Angeles County; **Mission Beach;** and the long, sandy beaches at the **San Diego Coronado Island Strand, La Jolla, Del Mar** and **Corona del Mar** in San Diego County. Grunion runs also take place on sandy beaches in Ventura and Santa Barbara counties.

South of the border along Mexico's Baja peninsula, most west-facing beaches are great grunion grounds.

16

When the Swallows
Come Back to Capistrano

It's tradition, they say. Every year on March 19, St. Joseph's Day, the swallows come back to Capistrano.

The song, "When the Swallows Come Back to Capistrano," written in 1939 by Leon Rene, says it's so. More than 12,000 tourists who flock to the Mission San Juan Capistrano every March 19 obviously believe in the swallows.

So is it true? Well ... sort of.

There's no question that sometime around mid-March of each year a large contingent of cliff swallows descends on the town of San Juan Capistrano on Southern California's coast between Long Beach and San Diego. They seem to concentrate at the Mission, founded in 1776 by Father Junipero Serra as seventh in the chain of California's coastal missions and once the major Roman Catholic outpost between Los Angeles and San Diego. The returning swallows build their jug-like nests under the eaves of the quadrangle and in the high arches of the ruins of the great stone church.

Their arrival, however, conforms to no timetable. Local residents in a position to observe say that from early March on the swallows trickle in, so that by mid-month a sizable number of the graceful, soaring creatures are in residence. The 5- to 6-inch bird, with a gray breast and dark wings, is easily recognizable by its long, elliptical glide pattern that ends in a steep, swooping jet-fighter climb.

A series of squeaking and grating notes, emitted while the birds are in flight, often is the first announcement that they're back. The sleek, rust-rumped harbingers of spring have spent the winter in warm, welcoming Argentina. They time their return to North America to take advantage of the winds and weather that can speed them on their way or slow their northward passage by weeks if it turns inclement. A single persistent coastal storm can delay their journey by as much as two weeks.

San Juan Capistrano welcomes the winged residents with the annual week-long Fiesta de las Golondrinas, or Swallow Festival, marked by a parade and other events. According to legend, the swallows leave Capistrano each year on October 23, the feast day of St. John (San Juan) of Capistrano.

Although serious birders disdain such sentiment and not a single major bird manual even mentions the word Capistrano in connection with the swallows, there's not much doubt that their annual migration is a celebrated occasion, authentic or not. After Disneyland and Knott's Berry Farm, it is the third most popular destination for tourists who come to Orange County, California. Bird books do verify that the cliff swallow winters in South America and has a range that includes Alaska, Canada and Mexico.

It's a pretty safe bet that whenever they want to return, the Mission, currently undergoing a massive reconstruction, will be there to welcome them.

Hot Spots

To reach the town of **San Juan Capistrano,** leave I-5 at the San Juan Capistrano exit and turn left onto Camino Capistrano. The Mission is at the intersection of Camino Capistrano and Ortega Highway. Called the Jewel of the Missions, Capistrano has lovely pools and endless beds of flowers. Tales of its four bells ringing by themselves to commemorate joyous or tragic love affairs have become almost as well known as the celebration of the return of the swallows. A self-guided tour will reveal exhibits representing eighteenth-century mission life and eaves full of nesting swallows. Wear a hat.

17

March Shorttakes

Wildflower Walks

This month and next, weekend wildflower walks at **Rancho Santa Ana Botanical Gardens** show off the best of California's spring wildflowers. The gardens have the most extensive collection of native plants in Southern California. Rancho Santa Ana is located at 1500 North College Avenue, Claremont, CA 91711-3157; (909) 626-1917.

Docent-led wildflower walks at the **Theodore Payne Foundation** take observers up Wildflower Hill for a look at native blooms as preserved by Englishman Theodore Payne. The foundation is at 10459 Tuxford Street, Sun Valley, CA; (818) 768-1802. Call the wildflower hotline at (818) 768-3533.

Rattlesnakes

Beginning this month, tread carefully in the desert. Rattlers are now coming out of hibernation, and although their intricate markings are fascinating to observe, it's no fun to be fanged. It may be more important to be informed about rattlesnakes in order to avoid them rather than observe them. When walking in the desert, wear long pants and high boots and don't put your hands on ledges or in places that you can't see. If you hear the telltale shake of a rattler's tail, your best move is none at all. Stand still and try to locate the source of the sound, then move slowly in the other direction. Rattlers try to avoid human contact and will not strike unless they feel threatened. Even if you're bitten, it is comforting to know that fewer than 2 percent of rattlesnake bites are fatal.

California has many different rattlers, including the Western, red, diamondback, speckled and sidewinder (easily identified by sideways S-curve movements) types and a few others. They generally hibernate during December, January and February and spend summer days dozing, becoming active only at night. In spring and fall they're most in evidence as they roam around looking for food and pursuing a mate. Eggs are hatched and the young are born late in the summer. Newcomers get no help from their parents. They're expected to learn how to use their fangs on their own. If they don't get picked off by a passing hawk, coyote or roadrunner, they will become predators in search of birds, rodents, lizards and young rabbits. They use heat-sensing organs on their heads to locate warm-blooded prey and are able to detect tiny temperature shifts at distances of more than a foot.

18

A Closer Look:
Earthquakes—Whose Fault Is It?

This is not the kind of stress that can be cured by a double dose of extra-strength Excedrin. California and all its faults have become a geological case study of earthquakes and why they occur. Some think of them as Mother Nature at her worst, while others are fascinated by these uncontrollable forces.

The state's devastating Northridge quake in the predawn hours of January 17, 1994, brought down freeways, toppled buildings and destroyed the homes of thousands of San Fernando Valley residents. A whole lotta shakin' went on for more than 24 seconds at the epicenter as the subterranean spasm killed 60 people and caused damage estimated to exceed $20 billion. The flurry of quakes that have shaken Southern California in the last few decades also have rocked the seismic world and have sent scientists scurrying to their labs to take another look at data that is, quite literally, shifting.

According to the theory of plate tectonics, the earth is covered with 50-mile-thick slabs, or plates, that shift relative to each other above a hotter, molten center. Until recently the surface disruptions they cause, better known as earthquakes, have been measured by the Richter Scale, invented in 1935 by California seismologist Charles Richter as a mathematical device to compare the size of earthquakes. The scale measures seismic waves, which are the energy released below the earth's surface. For scientific purposes, the Richter Scale has largely been replaced by what is considered a more accurate scale, the moment-magnitude scale. Part of its calculation is based on the area of the fault's rupture surface multiplied by the amount of earth movement along the fault.

The effect of a quake on the earth's surface is called the "intensity" and is commonly measured by the Modified Mercalli Intensity Scale.

An apartment building devastated by the Northridge earthquake in January 1994 in the San Fernando Valley north of Los Angeles.

It measures certain key responses ranging from I to XII, with II representing a quake felt only by a few persons at rest, especially on upper floors of buildings; delicate objects may move. An intensity of XII means total damage. Lines of sight and level are distorted and objects are thrown into the air.

Between 1987 and 1994, half a dozen strong quakes shivered the timbers of Southern California, each an unsettling surprise. The 6.7 Northridge quake was so completely unexpected because it occurred along what is called a "blind thrust fault" that was previously unknown. It started deep in the earth, then stopped 5 miles below the surface. This type of fault occurs totally underground and raises folded hills without breaking the surface. Many quakes leave a gash in the earth's crust. But postquake searches by air and land were futile as there was no telltale rupture. Because there is virtually no way to detect blind thrust faults, there is no way to predict when they might become active.

California's most famous fault is the San Andreas, emerging from the Pacific Ocean just north of the state's coastal "elbow" near Point Arena in Mendocino County in Northern California. It snakes southward for more than 800 miles, passing through great population centers as well as areas that are virtually deserted, under major freeways and interstates, bisecting peaks and valleys, finally to dissipate its fractious personality in the desert near the Salton Sea. It is named for a rift valley in Northern California somewhat south of the point at which it leaves the sea to become part of the land.

Along the San Andreas, two continental plates, the North American plate on the east and the Pacific plate on the west, move in opposite directions, gnashing against each other with tremendous force. The North American plate is under San Francisco; the Pacific plate is under Los Angeles. The plates move a couple of inches a year, about as fast as fingernails grow. Within 30 million years, Los Angeles will be a suburb of San Francisco, or vice versa, depending on your point of view. When the plates hit a hitch and are temporarily unable to move, tremendous amounts of energy begin to build. When they get unstuck and the energy is suddenly released, an earthquake occurs. Sometimes it happens in one big quake, but it also may be manifested in several smaller ones.

The San Andreas Fault is not a single unbroken line. Rather, it is made up of fault segments, each on its own particular quake timetable that is determined by the amount of stress that has built up. A quake on the San Andreas in Southern California probably does nothing to relieve stress on the fault in the northern part of the state.

Near the fault's northern parts, the quakes it causes are centered quite close to the fault. But in the southern part of the Golden State, quakes tend to spiderweb out from lesser-known faults. The unnamed fault that caused the Northridge quake is an example, as is the Elysian Park fault that runs through downtown Los Angeles. A fault map of Southern California looks like veins in an irritated eyeball. The Santa Ynez, Garlock, White Wolf, Imperial, San Jacinto, Elsinore and Owens Valley Faults are just a few that branch from the San Andreas.

If there is anything positive to say about earthquakes, it is that they have given shape to California's dramatic landscapes. Mountains, valleys and water courses are, over eons, the result of earthquakes. Today, landscapes are being altered and mountains are literally growing because of the San Andreas Fault. The Northridge quake added 1 foot to the mountains on the northern edge of Los Angeles. The San Gabriel and San Bernardino Mountains form a rocky spine that runs to the east of Los Angeles and continues south into the Mojave Desert. They are rising, by measurable inches per year, as a result of the San Andreas Fault.

Oil geologists have known for years that the precious petrol is trapped in pockets created by the folding action of blind thrust faults under the earth's surface. It was the search for oil that first located the potentially explosive Elysian Park Fault under Los Angeles.

So it would seem that Los Angeles is on a roll, quite literally. Many faults under the city, according to geologists and seismologists, haven't snapped in thousands of years and are long overdue. In the City of Angels' recent history, it has been rattled by 10 considerable quakes in the past 25 years, beginning in 1971 with the San Fernando quake. Since then the area has averaged one damaging quake per year.

Many earthquake faults are obvious if you know what to look for. By doing some homework (see the Selected Bibliography), surface evidence of faults will become readily obvious. At the eastern edge of San Luis Obispo County's **Carrizo Plain,** you can see the dramatic topography of the San Andreas's movement along its rumpled hills, which can be as much as 30 feet every few hundred years. Field trips that explore the fault and coastal ecology are offered monthly by the Bureau of Land Management. Call the Bakersfield BLM office, (805) 391-6000, for more information.

The fault can be explored on two driving tours by starting at the Goodwin Education Center, which is staffed during the winter and spring. From Bakersfield, take CA Hwy 119 west to CA Hwy 33, turn south through the town of Maricopa, then right on Soda Lake Road 7 miles to the Education Center. Pick up a driving guide that will direct you to the best views of the fault. At Wallace Creek you can actually stand on the fault. At one time the creek drained across the fault, but its drainage course has been offset by fault movement, which now places the downstream segment more than 400 feet northwest of the upstream segment. Scientists believe that the offset has developed over the last 3,700 years as a result of many very large quakes. Further downstream along the fault is a "beheaded" channel of Wallace Creek,

Carrizo Plain Natural Area

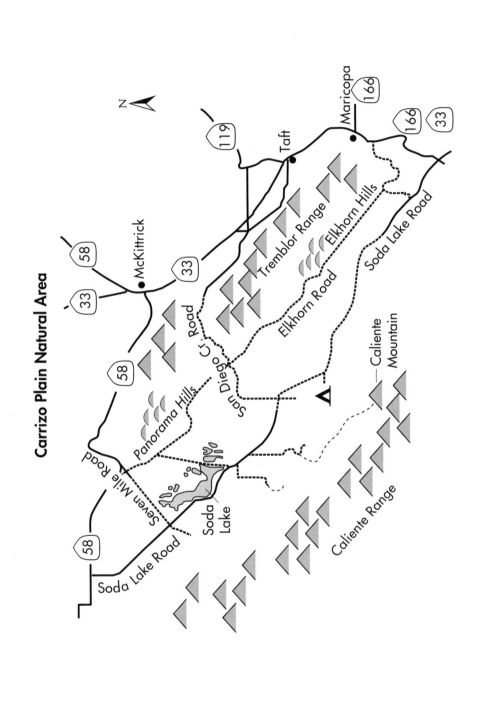

so-called because it has been completely separated from the upstream portion. Other offset gullies are clearly visible.

At another point on the drive, several miles past the road to KLC Ranch, the Elkhorn scarp pressure ridge marks an area where the San Andreas Fault changes direction slightly. Further along, the fault dominates the topography of the Elkhorn Hills. Photographers should try to get here in late afternoon when the light creates shadows that make the fault particularly obvious.

In Los Angeles, famed Sunset Boulevard follows the Hollywood fault. On a clear day, hikers who climb to the top of Mount Hollywood in Griffith Park can look down into the basin for an unobstructed view of its pathway.

Near Knott's Berry Farm in Buena Park, at the Ralph B. Clark Regional Park prehistoric fossil site, there are two earthquake faults that display 100 feet of vertical displacement.

The San Andreas Fault crosses CA Hwy 14 at Palmdale just north of the San Fernando Valley. Its movement is easy to see in a cut made during road construction. The Nature Conservancy's Hamilton Preserve at the base of the northern San Gabriel Mountains straddles the fault. It lies in a tectonically active structural trough between the San Andreas Fault on the north and the San Jacinto Fault on the south. Its striking geologic features tell of a complex history of folding and faulting. The San Andreas passes near the mountain village of Wrightwood in the San Bernardino Mountains, where some geologists believe a large quake is long overdue, then peters out as it crosses the Mexican border.

By riding the Palm Springs Aerial Tramway to the Mountain Station, you can take in a 180-degree view of the **Coachella Valley.** The San Andreas Fault is visible as an unmistakable lumpy ridgeline running across the landscape. The Nature Conservancy's Coachella Valley Preserve straddles the fault. Nearby, the San Jacinto Fault runs directly under the Indian Canyons on the Agua Caliente Indian reservation near Palm Springs.

In the same area in **Big Morongo Canyon Preserve,** construction of a gas line right-of-way has revealed a fault area. It exposes some of California's oldest rocks and can be reached via an easy hiking trail.

Ask for information at preserve headquarters. To get there, take Hwy 62 through the town of Morongo Valley, turn right on East Drive, then 200 feet farther turn left and enter the preserve.

The most readily observable evidence of earthquake faults is not, however, in the earth itself. Trendy boutiques with names like The Epicenter and My Fault often lodge directly on earthquake sites, defying the earth to try it again. In the town of San Juan Bautista, situated directly on the fault, a restaurant called the FaultLine serves home-made soups and stews. Further south, Parkfield experiences a quake about every 22 years, thereby encouraging residents to dub it the Earth-quake Capital. The Parkfield Inn and Cafe is papered with clippings attesting to its quake-prone status.

For a controlled look at a quake, visit **Universal Studios Holly-wood** and hop on the Earthquake ride. A couple of hundred times a day the magic of Hollywood simulates an earthquake that reaches 8.3 on the Richter Scale. A thunderous gas explosion, toppling telephone poles and smoke and flames are a bit too realistic for some.

Another safe way to view a quake is the interactive Create-a-Quake exhibit at the **Stephen Birch Aquarium-Museum** in La Jolla. By stand-ing on a platform and activating the display, visitors experience the rock and roll of an earthquake with no damage control needed. The display also explains how, in nature, plate tectonics creates the tem-blor.

Earthquake followers say that the ultimate way to observe a quake is to experience one, a problematic assignment since they are all but impossible to predict and adhere to no time schedule. Seismologists gathering in 1993 in the city of Parkfield in anticipation of a quake were disappointed. After a series of small temblors, a larger quake did occur. But it was smaller than expected and happened on a different portion of the fault than predicted. To get close-up and personal with a quake, the solution may be to spend as much time as possible in earthquake-prone areas, fully prepared, of course.

April

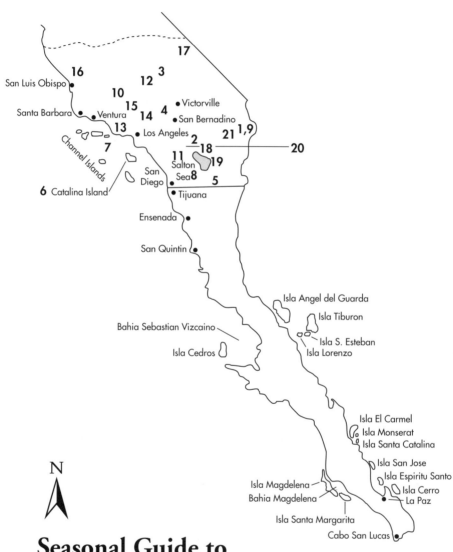

17

16
San Luis Obispo •

12 **3**

10

15 **4** • Victorville

Santa Barbara • **14** • San Bernadino
• Ventura

13 • Los Angeles **2** **21** **1,9**

Channel Islands **18** **20**

7 **11**

San **8** **5**
Diego

6 Catalina Island Salton Sea **19**

• Tijuana

Ensenada •

San Quintin •

Isla Angel del Guarda

Isla Tiburon

Bahia Sebastian Vizcaino

Isla S. Esteban
Isla Cedros Isla Lorenzo

Isla El Carmel
Isla Monserat
Isla Santa Catalina

Isla San Jose
Isla Espiritu Santo
Isla Magdelena Isla Cerro
Bahia Magdelena La Paz

Isla Santa Margarita
Cabo San Lucas •

N

Seasonal Guide to
the Natural Year

SITE LOCATOR MAP

LIST OF SITES
April

1. Colorado River Valley
2. Idyllwild County Park
3. Kern River Valley
4. Silverwood Lake State Recreation Area
5. Imperial Sand Dunes Recreation Area
6. Catalina Island
7. Channel Islands
8. Anza Borrego Desert State Park
9. Colorado River
10. Carrizo Plain Natural Area
11. Santa Rosa Plateau Preserve
12. Sand Ridge Preserve
13. Nicholas Flat
14. Antelope Valley California Poppy Reserve
15. Hungry Valley State Vehicular Recreation Area
16. Cerro Alto
17. Death Valley National Park
18. Coachella Valley Preserve
19. Thousand Palms Oasis
20. Dos Palmas Oasis Preserve
21. Living Desert

Notes

19

Migratory Birds

From April through June, and in September and October, California's position on the Pacific Migratory Flyway makes it an outstanding birding area. At these times of year rare, nonresident birds can show up in anyone's backyard, causing a rush to the bird book to identify the transient species. On any given spring or fall night, millions of migrants can be in the air over California.

In a state with a population that grows by thousands on a daily basis, migratory birds are continually challenged to find spots to rest and feed. Because they generally fly at night, covering several hundred miles and sometimes bucking strong opposing winds, it is essential that these feathered travelers find appropriate daytime places to replenish themselves. A pond that existed last year may now be a parking lot. A riparian area can suddenly become the site of a new home development.

A system of refuges and protected areas that provides a variety of habitat and cover can help keep up migratory bird populations. Many Californians have enjoyed the lovely, green-headed mallards that pause for a night or two on a golf course lake among the resident mudhens. It is an indication that country clubs and golf courses can play a part in preserving migratory birds. The Resort at Squaw Creek Golf Course in Olympic Valley has been designated an Audubon Sanctuary and commended for its efforts to provide a place of respite for wildlife. The course was built on wetlands that were largely preserved when the course was constructed. Reservoirs, manmade streams, subdivision greenbelts and local zoos and botanical gardens also provide temporary stopovers.

Although great numbers of birds are on the move during the months mentioned above, at almost any time there are birds going in one direction or the other. Spring migrants such as Costa's hummingbird will arrive in California in time to nest, lay eggs and raise a family.

Other species, such as the white-crowned sparrow, leave in spring. The process reverses itself as seasons change. In addition, there are great numbers of birds that use Southern California simply as a stop-over on their way somewhere else. These are the sought-after transients that serious birders strive to add to their Life Lists.

Migration can mean different things to different birds. Some, like the little coastal sanderlings, travel from the Arctic to Southern California's sunny beaches during winter months. Others, including some species of sparrows, simply move from higher elevations to lower as winter's chill sets in. All such movements, however, are a response to seasonal changes in the environment that signal breeding times. Some birders theorize that migration also has to do with adequate food supply.

Among the birds that begin arriving in April to summer in sunny Southern California is the gull-billed tern, which begins arriving at the salt marshes in the Salton Sea at the end of March. It often feeds on insects around the edges of the marsh. The Caspian tern, at 23 inches long America's largest tern, is abundant in coastal areas and along beaches and in bays and sometimes wanders to inland lakes. It is easily identifiable by its blood-red bill.

Graceful white-winged doves return to the Colorado River basin beginning this month, where they stay until early September. Larger than mourning doves, they have white wing patches that look like a thin horizontal stripe when the birds are at rest. This dove is plentiful and in many areas is hunted as a game bird. (Delicious!)

A number of hummingbirds make Southern California their summer home. The black-chinned, Costa's, little calliope, broad-tailed and Allen's hummingbirds usually are here when it's warm.

The dusky flycatcher returns to the pine forests of local mountains, as does the olive-sided flycatcher. The larger ash-throated flycatcher favors the mesquite bushes of the desert but also may be found among piñons and junipers. Although it is present in California the year around, the tiny house wren moves into the mountains for the summer, as does the larger rock wren; they prefer rocky slopes and canyons.

The elegant, glossy black phainopepla moves from the desert
and **Colorado River Valley** along California's border with
Mexico to the coastal lowlands and interior valleys this month,
where it looks for mistletoe and elderberries to supplement its
diet of insects. The phainopepla belongs to a group of tropical
birds; Southern California is the northernmost part of their range.
A whole host of warblers are common transients here as well. The
Townsend's, hermit, MacGillivray's, Wilson's, Nashville and black-
throated gray warbler are often seen in the spring.

Colored like a tropical drink with a red head and yellow body,
the Western tanager is a common summer resident in the pine
forests of the **Idyllwild** area near Lake Hemet. Also common in
summer is the black-headed grosbeak, another flashy bird with an
orange body and black head. There's a very good chance of spotting the shimmering iridescence of a tiny calliope hummingbird,
the smallest of all United States' hummers. The male is the only
hummingbird in the United States with streaky white and purple,
rather than solid-colored, throat feathers. From Hwy 74 in Riverside County, take Hwy 243 north to Rivco Playground Road and
park at the campground. Hike the campground trail to the visitors' center.

The **Kern River Valley** in the very southernmost end of the
Sierra Nevada in northeastern Kern County is a rewarding area to
bird any time of year, but in spring it is particularly exciting. Every April the Kern Valley Festival is held to celebrate the five of
the six bioregions that meet there. It is on major migration pathways and is able to sustain habitat for more than 300 bird species,
including up to 200 species that breed there. Bird walks, nature
games, nature photography workshops and moonlight nature walks
are part of the celebration. In April the orange-crowned warbler
and yellow-rump warbler can be spotted among the aspen groves
and underbrush of the area. Don't bother looking for the "crown"
on the orange-crown warbler. It's simply a small rusty streak and
you'll never see it unless you're looking down at the bird from
about three feet. For this year's dates, contact the Kern River Research Center, P. O. Box 990, Weldon, CA 93283; (619) 376-2629.

The gadwall, redhead, mallard and other ducks migrate through the **Silverwood Lake State Recreation Area** near Hesperia, where the west fork of the Mojave River is dammed up to form a reservoir. Great flocks of Canada geese often overwinter at the lake. It also hosts migrating least sandpipers, California gulls, Bonaparte's gulls, and an occasional Caspian tern. The area's marshes attract barn swallows who come here to breed. Call (619) 339-2303 for more information.

20

Spring at Its Bloomin' Best

In April the desert bursts into bloom with unrestrained exuberance and the state's mountains and valleys are covered with color. Precise timing and abundance depends on when and where winter rains fall—May and June also can be good months for some plants.

The term *wildflower*, meaning any naturally occurring plant that grows without cultivation, applies to a vast array of lovely growing things. Cactus flowers range from the palest translucent white to vivid, vibrant red, and wildflowers, bushes and trees do their best to assure visitors this month that wherever they turn there is something lovely to see.

Southern California's arid areas include the Mojave Desert and the Sonoran Desert, which also covers most of Baja California. The notion that desert is simply a large quantity of kitty litter is fantasy. The sands support one of the richest collections of plants and animals in the world and certainly some of the most interesting. Temperatures can dip well below freezing and soar as high as 120 degrees Fahrenheit, a range in which cacti as well as pine trees can flourish.

Everyone equates the desert with cactus, and with good reason. Perhaps the world's best example of water conservation, cacti have evolved to the point at which they no longer have leaves. Their spines protect fat green stems that store water between rains. When you look at one of the "armed" cacti such as a saguaro or senita, you'll notice pinched places on its appendages. This indicates a drought year, during which the plant pulled in its fleshy stem as it used its store of water. The "pleats" that make up the arms of many cacti are designed to expand as they store water during years of abundant rainfall. If cactus flowers look a bit like roses, it's because the two prickly plants are close relatives.

Along the Colorado River that forms California's border with Arizona, stately saguaro stand sentrylike on the horizon. California is

A prickly pear (beaver tail variety) in bloom. This cactus has no spines.

one of two states in which the saguaro grows. Its population is no-where near as great as in Arizona, where Saguaro National Monument near Tucson is a true forest of the "giants with arms," but there are certainly enough in California to provide good examples of the species. At maturity the saguaro can be massive and many-armed, reaching a height of more than 30 feet. Its first arms don't develop until it is close to a century old. Spectacular pale, waxy flowers appear on arms that are a year or two old, last just a few hours, then die.

Similar to the saguaro and also part of the Cereus family but not as common, the senita has arms that grow from a central base close to the ground. It blooms at night, producing huge 6-inch blossoms that are observable in early morning when bees snuggle deep into their fuzzy throats to emerge coated with pollen. They close by noon, never to reopen. If the bees, bats and moths have done their job, fruit will appear. When the fruit begins to blush (the birds will tell you when it's ripe), inside you'll find white fruit dotted with tiny black crunchy seeds similar to kiwi. Its flavor is bland and mild, rather like figs.

Short, fat and close to the ground, barrel cactus comes in many varieties. The one most common in the California desert is the compass barrel cactus, so called because of its tendency to lean to the south or southwest. Theories to explain this behavior are that it creates shade for itself by leaning into the sun, that its angle exposes its growing tip to the sun and that the north side grows faster, thus making it lean. Watch out for its main central spine that can make a nasty puncture wound. Its delicate blossoms are yellow or orange.

Flat, broad-leafed beavertail prickly pears are common in the desert as well as on dry slopes and in canyons. Their blossoms are reddish, with large petals and yellow hearts. Prickly pear fruit is considered so

A cholla cactus. It looks cuddly, but don't touch!

desirable that it is sold in some Southwestern food stores. Unlike its Arizona cousin, the beavertail prickly pear has no long, dangerous spines.

A cactus with a cuddly name, teddy-bear cholla, is anything but huggable. What appear to be gray, fuzzy covering are really spines much sharper than any needle. A relative, the jumping cholla, doesn't really jump (although many hikers beg to differ). Its spines are so loosely attached that when it is touched, no matter how lightly, spines immediately attach themselves to whatever has brushed by. This trait allows it to be propagated by the wind. Seeds blow off and take root nearby, so you often see cholla growing in a row. If you happen to brush against a cholla accidentally, take a fine pocket comb and gently comb your leg (where the spines most often get you) or your clothing. Don't try to pick them off or you'll end up with fingers and legs both in an aggravated condition.

One of the most common desert trees is the paloverde, its green trunk full of chlorophyll, which captures the sun's rays and processes them into sugars and starches even when it drops its leaves. In spring the tree is covered with tiny yellow flowers that form clouds of color.

Although they are not a cactus, yucca, or Our Lord's Candle, are particularly common in sandy areas below a canyon where cacti also thrive. From the heart of a cluster of sharp, pointed leaves a stalk rises as tall as 8 feet, bearing dozens of white and pale purple flowers that first appear in April and usually last into June. It is protected by law.

From March to May, paintbrush, or owl's clover, thrives in great masses in Southern California. Looking much like a thick painter's brush, clusters of flowers along a tall stem can be pale white melting into crimson at the top, and also may be a lovely purple. Paintbrush often is found growing among other wildflowers such as poppies and lupine. Sunshine, or gold-fields, is a small annual that often blankets open slopes beginning in March. Like a starburst, small flat leaves radiate out from a large yellow center.

Yellow-flowered creosote bushes once were a "desert drugstore" for Native Americans. Their distinctive smell, like railroad ties or burning electrical equipment, immediately identifies them. Lac, which occurs as a resin on branches, was used for mending pottery and fastening arrow points to shafts. The bush is easy to identify. Just rub its roundish leaves between your fingers and not only will you release the unmistakable creosote odor, but your fingers will be slightly greasy.

Hot Spots Pointing out wildflower hotspots is a bit iffy, especially for flowers that are annuals. They like sunny sites with little competition from other plants, but their growth depends on the whims of weather. Their seeds can lie dormant for decades until the precise amount of moisture and warmth coaxes them into bloom. So an area that one year was carpeted with color may remain dusty and barren for any number of succeeding years, until the weather gods once again cooperate. A good place to look is recently burned areas (see chapter 36). They are often best for dramatic flower displays because fire eliminates the grasses that compete with flowers for water. Perennials are more reliable but show varying degrees of enthusiasm depending on how the elements have treated them during their dormant periods.

The places listed here are likely to have flowers in April, and cacti will bloom into May and June, but it's always best to call ahead to be sure they're at their best.

An unlikely spot for desert flowers, but one that is eerily fascinating, is the **Imperial Sand Dunes Recreation Area** off CA Hwy 78 east of El Centro in Imperial County. Here a 40-mile-long system of sand dunes rises to heights of over 300 feet above the desert floor. It is thought they were formed from windblown beach sands of Lake Cahuilla, dry for more than half a century. Although off-road vehicle lovers have claimed a portion of the dunes as their own, other areas have been designated by the Bureau of Land Management as closed to all motorized vehicle use. Far from being lifeless, the dunes support an amazing amount of specialized plants and animals, including the colorful dune primrose and little yellow sand verbena. Looking a bit like a tall-stalked mushroom, the sandfoot is a parasitic plant that taps the roots of nearby desert shrubs for its food. It appears in the sand in the spring.

On **Catalina Island** off Southern California's coast, you'll find daisylike island ragwort growing on the island's damp eastern side. This species is found only on Catalina. The white clusters and gray foliage of the everlasting flower cover the island's hills beginning in early spring. A species of California poppy (see chapter 21) is hard to find, but you can look on the island's rocky seaside slopes for the small, four-petaled blooms. If spring rains have blessed the island, the tiny, rare woodland star will be growing in the damp canyons this month. Fragile and dainty, its tiny blossoms look like five-petaled celestial bodies. Only in the **Channel Islands** will you find a large 6- to 8-foot shrub called the wild apple. It is no relation to apples, but rather is named for its apple blossom–like, pale pink flower. Call Channel Islands National Park at (805) 658-5730 for more details. For information on getting to Catalina Island, call Catalina Express at (310) 519-1212.

The slopes and valleys within **Anza Borrego Desert State Park** (see chapter 27) range from an altitude of 15 feet to a high of

6,000 feet, giving this sprawling park a number of diverse habitats that support hundreds of blooming things. The show starts in late March and can continue through June. One attraction is the golden cholla, whose blooms actually appear as a pale green, surrounded by sharp spines. The large, 6-foot-high teddy-bear chollas are always crowd-pleasers. The crimson blossoms on the whiplike branches of the ocotillo, tiny yellow flowers on the green-bark paloverde tree, barrel cactus with vermilion crowns and pungent creosote are found in similar low-desert habitats.

Often intermingled with the cacti, little purple wild Canterbury bells bloom reliably from March through June. Orcutt asters with light purple petals and yellow centers sometimes carpet an entire area. Monkey flowers come in many varieties. The one in this park grows on bushes close to the ground and begins producing yellow-orange flowers as early as March. The small purple flowers of the verbena elongate after opening. To be notified two weeks in advance of expected peak wildflower dates, mail a self-addressed stamped postcard to Anza Borrego Desert State Park, P. O. Box 299, Borrego Springs, CA 92004. To get there, follow Hwy 22 (the road name changes to Palm Canyon Drive) through town half a mile to the visitors' center.

The only place to see giant saguaro in their natural state in California is along parts of the **Colorado River,** where a sprinkling of summer rains allows its seeds to germinate. Other portions of the California desert are too arid. From the little town of Earp, west of Parker, Arizona, a 12-mile strip of two-lane paved road called Parker Dam Road winds north to Parker Dam. The saguaro population is sparse but healthy. More saguaros dot the landscape further south, where CA Hwy 78 follows the Colorado River.

Saguaros that have been transplanted from Arizona, a practice allowed because of a loophole in Arizona state law, can be seen in the Palm Springs area at the Bighorn Golf Club. About 500 saguaros have been uprooted from Arizona and planted at the posh golf course. As with other native plants, it is illegal to remove saguaros from public lands in Arizona. But private-property owners are allowed to salvage and sell their saguaros with the proper permits. The law requires only that a "good-faith effort" be made to find in-state buyers before the plants can be sold out of state.

The **Carrizo Plain Natural Area,** 80 miles west of Bakersfield, has vast expanses of gold-fields, tidy tips and hillside daisies, all a rich, buttery yellow. Baby blue eyes, fennel, reddish-pink owl's clover, cream cups and patches of blue and white lupine also are abundant. Two flowers on the federally endangered list, the purplish California jewel flower that's part of the Mustard family and San Joaquin woolly threads, also grow in the area. The reserve is located in eastern San Luis Obispo County west of Bakersfield. Take Soda Lake Road south from Hwy 58, or north from Hwy 166.

Following winter rains, showy wildflowers bloom among the native bunchgrass, a rare plant community at the **Santa Rosa Plateau Preserve** near Temecula. Most common are blue dick, the tiny, pansylike Johnny jump-up, Mariposa lily, lupine (also occurring along roadsides because as a "disturbance plant" it thrives where earth has been turned), checkerbloom and shooting star. In late spring when water from the preserve's vernal pools is evaporating, their beds are often covered with colorful wildflowers. The reserve is located in Riverside County, about 40 miles south of the city of Riverside, along I-15 southwest of Murietta.

The Nature Conservancy's **Sand Ridge Preserve** on the southwest margin of the San Joaquin Valley is the only protected habitat for the rare and endangered Bakersfield cactus *(Opuntia treleasei)*. This beautiful plant, similar to a beavertail, has large shocking-pink blooms that appear in April and May. The cactus has a very limited distribution and in recent years has suffered loss of habitat because of development of the city of Bakersfield, 15 miles to the west. The sand ridge of the preserve winds along the northwest bank of Caliente Creek. The preserve is primitive, with no facilities. From Bakersfield take Hwy 58 through town 16 miles to Tower Line Road. Follow Tower Line Road south for 1.2 miles to a large road barrier and turn left. Continue 700 yards to a large red-and-white tower on the left, where you can park.

The Sand Ridge Preserve

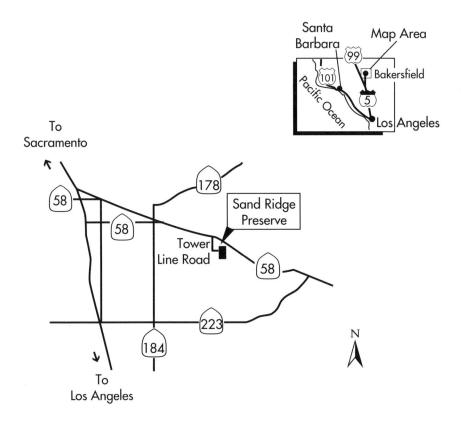

From there, walk south along the west base of the ridge where signs on fence posts identify the preserve.

In the Santa Monica Mountains about 25 miles north of Santa Monica, **Nicholas Flat** has unusually diversified wildflower viewing because four different plant communities come together there. Oak woodland, chaparral, grassland and coastal scrub all are represented. Look for yucca, lupine, purple nightshade, yarrow and sagebrush. From Pacific Coast Hwy 1 take CA Hwy 23 (Decker Road) about 2.5 miles. Bear left at the fork, then proceed 1 mile to a parking area and the beginning of a gentle trail to Nicholas Flat.

21

Proliferating Poppies Put On a Show

From mid-March to mid-May, along roadways north of Los Angeles, rippling fields of orange-golden blooms unfold in an annual spectacle that draws visitors from as far away as Japan and China.

California poppies *(Eschscholzia californica),* simple blossoms with just four silky petals and a maximum height of about 20 inches, carpet the hills in a breathtaking display of overachievement for so humble a plant. Their sheer mass is overwhelming. California's state flower, the poppy, similar to the Mexican poppy in Baja, unfurls in bright sunlight, then folds its petals inward in late afternoon as the sun disappears. This sleepyhead behavior caused the early Californians, from Spain, to nickname the prolific flower *dormidera,* meaning the "drowsy one." In some parts of the Midwest the poppies are called four o'clocks for the same reason. The California poppy is a relative of the opium poppy but lacks its heady narcotic effects.

On a weekend afternoon during peak bloom time, the area near Lancaster and Palmdale becomes a mass of cars snaking toward the Antelope Valley California Poppy Reserve, a state facility. Along I-5 north approaching Gorman, huge 18-wheelers, couples on motorcycles and cars crammed with parents and kids slow traffic to a crawl. But no one seems to mind, as the sheer overwhelming beauty inspires smiles that create a shared appreciation of the poppy-clad hills.

Visitors to the 1,700-acre poppy reserve, which is open mid-March through mid-May, can stroll among the flowers on five easy, well-marked hiking trails that total 8 miles, ranging individually from 1.2 to 1.7 miles. Some are paved to allow wheelchair access. Various viewpoints along the trails offer sweeping vistas of the San Gabriel and Tehachapi Mountains. Shaded tables invite picnicking. At the wind- and solar-powered interpretive center, rangers are on hand to answer questions, and poppy books, cards and paraphernalia are for sale. For more in-depth poppy appreciation, take time to view the wildflower video, then take a docent-led walking tour.

California poppies carpet the hills near Lancaster.

After its exuberant display, the poppy's polished petals begin to lose their intensity and fall away after pollination. An oval-shaped seedpod develops. As temperatures rise and summer nears, the seedpod ripens and dries, developing an audible rattle when shaken. In a last spurt of exhilaration the pod bursts open with a popping sound, scattering its seeds a good distance from the plant, thereby assuring another colorful season.

Many factors determine precisely when and how energetically the poppies will bloom each year. Ample sunshine seems assured in an area that boasts more than 300 sunny days per year. Rain is the prime motivator. Without its gentle nourishment the tiny black dots that are the poppy's seeds (yes, they do show up on poppyseed rolls, but from a different species) can succumb to the constant winds that blow over the high-desert hillocks.

Each year in late April the city of Lancaster celebrates the poppies with the California Poppy Festival. Entertainment, games and crafts are available, and during the festival it is possible to book a 20-minute helicopter ride over the blazing hills.

Although Southern California lays claim to the California poppy, the little flower flourishes as far north along the coast as Washington State, favoring open hillsides and grassy areas with its golden blossoms.

The Antelope Valley California Poppy Reserve

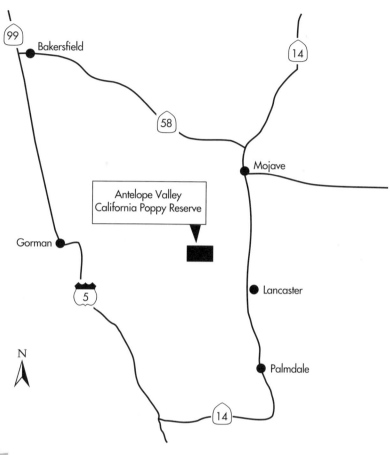

The **Antelope Valley California Poppy Reserve** near Lancaster in the Mojave Desert is about 13 miles west of CA Hwy 14 (the Antelope Valley Freeway). Drive west on Avenue I off Hwy 14. During the Poppy Festival held each April, shuttle buses pick up visitors at Lancaster City Park, 43011 North 10th Street West, in Lancaster. Call the reserve for precise dates, at (805) 724-1180.

The **Hungry Valley State Vehicular Recreation Area** hosts spring wildflower tours on weekends from the end of March through the beginning of June. The 19,000-acre recreational area is off I-5 at the Gorman exit. Signs direct visitors to the main gate.

In the northern part of the Los Padres National Forest, inland from Morro Bay, a mountain called **Cerro Alto** pokes 2,620 feet into the sky as part of San Luis Obispo County's coastal mountain range. In 1994 a devastating fire swept across the mountain, doing much damage. A consolation is that the fire stimulated the growth of wildflowers, which, depending on rainfall, have bounded back in abundance (see chapter 36). California poppies mingle with dainty white milkmaids and purple lupine. The mountain is off Hwy 41, 7.5 miles from Hwy 1 just north of Morro Bay. Call the Los Padres National Forest Santa Lucia District at (805) 925-9538 for more information.

The California poppy often grows with other wildflowers and may be spotted by its brilliant red-orange hue. Sharp-eyed nature lovers can see its elegantly simple blooms in many Southern California areas just by keeping a watchful eye. Call the Wildflower Hotline at (818) 768-3533 for current information on other Southern California wildflower sites.

22

The Desert Pupfish

It is able to withstand water temperatures of 100 degrees Fahrenheit and it can exist in water with salinity four times that of the ocean. The tiny desert pupfish *(Cyprinodon macularius)*, surviving in one of earth's least kindly environments, has adapted and endured for thousands of years. It is listed as endangered at both state and federal levels. Without a doubt it is one of the strangest aquatic creatures on earth.

During the Pleistocene epoch, huge lakes covered the area of Southern California that now is Death Valley. Remnants of that age, a few scattered patches of warm, salty water that dribble from splits in rocks to disappear into thirsty desert, are amazingly able to support the desert pupfish. When the Great Basin dried up 10,000 to 30,000 years ago, the little half-inch wigglers were left, not exactly high because Death Valley is 240 feet below sea level, but certainly dry. Today the Valley is home to five species of desert pupfish that exist in 20 separate populations.

One of their most interesting adaptive capabilities is that they can withstand temperature fluctuations of 70 degrees Fahrenheit, an important feature in a desert where scorching days give way to bone-chilling nights. They also can accommodate changing water salinity, a vital trait when evaporation leaves shallow trickles saltier than any ocean.

In March and April the tiny, 2-inch male pupfish turns a brilliant blue during spawning, driving off other males with animated movements and fierce behavior. They spawn furiously, engaging in jerky, stop-and-go antics that are exhausting simply to watch. Fifty years ago ichthyologist Carl L. Hubbs thought their antics looked playful, so he named them pupfish.

Hot Spots

In **Death Valley National Park,** pupfish spawn in Salt Creek. A wood boardwalk has been built over the stream for optimum viewing. The more flamboyant blue pupfish spawns at Saratoga Springs. The visitors' center is just south of Furnace Creek on CA Hwy 190. The Cottonball Marsh pupfish lives in the shallow,

99

California's Deserts

salt-encrusted pools of Cottonball Marsh south of Salt Creek and has developed into a subspecies because of its isolation from other desert pupfish. Although threatened in California, it lives in a designated wilderness area that will remain protected from future development. To get to Death Valley, take I-15 to Hwy 127 and travel north to Hwy 178. Turn west into the entrance.

You can see pupfish in the artificial pond habitat at **Anza Borrego Desert State Park** at the visitors' center. They also live in a pond along the Borrego Palm Canyon Trail. The park is just west of Borrego Springs. Follow Hwy 22 (the name changes to Palm Canyon Drive) through town 0.5 mile to the visitors' center.

The pleasant trail that winds through the fan palm oasis at the **Coachella Valley Preserve** passes through the last undisturbed watershed in the Coachella Valley. In this rare combination of desert and aquatic habitats there are shallow pools along the trail that contain the little pupfish. Among the fan palms at the Thousand Palms Oasis (in the center of the Coachella Valley Preserve) near Thousand Palms, pupfish are at home in cool pools. From Palm Springs take Ramon Road east to Thousand Palms Canyon Drive to the preserve entrance. At **Dos Palmas Oasis Preserve** near Indio, artesian water has helped revitalize the pupfish habitat and now supports a population that is active and viable. The preserve is 25 miles south of Indio via Hwy 111. Turn left on Parkside Drive, 1 mile to Desertaire Drive, and turn right to the entrance.

Near Palm Desert in the **Living Desert Botanical Garden and Wildlife Park** the desert pupfish is observable in a comfortably protected environment of palm oasis pools. Living Desert is 2 miles from Palm Desert, 1.5 miles south of Hwy 111 on Portola Avenue.

23

April Shorttakes

Window on the Desert

A first-class way to get a close-up look at the desert environment with very little effort is with a visit to the **Living Desert** near Palm Desert. It is in full bloom this month. The 1,200-acre interpretive center, cradled by the Santa Rosa Mountains, features botanical gardens that replicate North American deserts. An "after-sundown" exhibit of live native mammals and reptiles gives a glimpse of the desert's nocturnal activity. The museum is 2 miles from Palm Desert, 1.5 miles south of Hwy 111 on Portola Avenue.

Mockingbird Mania

If the mockingbirds in your neighborhood have turned into fighter pilots (shrieking, screaming kamikaze gray torpedoes), you know it's spring and the nesting season has begun. Never exactly mild-mannered, the talkative birds become screeching terrors that will attack anything that moves near their chicks. They'll even attack cats, their principal enemy, and win, driving a slinking tabby to the safe cover of a nearby oleander.

Known mostly for their skills in mimicry, they can imitate anything from another bird to a baby's cry to a cat's meow to a soprano's trill. One talented bird was even heard to duplicate the sequential blarings of a car alarm. Why? Some ornithologists believe it has to do with competition, with the alert gray birds vying for food, territories and mates through the extent of their repertoires.

Mockingbirds are family-oriented, with both parents sharing nest-building chores. They also share feeding duties, and may continue to feed their chicks for as long as a month after they've left the nest and are on the ground.

Mockingbirds thrive in an urban environment and are quite comfortable in human habitat. Their expanding population verifies their hardiness. In general they coexist happily with humans, but there are two schools of thought on their mellifluous song. From some the

Santa Monica Mountains Hiking Trails

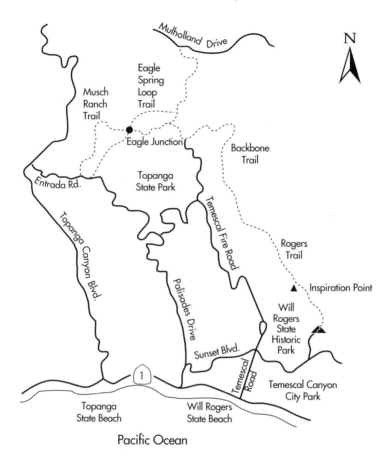

serenade elicits "ooohs" and "ahs" of appreciation. Others find it objectionable, especially when their proclivity to burst into song hours before dawn, a mockingbird specialty, becomes an unwelcome wake-up call.

In addition to its characteristic song, the northern mockingbird *(Mimus polyglottos)* can be identified by the large white patches on wings and tail, easy to see when it is in flight. Look for them almost anywhere in Southern California, especially in urban areas, along roadsides and on farms and ranches.

Along the Backbone Trail

Just an hour away from a metropolis of more than 10 million people, the **Backbone Trail** north of Los Angeles follows the ridge line of the

Santa Monica Mountains in relative isolation. When complete, it will total a rugged 65 miles. In the meantime, various stretches are at their best in April. Winter rains have had their effect, and wildflowers are beginning to emerge. A significant area of the trail burned in 1994, inspiring dramatic wildflower displays including the delicate blue blossoms of the phacelia. The California lilac, a large showy shrub, ranges from deep blue to lavender and light blue. Spring's burgeoning brush and plants also bring out mule deer that have become quite tame in this protected environment. Their presence, in turn, attracts coyotes and bobcats. Red-tailed hawks are easy to spot overhead, as are kestrels. The trailhead can be accessed from Will Rogers State Historic Park, 4.5 miles inland from the Pacific Coast Highway.

Orange Blossoms

The fabulous fragrance that permeates Riverside County and much of Southern California this month is orange blossoms. This is the month that oranges-to-be have their beginnings in aromatic white waxy blooms that cover citrus trees. (See chapter 10 for more information on oranges ready to harvest.)

24

A Closer Look:
State Fish—Golden Trout
and Garibaldi

Until 1996 the golden trout was the Golden State's sole and official finny symbol. Prized for its exceptional color—orange-red belly, deep olive back, lemon yellow sides—and attractive spotted markings, it is at home in the chilly rivers and streams of the southern Sierra Nevada. Two separate but similar species, the California golden trout *(Oncorhynchus aguabonita)* and the Volcano Creek golden trout *(Oncorhynchus roosevelti aguabonita)* are together considered the state fish. Both are listed as threatened at the federal level.

Trout are important measures of the environmental health of a stream because they flourish only where the water is the cleanest and clearest. Chemicals used in agriculture, logging that denudes stream banks and denies shade that keep waters cool, acids and chemicals used in old mines and development that allows rain to run off into streams without the purification process of filtering through soil all can spell death to trout.

The Department of Fish and Game (DFG) theorizes that the trout developed its colorful countenance to blend in with the red and orange rocks that commonly line mountain streams. It also is thought that because it lives in lakes and streams at altitudes above 6,000 feet, in some of the clearest waters anywhere, its bright colors help attract mates and scare off predators. Females excavate shallow depressions in creek bottoms in which they deposit their eggs.

The DFG stocks the Volcano Creek golden trout in many High Sierra lakes, much to the delight of serious anglers. Their usual mature size is 5 to 8 inches, but a 12-inch fish living in a lake rather than a stream is not unheard-of. The California record for a golden trout is believed to be 9 pounds, 14 ounces. Fingerlings are raised from eggs taken from Cottonwood Lake in Inyo County in Northern California and then used for stocking. Unfortunately, because the streams and lakes in which they live are so remote, few observers other than intrepid anglers ever glimpse the state's aquatic icon. But in the Cottonwood Creek area of the Sierra Nevada the fish is quite easily viewed during summer months. And in Sequoia and Kings Canyon National Parks the fish usually can be found in the Little Kern River.

Forty years ago rainbow trout were introduced into much of the golden trout's habitat, creating hybrid fish and endangering the golden's pure strain. With the establishment of the Golden Trout Wilderness in 1978, programs began to reclaim the golden's original home. The DFG has succeeded in removing many of the introduced fish and is undergoing a restocking program that is successfully returning pure stocks of golden trout to their original habitat.

It is a long trek to see the state fish in its natural surroundings. To get really close-up and personal with the colorful fish without braving the wilds, it is probably easier to make a trip to **Monterey Bay Aquarium** south of San Francisco, where a tankful of the graceful beauties dazzle onlookers alongside tanks that hold their saltwater brothers and sisters.

The glorious golden trout now shares its throne of distinction with the garibaldi, a longtime symbol of Southern California's spectacular underwater coastal beauty. As of January 1, 1996, the California legislature designated it the official state marine fish. Depending on your point of view, California either has two state fish, or it has one marine state fish and one freshwater state fish.

The garibaldi, named for the flamboyant crimson garb favored by nineteenth-century Italian General Guiseppe Garibaldi and his redshirts who are credited with unifying Italy, is a dazzling orange-red fish that has electric blue spots as a juvenile. The spots disappear when the fish is 6 to 8 inches long, on its way to becoming as big as 14 inches. It belongs to the Damsel family of fish, familiar to divers and snorkelers who frequent tropical waters. The garibaldi, however, prefers the chillier climes of the California coast and can be found from Monterey Bay south to Baja. It is particularly fond of the rocky crevices and kelp forests surrounding **Catalina Island** 26 miles off the coast of Los Angeles (see chapter 54 for more information on Catalina).

The fish's brilliant color has made it popular with aquarium aficionados, which is what spurred its inclusion as a state fish and also provides for a three-year ban on its commercial collection. It has been protected from sportfishing for more than half a century, although commercial divers with a marine aquarium collector permit could catch them, provided that they submitted a catch record to the DFG of the number of fish taken. Sport divers who frequent Catalina waters reported a noticeable decline in its numbers, and surmised that dealers in aquarium stock were netting substantial numbers of the flame-colored fish beyond what was reported. Marine biologists note that garibaldi require many breeding cycles to recover once they are removed from a reef.

Other than donning scuba gear (see chapter 48), the easiest way to spot a garibaldi is to stroll the green Pleasure Pier on Catalina Island. You'll spot their flashes of color among the rocks that support the pier. From Catalina you also can take a glass-bottomed boat tour (see Appendix) for guaranteed close-up views of the fish that some have called the "butterfly of the ocean."

May

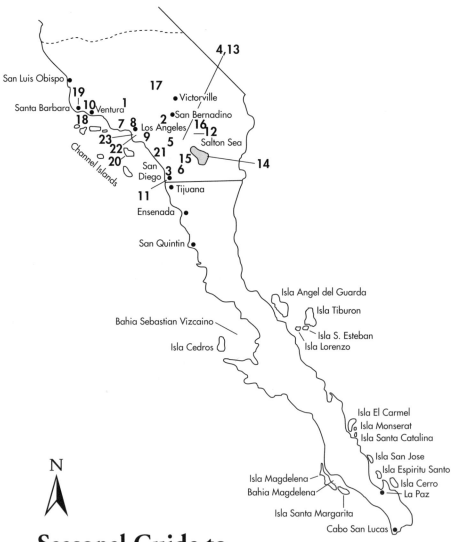

4,13

San Luis Obispo

17

19

Santa Barbara
10
Ventura
1

18

San Bernadino
Victorville

2
7
8
Los Angeles
16
12

23
9
5
Salton Sea

22
21

20

15

14

San Diego
3
6

11
Tijuana

Channel Islands

Ensenada

San Quintin

Isla Angel del Guarda

Isla Tiburon

Bahia Sebastian Vizcaino
Isla S. Esteban

Isla Cedros
Isla Lorenzo

Isla El Carmel

Isla Monserat

Isla Santa Catalina

Isla San Jose

Isla Espiritu Santo

Isla Magdelena
Isla Cerro

Bahia Magdelena
La Paz

Isla Santa Margarita

Cabo San Lucas

N

Seasonal Guide to
the Natural Year

Site Locator Map

LIST OF SITES
May

1. Pine Mountain and Mount Pinos
2. Idyllwild County Park
3. Torrey Pines State Reserve
4. Mount San Jacinto State Park
5. Silverwood Lake State Recreation Area
6. Cuyamaca Rancho State Park
7. Malibu Lagoon, Malibu
8. Rancho Santa Ana Botanic Gardens
9. Tucker Wildlife Sanctuary
10. Camino Real Park
11. Cabrillo National Monument
12. Joshua Tree National Park
13. Coachella Valley Preserve, Indian Canyons
14. Dos Palmas Oasis Preserve
15. Anza Borrego Desert State Park
16. Big Morongo Canyon Preserve
17. Desert Tortoise Natural Area
18. Ventura (Santa Clara Estuary Natural Preserve), Oxnard
19. Santa Barbara Botanic Garden, Nipomo Dunes Preserve
20. Catalina Island
21. Upper Newport Bay Ecological Reserve, Bolsa Chica Ecological Preserve
22. Venice Beach, Marina Del Rey, Ballona Lagoon
23. Terminal Island

Notes

25

Birding Among the Pines

May is a good birding month among the tall pines because of the great number of species that can be observed. Winter birds may be lingering, summer residents have begun to arrive and migratory birds may be passing through.

Don't overlook your own backyard as a source for exciting sightings. Attracting birds can be as easy as supplying the right type of food and habitat. Sunflower seeds, especially the black-oil type, will lure the greatest variety. They are a high-energy food, and the black-oil type is easier for small birds to crack than are the bigger, striped sunflower seeds.

Doves love milo and millet, which often are the primary component of commercial seed mixes offered in Southern California. Jays and quail like dried, whole-kernel corn. You also can save seeds from squash and melon, air-dry them, then put them in feeders. Insect-eating birds like woodpeckers and nuthatches are attracted to suet and peanut butter. At higher elevations in Southern California, where it gets quite cold, these are good wintertime choices. Don't put them out in the summer because they quickly turn rancid. If you put out fruit you may attract bluebirds and mockingbirds.

Birds' habitat isn't tidily trimmed and mowed. The less manicured you leave your yard, the more birds it will attract simply because it is more like their natural home. Some plants become a source for nesting materials; others furnish shelter and nesting sites. Others, such as black-eyed Susans, daisies and sunflowers, provide seed, and still others attract the insects that become meals for birds. You can plant trumpet vine and honeysuckle to attract hummingbirds and goldenrod to please goldfinches, juncos and sparrows. If you have space for a thicket of raspberries and blackberries, you'll be providing shelter for sparrows and food for grosbeaks, orioles and woodpeckers.

The **Pine Mountain** and **Mount Pinos** areas harbor an abundance of pine siskins, scrub jays, chickadees, nuthatches, Clark's nutcrackers and even a mountain bluebird or two. At higher elevations you'll see soaring golden eagles and other raptors. Take I-5 north from Los Angeles about 50 miles to the Frazier Park exit. Turn left, through Frazier Park, to the forest.

At **Idyllwild County Park** the visitors' center supplies trail maps for an easy half-mile or 2-mile loop that wanders through a second-growth yellow pine forest mixed with black oak, incense cedar and the sun-loving manzanita. It provides habitat for three easy-to-spot bright-blue jays—pinyon, scrub and Steller's—as well as half a dozen woodpeckers, including the uncommon Nuttall's. The white-headed woodpecker is often the most-seen bird. Flycatchers and gnatcatchers flit among the pines in abundance, and red-tailed and Cooper's hawks hover above rocky ledges. The lilting song of the hermit thrush is commonly heard. It's a pleasant way to spend a day in cool pine country. From Hwy 74 in Riverside County, take Hwy 243 north to Rivco Playground Road and park at the campground. Hike the campground trail (clearly marked) a few minutes to the visitors' center.

Although not typically equated with whispering pines, **Torrey Pines State Reserve** just north of La Jolla offers interesting birding in the state's smallest pine forest. Don't be fooled when you look into the distance toward Torrey Pines State Beach and glimpse what appears to be very large birds chasing small birds. Get out your binoculars and you'll see that the large birds are wearing goggles. Aficionados of hang-gliding and those with radio-controlled minigliders love this area for the updrafts that develop off the 100-foot cliffs above the beach. Glider pilots report that interaction with the hawks, eagles and other raptors that live in the area can be a bit dicey. The birds are very territorial during mating season and are not a bit shy about attacking a glider many times their size. Glider pilots also report dogfights with seagulls that apparently perceive the little planes as a threat. However, some pilots like the birds, because the birds know where to catch the best updrafts. To reach the reserve, exit I-5 at Carmel Valley Road and head west. At Camino Del Mar, turn left. Drive along the beach for about 1 mile, then head right uphill to Torrey Pines.

Wear a jacket for birding in **Mount San Jacinto State Park** near Palm Springs. Take the tram up to 6,000 feet above the desert floor, where you'll see traces of snow even in May. Look for Cassin's finch, mountain quail and other mountain birds. A bird list is available at the information center and small museum on the lower level of the tram building. From the north edge of Palm Springs take Tramway Road off CA Hwy 111 for about 3.5 miles up the hill to the park entrance.

Silverwood Lake State Recreation Area in the San Bernardino Mountains centers around 976-acre Sherwood Lake that has 13 miles of shoreline. At an elevation of 3,378 feet, it is surrounded by forest that includes Ponderosa pine, big-cone Douglas fir and incense cedar. On the southeast side of the lake near Miller Canyon look for juncos, mountain chickadees and Steller's jays. Acorn woodpeckers and western bluebirds are common among the black oaks. In chaparral areas northeast of the lake, scrub oak and manzanita at lower elevations provide a home for brown and rufous-sided towhees, California thrashers, wrentits and mountain and California quail. It's a pleasant birding area with facilities, about two hours southeast of Los Angeles. Take I-15 from the city of San Bernardino to winding CA Hwy 138, turn left and proceed to the recreation area.

Magnificent stands of coulter, sugar, ponderosa and Jeffrey pine as well as cedar and oak in **Cuyamaca Rancho State Park** in San Diego County on Hwy 79 draw more than 100 species of birds that either live there permanently or migrate through. Birds of prey include red-shouldered hawks, golden eagles, acorn and white-headed woodpeckers, Steller's jays, white-breasted nuthatches and migratory songbirds. Take Hwy 8 east 40 miles from San Diego to Hwy 79 and go north 4 miles to the park entrance.

26

Hummingbirds:
Nature's Iridescent Jewels

Their movements are so swift and precise they look computerized. Their colors are as brilliant as precious gems, displaying jewel-like iridescence that seems to come and go depending on the source of light and the angle from which you view them. They'll attack a bird many times their size and can beat their wings at more than 80 flutters per second. They can fly sideways and backwards, hover in place and execute amazing aerobatic displays that are the envy of pilots everywhere. Since ancient times hummingbirds have fascinated people, and with good reason.

During the Victorian era hundreds of thousands of the tiny, colorful birds were killed and stuffed to adorn women's hats. Fortunately the whims of fashion changed and protective legislation was put in place, so successive generations of hummingbirds were spared further devastating indignities.

Most of the world's 300-plus species of hummingbirds are concentrated near the equator. But at least eight species have been spotted in California and Baja. Adaptable birds, hummers can survive happily in the tropics, high-altitude forests, coastal areas and deserts.

You may sometimes see them repeatedly hovering and darting. This is feeding behavior. They are going after insects that probably are too tiny for you to see, straining gnats and white flies from the air as they circle.

Hummers are not just flights of fancy. They have a special job in nature. In many areas they are considered essential as pollinators. When feeding, they draw nectar from various blossoms with their long, slender bills. In the process their heads and bills become dusted with pollen from protruding stamen, which they inadvertently brush on the next blossom they visit. Usurping what many people think to be the exclusive province of bees, hummingbirds therefore can take over pollinating tasks for many lovely flowers. Hummingbirds are responsible for the blooms on the rich, red claret cup hedgehog cactus of southeastern California, as well as the red, tubular flowers of the hummingbird trumpet. They also pollinate the scarlet creeper, skyrocket, betony and scarlet penstemon.

With a body weight of 2 grams, a hummingbird that lives in Cuba is among the smallest vertebrates known. The largest hummer is native to the Andes and is 8.5 inches long. Those observed in California are usually between 3 and 4 inches long. If you can imagine the sound made by Woodstock, the bird in the "Peanuts" comic strip, you'll recognize the high-pitched squeaks of a hummingbird.

Costa's hummingbird can be identified by its violet-purple crown and long side feathers. It is a year-round resident of Baja California but may spend summers in California, arriving from Mexico as early as February, moving north as the weather warms. The rufous hummingbird spends summers in Washington, Oregon and Canada, passing through California on the way to Baja California and mainland Mexico to winter. Its head is noniridescent and it has a white tummy. The black-chinned hummer visits California's coastal areas April through August and also is at home along the Colorado River that borders Arizona. The tiny calliope, at 2.5 to 4 inches in length the smallest hummingbird normally found in the United States, visits the higher mountain areas during May, June and July, and the rufous hummingbird can be spotted in both coastal and mountainous areas throughout the summer. Allen's hummingbird is abundant and easy to spot from March through July in coastal areas.

If you see a hummingbird in California in midwinter, it will most likely be an Anna's. It is the most abundant California species, easily spotted along coastal areas and northern Baja all year. It is the only hummingbird in the United States with a red crown.

It's not true that hummingbirds hum because they don't know the words. Their hum is produced by their wings, with each species having its own particular note. Some ornithologists believe these distinctive wingbeat sound pitches may help the tiny creatures communicate.

Hummers are found in many habitats, from coastal areas to the desert. They're equally at home in an urban garden and a remote woodland.

North of Los Angeles, 1.5 miles east of Malibu Canyon Road on Pacific Coast Highway 1 and just a few blocks west of the Malibu Pier, **Malibu Lagoon** is an important stop for birds navigating up and down the Pacific Flyway. From Pacific Coast Highway, turn left on Cross Creek Road just after the creek, where there is public parking. Stroll around to the shrubby area on the lagoon's east side to see Allen's hummingbirds that are permanent residents. The 3.5-inch Allen's has a bright red throat and iridescent green back.

In Claremont, at **Rancho Santa Ana Botanic Gardens,** three species of hummingbirds are permanent residents. Anna's like the mesa area of the 86-acre garden, Costa's nest in the cactus garden, and the black-chinned hummers pretty much rove all over. In addition, many migrant hummingbirds pass through during spring months. Audubon Society members conduct bird walks through the garden every Sunday morning at 8 A.M. From I-10 take Indian Hill Boulevard north to Foothill. Turn right to College Avenue and the garden is just to the north.

Santiago Canyon Road (CA Hwy 18) south of Santa Ana winds through some prime birding areas. If you bear left on Modjeska Canyon Road you'll come to **Tucker Wildlife Sanctuary,** a private refuge that is affiliated with California State University at Fullerton and is a prime observation area for large numbers of hummingbirds. In April and May Costa's and black-chinned are found on the surrounding slopes as they pause on their migration north. Anna's are in residence the year-round. Allen's are common, and an occasional calliope will sometimes stray off course and end up at the sanctuary for a day or two. North of Los Angeles, in **Camino Real Park** in Ventura you'll find Allen's hummingbirds almost all the time. From Hwy 101 take the Main Street off-ramp to Mills Road. Go north to Dean Drive and the park is to the right. If hummers aren't plentiful on the day you visit, you won't be disappointed because the number of migrants you'll find there in spring and fall is enormous.

Coastal sage scrub and wooded thickets near the visitor center at **Cabrillo National Monument** in San Diego provide habitat for several hummingbird species. As long as you're there, wander toward the water to see black turnstones, surfbirds and Brandt's and pelagic cormorants.

At **Idyllwild County Park** Anna's hummingbirds are commonly seen residents the year around, and the calliope is common in summer. Passing through on migration are Allen's, black-chinned, Costa's and rufous. From Hwy 74 in Riverside County, take Hwy 243 north to Rivco Playground Road and park at the campground.

Endemic to Baja California is Xantu's (black-fronted) hummingbird, with a green throat, cinnamon belly and white stripe behind the eye. They are quite common along the peninsula once you get away from towns. If you're going to a resort city such as Cabo San Lucas, rent a jeep for half a day, bounce around the surrounding desert, and sightings are almost guaranteed. Costa's also prefers Baja's arid climate and is a year-round resident.

If you possibly can slip over to southern Arizona near Sierra Vista, **Ramsey Canyon Preserve** is perhaps the nation's consummate hummingbird-watching site. More than 14 species congregate there from spring until early autumn. April and May are prime months. This cool green gorge in the Huachuca Mountains is managed by the Nature Conservancy and has six creekside cabins for which reservations must be made. Contact Ramsey Canyon Preserve, 27 Ramsey Canyon Road, Hereford, AZ 85615; (520) 378-2785 for information.

27

Desert Oases

Lawrence of Arabia gallops dashingly toward the skeletal desert outcasts as they crawl their way across blazing sands to find life-giving waters. Exotic beauties recline on silken robes underneath gently waving palms. That's what an oasis is, at least to Hollywood.

In reality an oasis is a small fertile or green area in a desert, usually with a spring or well. The deserts of Southern California have a number of lovely examples, certainly as picturesque and refreshing as any Lawrence might have encountered, minus the camels. Spring is a particularly good time to visit an oasis because wildlife activity is high. Migrating birds are passing through, resident birds are breeding and wildflowers are in bloom.

The palms at oases provide a dense canopy that shades vegetation growing at the edges of pools or in earth kept damp by water seeping from underground. Because these skirted, swaying sentries often grow to a height of 75 feet, they are visible from miles away. Besides sheltering humans from the desert heat, they are a rich haven for wildlife. The hooded oriole weaves his nest from palm fibers, suspending it to hang freely from the underside of a frond like a natural, breeze-rocked cradle. Maidenhair fern, the little California tree frog, the red-spotted toad, the delicate Venus hair fern and much more depend on the cool, damp habitat for survival.

For years naturalists were puzzled at how the palms came to grow in such diverse locations. Growing conditions in oases are ideal for the stately trees, but how were the first ones planted? Studies of wildlife found that birds and small mammals do not ingest the seeds, so they could not be credited with dispersal. But then a coyote was observed eating the marble-sized palm fruit, and the problem was solved. In fact, it has been documented that seeds that have passed through a coyote will germinate twice as often as "un-coyoted" seeds.

Human interference in the delicate natural balance of oases has created complicated problems. The years since the mid-1950s have

Hikers enjoy shady Palm Canyon near Palm Springs.

been particularly short on rainfall, and in many areas heavy pumping from underground wells has lowered the water table. Palms can send roots that extend just 20 feet. If a permanent water supply is not available, they will die.

The availability of water at an oasis often can be credited to the same geologic faults that cause devastating earthquakes. The fracturing of underlying bedrock material creates a barrier to water flowing underground from a higher elevation. This forces water to the surface to create a unique aquatic environment. It also means that an oasis may sit directly on top of an exceptionally active earthquake fault.

Caution: Do not drink the water at oases. Usually it is not potable. Remember that you are in the desert, and be sure you have plenty of water with you when you set out.

Hot Spots Within **Joshua Tree National Park** are five places where native California fan palms flourish in dignified grandeur. A 4-mile trail through canyons and washes leads to Lost Palms Oasis, one of the most beautiful. The hike (not for beginners) leads through a deep canyon to a stand of more than 100 California fan palms surrounded by majestic walls of quartz monzonite. The palms are sustained by an underground spring. At one time there was sufficient water from the spring to create a series of permanent, still pools. But in the last few years there has been little surface water. What moisture remains is sufficient for the health of the palms and other vegetation, and the oasis is still a cool, pleasant place for a respite after the hike.

Adjacent to Lost Palms Canyon in an upper canyon is a smaller group of palms, not considered a separate oasis, called Dike Springs. Although unspectacular by comparison with Lost Palms, it can add a little extra challenge to what most view as an already tough hike.

Nearby, in Munsen Canyon Oasis, water comes close to the surface but does not quite break through. Small palm groves line the canyon bottom for several miles. The Oasis of Mara and Fortynine Palms Oasis are the northernmost stands of native fan palms in this hemisphere. They would easily succumb to the frequent frosts further north. At Fortynine Palms water pools at the surface, providing increased habitat for amphibians and water dwellers. The blackened trunks of the trees here tell of three fires in the last half-decade. It once was the habit of Indians to burn oases periodically in religious rituals, which also got rid of undergrowth and stimulated seed production (see chapter 36). Because the bud from which palms grow is protected deep in the tip of the stem, fires of moderate heat do no permanent harm and in fact perform a service to the tree by burning away dead leaves from the trunk. The recent fires are of unknown origin and have done no lasting damage.

The fifth and southernmost oasis in Joshua Tree National Park is Cottonwood Spring Oasis, the only one that is man-made. Near the turn of the last century, Cottonwood Spring gushed thousands of gallons each day. Homesteaders planted the palms and the cottonwoods that give the oasis its name near the natural spring. Through the years the spring slowed to a trickle, until nature intervened with the 1971 San Fernando earthquake. The spring's output immediately jumped to 30 gallons per hour, perhaps one of the few fortuitous effects of the quake. Unfortunately, this is also the only oasis of the five that is not holding its own. Although still beautiful, several trees have died of unknown causes, and few new trees have sprung up to replace them.

Joshua Tree National Park is about an hour's drive from Palm Springs. Take I-10 north to Hwy 62 to the town of Joshua Tree. Turn south on Park Boulevard to the Oasis Visitors' Center. By taking I-10 south, you can reach the Cottonwood Visitors' Center for access to the park.

A waterfall in Palm Canyon Desert Oasis.

A rare combination of desert and aquatic habitat, palm oasis woodland, is found in a number of cool groves within the **Coachella Valley Preserve** in Riverside County, north of I-10 about 10 miles east of Palm Springs off the Ramon exit. Thousand Palms Oasis, in the center of the preserve, has the state's second largest grove of *Washingtonia filifera,* the only palm native to the North American continent. Here, it is the San Andreas Fault (see chapter 18), straddled by the preserve, that is responsible for the faulting and fracturing that have created this oasis.

North America's largest group of natural *Washingtonia filifera* is hidden away amid the lush greenery of the **Indian Canyons** (Andreas, Murray and Palm Canyons), which were home to the Agua Caliente Indians for decades and are still owned by the tribe. Years ago they helped provide food, medicine, housing and, of course, a reliable water source for the Indians, who were hunter-gatherers. You'll immediately notice that the palms here have smudged and darkened bark that tells of past burnings. The Indians deliberately set occasional fire to the trees' "skirts," the dead fronds that droop and cluster immediately under the green, living fronds. This increases production of the tiny, grape-size dates that grow on these trees and reduces the habitat of spiders and lizards that would drop unannounced into the Indians' living quarters below. These decades-old burnings have not harmed the trees but have ultimately made them more productive.

Palm Canyon is a spectacularly beautiful gorge lined with 200-year-old palms and other flora growing along a flowing stream that is a sharp contrast to the arid desert just beyond. A paved footpath winds into the canyon for easy access to strolling and picnicking. In Andreas Canyon, more than 150 species of plants within a half-mile radius create a cool, still environment even during the heat of summer. Along Andreas Creek, look for the bedrock mortars and metates used centuries ago for preparing food. Birdwatching is excellent here. Murray Canyon is an easy hike south from Andreas Canyon. Watch for peninsula bighorn sheep and wild ponies that still roam the high ground above the canyon. The endangered least Bell's vireo commonly nests here.

Entrance to Tahquitz Canyon is restricted by the Cahuilla tribe, but with a permit it is possible to roam the magnificent waterfalls and pools of this flourishing oasis. There is an admission fee to all the Indian Canyons. Guided jeep tours can be arranged through Desert Jeep Tours, (619) 324-5337. For admission to restricted areas, contact the Cahuilla Tribal Council Office, 960 E. Tahquitz Canyon Way, Palm Springs, CA 92262; (619) 325-5673.

Much of the Palm Springs area near Indian Canyons is covered with commercial date palms (see chapter 49). Irrigation has made it possible for them to flourish in tidy rows without the support of a natural oasis. The ancestors of these sturdy trees were imported from the Far East and planted by the Department of Agriculture in the late 1800s.

Located about 50 miles from Palm Springs, northeast of the Salton Sea at the base of the Orocopia Mountains on the Riverside-Imperial county line, the **Dos Palmas Oasis Preserve** is a low-desert (as much as 120 feet below sea level) habitat of small hills and sand dunes. Streams fed by faults form the Salt Creek watershed that drains into the Salton Sea. Fan palms and Orocopia sage *(Salvia greatai)*, which is on the federal list of endangered species, are among the interesting flora. It's a favorite resting spot for migrating birds.

At the end of Borrego Palm Canyon Trail in **Anza Borrego Desert State Park,** the cool oasis is a welcome relief after a 40-minute trek through the desert. The 3-mile round-trip walk is pleasant and easy, with placards along the way coordinating with a self-guided trail map available at the trailhead. Park staff and volunteer naturalists do frequent oasis hikes. Look for tiny darting lizards, noisy blue scrub jays, hummingbirds and perhaps a covey of soft, round California quail. Scan the ridges and rocky slopes for a glimpse of bighorn sheep (see chapter 46). Stop at the visitors' center for a brief slide presentation on what the oasis and surrounding desert has to offer. Visual exhibits explain the rocky, layered, earthquake-rocked terrain that has helped create the oasis. The park is just west of the city of Borrego Springs. Follow Hwy 22 (the name changes to Palm Canyon Drive) through town 0.5 mile to the visitors' center.

Other examples of oases exist in **Big Morongo Canyon Preserve,** where snowmelt from nearby San Gorgonio Mountains bubbles to the surface as a result of uplifting caused by the Little San Bernardino Mountain Fault. Almost 100 acres are classified as cottonwood willow riparian woodland. A stream ribbons through Upper Big Morongo Canyon and flows for almost 2 miles before disappearing into the sandy soil. Boardwalks and benches provide pleasant places to enjoy the oasis, even on summer's hottest days. The preserve is in San Bernardino County, off Hwy 62 at the northeast end of the business district of the town of Morongo Valley. Turn right on East Drive, then left after 200 yards to go into the preserve.

28

Slow and on the Go: The Desert Tortoise

In sharp contrast to the freeway-frenzied, life-in-the-fast-lane, Type-A personality that has come to characterize Southern California, the desert tortoise *(Gopherus agassizii)* the official state reptile, takes things at a more leisurely pace. Everyone knows that the steady-going tortoise always beats the hare, but today it is in another sort of contest, a race for survival. Its numbers have dwindled to the point that it has been placed on the federal list of threatened species.

Desert tortoises, the largest reptilian herbivores in the state, were around during the dinosaur days 67 million years ago. But while the larger creatures succumbed to a changing environment, the clever tortoises survived. Their ability to go long periods without water or food and to withstand the heat and the cold of the desert has helped them endure.

They live in the West Mojave Desert, and the best times for sightings are early morning or late afternoon during the spring from mid-March through mid-June, when they emerge from six months of hibernation to feed. These reptiles may hibernate for as long as nine months each year. They usually stay quite close to their burrows, so best bets for sightings rely on finding their holes or asking a resident ranger where to look.

Another indicator that the lumbering reptiles are in the area may be the growth of yellow wildflowers. Although no hard scientific evidence exists to verify that golden blooms especially attract tortoises, observers point out that sightings often occur as the creatures munch contentedly on desert wildflowers, seemingly preferring the amber to the azure. Grasses and leaves also are favored delicacies.

Just 2 inches long at birth, a male tortoise can grow to be longer than 1 foot at maturity. In the wild a natural lifespan is 60 to 100

126

years, or even older. They can completely draw their elephantlike legs and feet inside their shells so that enemies have only rough scales and a hard shell left to attack.

The vast Mojave, covering more than 15,000 square miles, at one time supported a desert tortoise population of 2,000 of the shelled reptiles per square mile. Today its numbers have dwindled to a fraction of that. According to the Bureau of Land Management, there may be no more than one tortoise every 2.5 acres, and densities of one tortoise every 100 acres are far more common.

From ancient times the tortoise has managed to adapt and adjust, until the last century when competition with man's encroachment took a serious toll. Off-road vehicles and grazing animals crush their burrows, and they die from the desert heat before they can dig new ones. Development robs their habitat, and some are shot simply for sport. They are just too slow to be able to find enough food when grazing cattle strip their desert habitat of vegetation. A turtle's shell, its only defense, can protect it against fire, predators, drought and extreme heat. But it cannot protect against a 2-ton vehicle or a bullet.

A secondary scourge plaguing the tortoises are ravens. Scavengers by nature, the birds have been lured in great numbers to the desert to thrive on the garbage that visitors strew across the Mojave's once-pristine dunes. Turtle eggs are laid in a small hole dug by the female, with hatchlings appearing in about 70 to 120 days. Young tortoises are easy prey for the swift birds, and in some areas virtually all hatchlings are devoured within hours of birth.

Additionally, genetic factors work against the creatures when it comes to replacing their numbers. Although the hardy reptiles can live to 100 years, they don't attain sexual maturity with the ability to breed until they are 15 or 20 years old. These early years can be the most critical in terms of survival.

The imperiled survivors are getting help from a number of quarters. In 1971 the U.S. Bureau of Land Management established a 38-square-mile desert tortoise sanctuary near California City. Within its fenced boundaries the tortoises are doing well.

And in October 1994 Congress passed the controversial California Desert Protection Act that transferred the East Mojave National

Desert Tortoise Natural Area

Scenic Area from the Bureau of Land Management to the National Park Service. This established the new Mojave National Preserve. Implementation of protective measures continues to be a bone of contention between environmentalists and those who would bring their off-road vehicles to the desert.

But even in their own protected environment the hard-shelled survivors succumb to man-made influences. Thinking that they are doing their pets a favor by returning them to the wild, people release captive tortoises in the natural area. This introduces a difficult-to-cure upper respiratory condition that spreads rapidly among the wild tortoise population.

However, positive influences may yet prevail. The plight of the plucky reptiles could have a happy ending, if public awareness increases and if the little creatures themselves can withstand man-made perils until their environment can be once again made safe.

Hot Spots

Although the entire Mojave Desert is home to the desert tortoise, with the guidance of a ranger they are easiest to spot in the **Desert Tortoise Natural Area.** From CA Hwy 14 (Antelope Valley Freeway), 5 miles north of the town of Mojave, exit on California City Boulevard. Through California City, about 10 miles east, turn left on 20 Mule Team Parkway. Within 1.5 miles turn left onto Randsburg-Mojave Road. The Desert Tortoise Natural Area is not quite 5 miles further on a graded dirt road.

Walking trails crisscross the preserve, inviting leisurely exploration. Pick up trail guides in boxes at trailheads. Along the Animal Loop Trail, marked placards point out an old tortoise burrow, tortoise bones, shells of hatchlings killed by predators and possibly a tortoise itself. Other trails include the 0.5-mile animal habitat loop and plant loop trails.

With a great deal of patience you may be able to spot tortoises anywhere in the desert, if you get up early and walk slowly among the vegetation. Their favorite places are at the base of bushes and scrubs just outside their burrows, which in spring or summer are just a few inches under the surface and range from 18 inches to 5 feet long. When the temperature is 100 degrees Fahrenheit on the surface, a tortoise burrow may have a temperature of 75 degrees or less. Tortoises usually have a "neighborhood" that they stay within, sometimes no more than 150 feet from their burrow. Older, bolder tortoises have been known to travel almost 1 mile from home in a single day.

Because they move slowly and deliberately, there is no flash of movement to catch the eye. And their neutral shell color blends perfectly with the rocks and boulders of the desert. More than one visitor has extended a hand to a foot-long boulder, only to have it walk away under his touch. But if you spot one and sit very quietly 10 or 20 yards away, you could be lucky enough to see a female digging a nest for her eggs in late spring or a tortoise munching the leaves of a pretty wildflower.

29

May Shorttakes

Strawberry Fields Forever

This is the month when delicious, sweet strawberries are ripe for picking in the vast fields of **Oxnard** and **Ventura,** in Ventura County, about an hour north of Los Angeles. This close to the Pacific coast, a serendipitous merging of amiable climate, rich soil and morning fog helps keep the plump berries from ripening too quickly, producing outstanding crops. Visitors come to purchase just-picked berries for shortcake, to top cereal, and to simmer gently into delicious jams. More than 5,000 acres of the low-to-the-ground plants supply strawberries that are shipped worldwide. California produces 75 percent of the country's strawberry crop. For years the most popular berry was the Chandler, reliably sweet and firm. But in the last few years its widespread cultivation has been displaced by a new hybrid called Camarosa. Large-scale grocers love them because they are large, grow abundantly, and stay firm from the time they are picked until they finally end up in a supermarket. The downside is that consumers say they lack taste and have an unpleasant crunchiness that belongs in apples, not strawberries. If you go to Ventura County for strawberries, look for roadside stands (there are many) or farmers' markets. Ask for strawberry varieties like Oso Grande, Chandler, Seascape, Douglas or Sequoia. If you find them, they will be freshly picked, reliably sweet and flavorful, and sold locally only because they do not withstand shipping. Take the Ventura Freeway 101 or PCH 1 north to Oxnard.

Santa Barbara Botanic Garden

Among more than 65 acres that include 5 miles of creekside canyon paths and flowering meadows are some of the state's most interesting native flowers and plants, all decked out for visitors this month. Apache plume, white meadow-foam, scarlet bugler, lupine and blue lobelia are among the favorites. Garden docents help you get acquainted with their charges. The garden is 1.5 miles north of the Santa Barbara Mission. Take Mission Canyon Road toward the mountains from the Mission. Jog right on Foothill (Hwy 192), then left to rejoin Mission Canyon, bearing right at the fork. Half a mile up on your left you'll see the entrance.

California Quail

This small, plump bird with a short black plume that curves forward is the California state bird, whose range extends into most of Baja. Its habitat is mainly chaparral, coastal areas and woodland edges where it scoots along the ground, but in recent years it often is seen bobbing among the plants and trees of urban parks. In some areas where new construction has intruded on habitat, it visits backyards, sometimes feeding on seeds that fall from bird feeders. When spring warms the ground sufficiently for nesting, it's just a matter of weeks until mother quail appear, trailed by an entourage of up to a dozen downy chicks.

Depending on weather, May is often a good time to spot quail families in city wildlife refuges, on farms and in suburbs with adjacent desert or wooded areas. Quail seen in the desert in the eastern part of the state are Gambel's quail, almost identical to the California species except that they have a black breast patch. At higher altitudes you'll see the mountain quail, easier to distinguish because its plume stands straight up. When a quail family is feeding on the ground, a male acts as lookout from a tree branch or other high vantage point, emitting a warning cry that some say sounds like "To-PE-ka! To-PE-ka!" Quail are gregarious by nature, and often are seen in coveys as they search for food. California quail almost always are in residence in **Solstice Canyon Park,** a coastal canyon habitat just off Pacific Coast Highway 1 on Corral Canyon Road in Malibu. Call the park to check on that day's probability of cozying up to a quail. An endemic quail subspecies is in residence on **Catalina Island,** commonly seen as soon as you leave the city of Avalon for the island's interior. Call the Catalina Island Conservancy at (310) 510-2595 for advice on best current sighting areas.

International Migratory Bird Day

The second Saturday of May marks the observance of the passages of migratory birds with a special day set aside for winged commuters. It is the hallmark event of Partners in Flight, the international coalition whose mission is to stem declines in populations of migratory birds. Although most migratory birds are still abundant, some species are at risk because of habitat destruction and use of chemicals in the areas to which they migrate. Programs and activities are scheduled in many areas that include bird walks and bird counts and restoring local habitats to provide homes for birds. For information on what's happening in Southern California to celebrate the day, call the U.S. Fish and Wildlife service nongame bird coordinator in Portland, Oregon, at (503) 231-6235.

30

A Closer Look: Endangered Least Terns and Clapper Rails

Two of Southern California and Baja's most interesting birds share much of the same habitat as well as the distressing distinction of being on both the federal and state lists of endangered species. They live along the coast, depending on the water and salt marshes for safe nesting habitat and for food. Recent protection of habitat is helping keep both populations stable, but their range has been severely limited by construction along the coast and the continued disappearance of wetlands. More than 90 percent of California's coastal wetlands south of Santa Barbara have been drained, dammed up or filled in. More than 99 percent of the marshland that once existed between Los Angeles and Long Beach and that surrounded Mission Bay in San Diego is no longer intact.

The California least tern *(Sterna albifrons browni)*, at about 9 inches long the smallest of the terns, is making a slow but steady recovery and now numbers about 3,660, up from 1,200 in 1970. It is a dainty, fluttery white creature with a gray back and wings whose diving antics are a delight to watch. During courtship the male tern typically offers the female a choice little fish, followed by an intricate display of aerobatics. When the female accepts the male's fishy gift, it's pretty much decided that the two are an item.

Beginning in April, the terns return from South America and Mexico to the same sunny California beaches each year to breed and nest. They lay several pale beige eggs in shallow depressions in the sand, one of the habits that makes them particularly vulnerable. With almost every square inch of beach between San Diego and Santa Barbara now chockablock on warm spring days with volleyball players, sunbathers, Frisbee tossers and other beachgoers, the birds' open nests hardly have a chance. Add the hazards posed by frolicking dogs during the day and feral cats at night, and it is amazing the terns survive at all.

Some of the wary birds have forsaken sandy beaches to deposit their eggs on man-made surfaces such as landfills, airport runways and service roads. This, however, can bring the problem of chemical pollutants from vehicles, as well as the likelihood of eggs being smashed by traffic. The California Coastal Zone Act now protects some of the habitat essential to the terns' successful mating and breeding.

The light-footed clapper rail *(Rallus longirostris)* is even worse off. It is estimated that there are fewer than 300 nesting pairs of the subspecies in the United States. This pretty, 16-inch tan and gray marsh hen with a tawny chest and dappled back is shaped much like a domestic chicken except for its long beak, which it uses to excavate clams, striped shore crabs and its favorite California horned snails out of mud flats.

Clever clapper rails, so-named because of their staccato "clapping" call, build an ingenious platform nest in the marsh's cordgrass. It is "hinged" so that it can rise and fall with the tide, keeping eggs and fledglings dry despite the vagaries of the water's flow.

All this doom and gloom should not deter you from observing these two enchanting birds. Kayakers who ship their paddles and simply drift along the **Upper Newport Bay Ecological Reserve** beneath weathered diatomaceous cliffs report watching in fascination as the little terns hover, then plummet into the water to emerge with a wiggling anchovy or silversides grasped firmly in their yellow bills. Recently the terns have begun nesting in the reserve on one of two islands created especially for them. An active nesting colony of 75 pairs recently has been verified. Continual dredging keeps their nesting habitat isolated so a land bridge can't form to allow access to predators such as foxes and coyotes. Although the reserve is completely encircled by homes, freeways, hotels, businesses and other badges of civilization, the now-protected 752-acre wetland manages to survive. On any given summer day, as many as 30,000 birds find refuge there.

The reserve also shelters more than two-thirds of the remaining population of light-footed clapper rails. It is believed that 116 breeding pairs are at home in the Newport Reserve. They are in residence the year around, and are easiest to see at high tide (see end of the Appendix for where to get a tide chart). Look for them in the salt marshes near the beginning of Back Bay Drive and in nearby tidal

Clapper Rail Trail

1. A Bedroom that floats, *nesting platform*
2. A Supermarket called "Food Chains Plus," *Shellmaker Island*
3. Healthy native plants are critical for survival.
4. Humans need estuaries to survive, *wickiup*
5. Standing on History, *artificial sand dune*
6. Why are estuaries important to us today?

creeks. The reserve is a unique, wildly beautiful estuary where saltwater from the ocean mixes with fresh water from San Diego Creek.

There even is a Clapper Rail Trail that begins at the visitors' center. Pick up a self-guiding map that directs you to stands of cordgrass that are typical rail habitat and to Shellmaker Island where plants and animals depend on nature to help their life cycle flourish. It explains the critical functions of estuaries as nurseries and nesting areas for countless species of fish and birds. The Upper Newport Bay Ecological Reserve is in the city of Newport Beach just off Jamboree Road.

The California least tern also nests in the northern half of McGrath State Beach at the 160-acre **Santa Clara Estuary Natural Preserve** in Ventura. The preserve was established primarily to protect the tern, which nests on the sand bars at the mouth of the Santa Clara River, and the Belding's savannah sparrow that sometimes is spotted among the willows and reeds growing on the river banks. As of this writing the preserve is being eyed by developers who see the valuable sea-related property in terms of dollar signs rather than protected habitat.

Impressive coastal beach dunes in **Nipomo Dunes Preserve** near the town of Santa Maria in Santa Barbara County attract terns that nest south of the Santa Maria River, foraging for fish at the river's mouth. They are in residence from April though August. At the **Bolsa Chica Ecological Reserve** near Huntington Beach, groups of as many as five tern species may be observable from the boardwalk. Take your time, use your binoculars and you may be able to pick out a California least tern.

Torrey Pines State Reserve and the adjacent **Los Penasquitos Marsh** north of San Diego provide sanctuary for both the rails and the terns. In one of Southern California's few remaining salt marshes, look for these two species in the pickleweed that also hides the endangered Belding's savannah sparrow.

On the north side of Ballona Creek at **Venice Beach** in Playa del Rey in Los Angeles, there has been a least tern colony for a number of years. Unless the volleyball players have driven them out, beginning in May they should be there. Nearby, they also can be spotted in the **Marina del Rey Channel, Ballona Lagoon** and on **Terminal Island.**

A subspecies of the rail, the Yuma clapper rail, is so similar to the light-footed clapper rail that even expert birders are often fooled. The defining factor is that the Yuma rail lives along the lower Colorado River that defines California's southeastern border with Arizona. There also are a few spotted occasionally at the Salton Sea. Like their coastal brethren, the Yuma rails like marshy land. Look for them wherever you see stands of cattail, but also check reeds and bulrush. Seasoned birders say the best chance of luring them into your sight is to play a taped recording of their call. Yuma rails are on the federal list of endangered species and are considered threatened in California. Dredging and channeling the Colorado, which goes on constantly, destroys their habitat. Their numbers, however, do not seem to be declining, and with a combined U.S. and Mexican population of an estimated 1,000-plus birds, their future seems bright.

June

June Hotspots

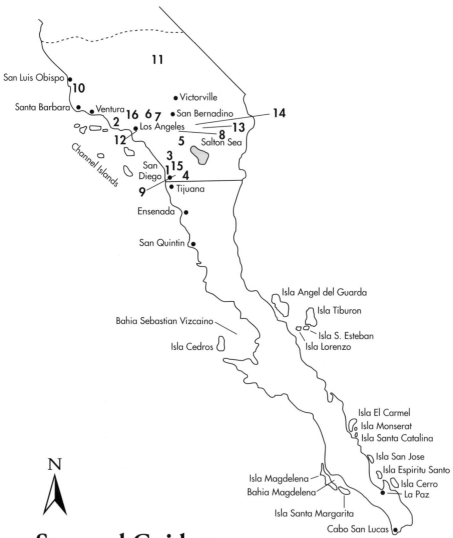

San Luis Obispo

10

Santa Barbara

Ventura **16 6 7**

11

Victorville

San Bernadino

14

2

Los Angeles

13

Channel Islands

12

8

5

Salton Sea

3

San Diego

1 15

4

9

Tijuana

Ensenada

San Quintin

Isla Angel del Guarda

Isla Tiburon

Bahia Sebastian Vizcaino

Isla S. Esteban

Isla Lorenzo

Isla Cedros

Isla El Carmel

Isla Monserat

Isla Santa Catalina

Isla San Jose

N

Isla Espiritu Santo

Isla Magdelena

Isla Cerro

Bahia Magdelena

La Paz

Isla Santa Margarita

Cabo San Lucas

Seasonal Guide to
the Natural Year

Site Locator Map

LIST OF SITES
June

Notes

31

Going to Bat for Bats

On a balmy summer evening as dusk crept into the Los Padres National Forest, a group of us were enjoying after-dinner coffee on the deck of a friend's mountain cabin. Besides our murmured chitchat, I became aware of a whispery flutter in the air above us. It was so subtle I wasn't even sure I'd heard it.

"Bats," smiled our host. "They're quite numerous this time of year." One of the women shrieked and covered her hair while her husband joked about vampires. "You've got the wrong idea," said our host. "You should thank the bats for the lack of mosquitoes here this evening."

According to fossil records, bats have been around for 55 million years, looking pretty much the same as they do today. Somewhere along the line they began to be maligned as evil spirits, carriers of horrible disease and (eeek!) suckers of human blood. It's all fantasy and folklore. The benefits they provide far outweigh any negatives.

Bats are the only true flying mammal, belonging to the second largest animal order, Chiroptera, which contains almost 1,000 species. Bats make up nearly one-quarter of the world's mammals. Researchers now are verifying the vital role they play in maintaining the world's ecological balance.

All 24 species of southern California bats (about half are common) are insect eaters. They include the big brown, little brown, long-eared myotis and Western big-eared bats. They help control the aforementioned mosquitoes and protect crops from pillaging insects. A lone little brown bat can consume up to 600 insects in just an hour. Some species are essential for pollination and seed dispersal. Bats routinely pollinate a variety of cacti, including the saguaro, as well as the agave and century plant.

Bats are not blind. Although some species have eyesight that isn't particularly sharp, the suborder Microchiroptera, to which most Southern

California bats belong, navigates at night using echolocation. They can hear the footsteps of a moth and sense changes in air currents made by fluttering mosquito wings. The squeaks and squeals they emit are on a frequency so high they are inaudible to the human ear.

The creatures can become airborne because they have a thin, hairless skin stretched over their "fingers." Their "thumb" has a sharp claw that helps them to climb and to crawl into tiny crevices. An adult female bat mates at the end of summer before hibernating, producing one and possibly two pups the following spring. The baby can weigh as much as one-quarter of the mother's weight at birth and nurses from its mother's pectoral mammary glands until it is almost full-grown. Scientists say the young bats need this long-term tending in order to develop the large wingspan and surface area they must have to fly.

Those who study the winged creatures report that bat populations have declined over the past three decades, largely because of human-induced factors such as destruction of foraging and roosting habitat and deliberate killing. In other states, the caves that bats roost in have become popular as recreational sites. A bat in hibernation, aroused by spelunkers more than once, can burn up so much stored fat that it may not have the resources to make it until spring and will starve to death. In California, old mines may be closed in the name of hazard abatement, thereby taking away a roosting site. Pesticides that knock out insects also may kill bats directly.

So what about the legends of vampires, and the ghoulish Dracula tales about bats taking on human forms? There are three species of blood-feeding bats that live in the New World tropics (nowhere near Southern California). Although it is true they feed on mammals and birds and have been photographed at night attaching themselves to cattle in remote areas of Mexico, human contact is undocumented.

Bats roost in caves, old mines, buildings with high rafters, trees, under eaves and wherever else they believe they can rest undisturbed.

Hot
Spots

There is no commercial spot in Southern California, such as New Mexico's Carlsbad Caverns, where it is possible to watch a massive bat outflight. The California Department of Fish and Game protects bat information because of recent vandalism of their roosts. Much of the destruction stems from a misunderstanding of bats' purpose in the ecosystem. Some people think that all bats carry rabies and should be destroyed. But even the less than half of one percent of bats that do bite, normally do so only in self-defense and pose little threat to people who do not handle them.

To watch bats that are active at night, any large reservoir area is a good venue. At **Lake Hodges** in Escondido in San Diego County, just off Hwy 15, there are many little brown bats that roost in the dam. At dusk you'll find them flying out to forage over the lake. Because there is no access to their roosting site, the bats are observable but cannot be harassed.

Bats often can be seen around ballfields, where they are attracted to the insects that collect around the lights.

32

Mountain Lions

They're everywhere in California but rarely seen. And when they are, it's usually because they have been killed in the name of protecting humans or they are trapped and living in a cage. Reclusive loners, these sleek, lovely creatures will avoid contact with humans and civilization if at all possible. They can adapt to a wide variety of habitats, as studies of radio-collared lions have shown. They've been observed using areas immediately adjacent to urban residential centers and exist on the outskirts of urban areas. Recent encounters between lions and humans are pointing to an unavoidable, unfortunate conflict of habitat.

Mountain lions *(Felis concolor concolor)*, also called cougars, panthers and pumas, are the largest pure carnivore in California. They are tawny colored with black tips on ears and tails. Black stripes extend from the corners of the mouth to the eyes. They cannot roar, but they can purr. An adult male can weigh up to 200 pounds and be more than 8 feet long. Smaller females weigh between 65 and 90 pounds. They live about 12 years in the wild and up to twice that in captivity where they are fed regularly and face no danger from predators or hunting humans.

A female mountain lion can have a litter with as many as five cubs every other year, but the usual number is three. They are born spotted and with blue eyes. Because of the rigors of growing up in the wilderness, two cubs out of three will not live to be a year old. Unlike coyote fathers (see chapter 50), male mountain lions have little to do with raising the litter. At age two or three, cubs leave their mother's home range to establish territories of their own.

Their habitat includes all parts of the state, but they are most heavily concentrated in Northern California and in areas where there are deer, their natural prey. In the southern part of the state, the coastal mountain range and inland mountain ranges provide suitable habitat, although they survive in deserts, humid forests and from sea level to elevations of 10,000 feet.

Ninety years ago the mountain lion in California was much sought by hunters because it was a bountied predator that brought monetary rewards for each kill. It was hunted for sport and shot by ranchers because it killed their cows and sheep. In 1963 California ended its bounty program but not until 12,500 mountain lions were killed in slightly more than half a decade. By 1969 the mountain lion's status had changed to that of "game mammal," and shortly thereafter all mountain lion hunting was stopped. By 1990 California gave it the status of "specially protected mammal."

Mountain lion populations in California have grown recently. A probably inaccurate 1920 estimate put their numbers at about 600. In the 1970s a more precise study reported approximately 2,000 in the state. Today's population estimate is between 4,000 and 6,000. This increase, plus recent interactions with humans, have caused a movement by hunters to create an open season. A jogger in one of Southern California's state parks recently was attacked by a mountain lion. The animal was tracked and killed. Later, it was found that the cat was apparently protecting her pair of cubs.

In another incident, a camouflaged turkey hunter was calling turkeys when a mountain lion appeared. As soon as the lion realized that the hunter was not a turkey, it ran away. The Department of Fish and Game concluded that if the hunter had not been camouflaged and sounding like a turkey (a favorite lion meal), the lion would have avoided him.

These sorts of incidents help spur the open-season idea. Then too, deer hunters are unhappy with the mountain lion's stalking skills, resenting the competition and pointing out that a single mountain lion can kill up to a deer a week for survival. In defense of the tawny creature, some biologists say that the lion takes only the weak, sick and infirm deer, thereby increasing the health and strength of the entire deer population. If sick deer were not predated upon, goes the logic, a single diseased deer could infect an entire population and wipe it out. In areas where deer have been reintroduced but mountain lions have not, deer have multiplied to the point where they strip entire areas of vegetation and frequently starve. Without natural predators, the balance of nature is badly upset. It is an issue unlikely to be resolved soon.

Wildlife experts say that mountain lions will never overrun the countryside because only so many lions can live within a particular area. Their numbers are determined by the food supply, a self-limiting restriction that nature enforces. Because they are large animals and their prey is large, it requires the resources of a sizable area to support a mountain lion. An adult male's home range can cover 100 square miles while females generally can survive on 20 to 60 square miles.

You'll probably never see a mountain lion in the wild. They are secretive and elusive, preferring to hunt alone at night and sleep during the day. They'll ambush a deer, often dropping from a tree limb to deliver a crushing bite at the base of the skull to break its neck, then feed at leisure. Sometimes they cover a carcass with leaves and brush and return to feed on it for days.

The natural conditions that support an increasing mountain lion population can exist in mountain communities and on the fringes of suburban developments. As with much of nature, people are moving into their habitat and are using their territory for hiking, camping and mountain biking. Lions are predators, and humans can serve as their prey. A March 1996 ballot measure that would have deleted the "specially protected mammal" status for mountain lions was defeated by California voters. The measure noted that mountain lions are neither an endangered nor a threatened species. Current law makes it illegal to kill mountain lions unless it is in the act of self-defense, or after wildlife officials issue a permit to kill a lion that has attacked livestock or pets.

Hot
Spots

The closest you may ever get to a mountain lion is its tracks. They're distinguishable from those of a domestic dog because you can see a dog's claw marks but you can't see a mountain lion's. Also, the pad part of the lion's track has a distinctive **M** shape. If you want to try your hand at tracking, these are the places to give it a try.

Malibu Creek State Park, 12 miles north of Santa Monica on Hwy 1, has a mountain lion population, as does **Palomar Mountain State Park,** where some sightings have been reported in this mile-high wilderness. To get to Palomar, take I-15 14 miles north of Escondido to Hwy 76. Then go east for 21 miles to County Road 56 and head north for 7 miles to a mountaintop intersection. Here, turn left, then left again onto State Park Road.

Within **Cuyamaca Rancho State Park** are many habitats designated as wilderness areas that support a substantial mountain lion population. From San Diego take Hwy 8 east 40 miles to Hwy 79/Japatul Road exit and turn north 4 miles to the entrance. **Mount San Jacinto State Park** near Palm Springs shelters mountain lions in its subalpine forests and mountain meadows that form a designated wilderness area. From the north edge of Palm Springs take Tramway Road off CA Hwy 111 and follow it 3.5 miles up the hill to Palm Springs Aerial Tramway.

An excellent place to see mountain lions happy and well taken care of in captivity is the **Wildlife Waystation,** a unique facility west of Los Angeles in the Angeles National Forest that's part hospital and part orphanage. It rescues, rehabilitates and relocates wild and exotic animals. At any given time it will have two dozen mountain lions in residence, many of them destined to remain there for life because they cannot be returned to the wild. Some are injured or maimed, and some have never lived in the wild so they have no survival skills. Kiowa, a recent arrival at the Waystation, is typical of the mountain lion population. She was purchased in Minnesota as a cub by California residents who didn't realize they couldn't get a California permit to keep her, so she was brought to the Waystation where she is quite tame and participates in area educational programs. The Waystation is at 14831 Little Tujunga Canyon Road, Angeles National Forest, CA 91342; (818) 899-5201.

33

Butterflies

When the weather warms and flowers are at their best, butterflies are also found in greatest abundance. One of the most ancient life forms, butterflies and other nectar-feeding creatures evolved during the Cretaceous period in response to the era's production of flowers. The abundant food source forged a new and beautiful link in the evolutionary chain.

Butterflies live just a few weeks, but during that short span they display an amazing array of spectacular colors and interesting behavior. Some flowers have become so united with the butterfly, depending on them for pollination, that one would be hard pressed to exist without the other. Many species are threatened or endangered, mainly because of the destruction of habitat. During developmental stages—from caterpillar to chrysalis to butterfly—the environment, weather and other surrounding conditions must be just right for all three stages to form properly.

Like moths, butterflies belong to the order Lepidoptera, characterized by wings covered with tiny scales. There are more than 15,000 species throughout the world. Southern California is generally thought to have more than 100 distinct species, although some haven't been observed for more than a decade. The Palos Verdes blue butterfly hasn't been seen since 1983, yet the Fish and Wildlife service is reluctant to declare it extinct because butterflies have the ability to remain in a dormant state for years, emerging when conditions are right.

The North American Butterfly Association conducts annual Fourth of July counts, similar to the Audubon Society's Christmas Bird Count, in an attempt to assess butterfly populations and gather useful long-term data and also to increase public awareness and enjoyment of butterflies. Counts are conducted within a circle 15 miles in diameter at approximately 300 sites in the United States and have been going on since 1975. Even if you can't get out, a special category called "garden watcher" lets you contribute to the count without leaving your home.

By June, chaparral habitat in the Golden State has been in flower for a month or more, and pine forests mixed with oak and shrubs have produced the flowers that attract butterflies. Flowers upslope, at higher mountain elevations, are in bloom in June and July, providing a food supply for the delicate winged creatures. If you can spot wildflowers, you'll surely find butterflies.

Although butterflies in general are benign, a small pale specimen called the cabbage white butterfly can be very destructive to crops. In the 1800s it made its way from Europe to Quebec and spread rapidly because it produces three generations in a single year. Anyone with a backyard garden no doubt has seen more than one of the creatures, white-winged with black dots, flitting among the squash and tomato plants. *Smithsonian* magazine referred to them as "the English sparrow or kudzu of the butterfly world."

You can tell a butterfly from a moth because butterflies have club-shaped rather than feathery antennae. When alighting, their wings are held vertically, not flat or sloping.

To attract the winged delights to your yard, try planting daisies, chrysanthemums, zinnias, marigolds and cosmos, all of which supply nectar that is palatable to most butterflies. Lantana and pentas also are butterfly favorites.

Tips for viewing butterflies include choosing a warm, still, sunny day when the winged beauties are most active and flowers are blossoming exuberantly. Bring binoculars. Because butterflies have compound eyes, they'll spot you long before you spot them and will flit irritatingly away, always seeming to stay just out of range. Call the Southern California Wildflower Hotline at (818) 768-3533 for recorded information on where to view the best blooms during spring and summer months. And if all else fails, simply enjoy the flowers.

If you're serious about butterfly observing, the North American Butterfly Association (see Appendix) publishes newsletters and a magazine that aid in successful butterfly gardening and identification and give detailed site guides for butterflying hot spots. It's a good source of information about these ephemeral spirits.

Take the Angeles Crest Highway from Los Angeles up into the **San Gabriel Mountains,** and you're likely to see pale and western tiger swallowtail and California sisters that are black and white with orange wingtips. Their caterpillars feed on live oaks that are abundant in the mountains. Along mountain streams a similar butterfly, the Lorquin's admiral, also with orange-tipped wings, feeds on willows. You'll see a number of species of blue butterflies including Acmon's and lupine (named for its color, not because it feeds on the lupine flower).

In the Little San Bernardino Mountains southeast of the town of Morongo Valley, the Nature Conservancy's **Big Morongo Canyon Preserve** is home to the western tiger swallowtail and Lorquin's admiral. The preserve has several short trails as well as the Canyon Trail that extends for 5 miles into the canyon. Take I-10 to its junction with Hwy 62, then go north about 10.5 miles. At the northeast end of the business district of Morongo Valley, turn right on East Drive. The preserve entrance is about 200 yards ahead on the left.

Although most people go to the Hidden Jungle aviary at the **San Diego Wild Animal Park** to see the tropical butterflies imported from exotic places, a wonderful collection of California resident butterflies are there as well. A lush garden around the exhibit is planted with lantana and other nectar plants to entice clouds of local butterflies. You'll find lovely reddish orange gulf fritillaries, monarchs, queen butterflies that closely resemble monarchs and spectacular yellow and black swallowtails. Small white triangular-winged skippers are not so pretty as they are interesting for their active behavior. Among the real crowd-pleasers are the brown buckeyes, beautifully marked with an eye-shaped pattern that nature supplies to help frighten off the birds that would be the buckeye's natural predators. The park is located 30 miles north of San Diego. Take the Via Rancho Parkway exit off I-15 and follow signs to the entrance. Call (619) 234-6541 for more information.

Pismo State Beach, just south of San Luis Obispo, has an abundant butterfly population among its giant eucalyptus trees and coastal sand dunes, attracted by flowers and the giant yellow coreopsis.

An annual butterfly count is conducted at the Nature Conservancy's **Kern River Preserve** near Bakersfield under the guidelines of the Xerxes Society. The preserve is northeast of Bakersfield in Kern County, 1.5 miles east of Sierra Way on Hwy 178. Call (619) 378-2531 for more information.

The endangered El Segundo blue butterfly is found exclusively in the dunes west of **Los Angeles International Airport,** an unlikely place for such a fragile creature, but the one that it likes because it is uniquely adapted to the dunes vegetation. In 1984 its numbers had declined to fewer than 400, but today 10,000 of the lovely butterflies flutter over the dunes. Its recovery is attributed to the rehabilitation of the dunes habitat, and to restricted public access. You may not be able to wander the dunes but you should be able to approach their periphery and spot the El Segundo blue. (See chapter 69 for more on monarch butterflies.)

34

Tarantulas

Those hairy, scary creatures you see scurrying across quiet desert backroads during warm summer months are tarantulas. Best sightings are usually at night, between June and October, when the male leaves its burrow and sets off to find a mate. In some areas it's not unusual to spotlight a dozen or more scuttling in the beam of your headlights.

They may be the largest and hairiest spider in the United States, but they are not lethal. Their venomous reputation, and their name, date back to the fifteenth century when people sometimes suffered from a form of hysteria that was thought to be caused by the bite of a large wolf spider named after the town of Taranto in Puglia, Italy. The only cure for the afflicted one was to dance into a frenzy, therefore purging the effects of the spider's bite. Modern-day medical professionals have speculated that, once injected with the irritating venom of a tarantula, the gyrations of the dancer caused body sweat to dilute and wash away the toxin, thereby appearing to effect a cure. The Italian folk dance called the tarantella is said to be named for this bizarre remedy. When Italian explorers discovered the North American tarantula, they named it for the scariest spider they knew.

Tarantulas are members of the family Theraphosidae, which also includes trapdoor spiders and funnel-web spiders. They are interesting and quite beautiful when viewed from an aesthetic perspective. They range from a rich, dark brown to a reddish color that blends with desert habitat. Although they have eight eyes, when hunting they rely on their hairs as sensory perceptors to locate prey.

The fuzzy arachnids don't spin webs to capture food. They seize their quarry by emerging cautiously from their burrows at night to pounce quickly on any insect, or possibly another spider, smaller than they are. Some very large South American tarantulas have been known to kill small birds. The tarantula has a beaklike mouth from which it ejects a venom fatal to small creatures, along with enzymes that begin the digestive process. Thus disabled, hapless insects become a meal.

Tarantulas have been kept successfully as pets for many years. A female may live to be as old as 30, and a male has a life span of about 10 years. If you hold one in your hand you'd expect it to weigh more than the half-ounce it does, because the 5-inch span of the hairy legs that extend from a 2-inch body makes it appear larger than it really is.

Most of a tarantula's life is spent in its burrow, which may be an abandoned animal hole or a remote ledge. Males don't leave the sheltered hollow until they are sexually mature, at about eight years of age. That is when you're most likely to see them scampering about the desert, so please don't deter them and put a damper on their romantic quest. Their mating process is complication enough.

Although they don't spin webs for food catching, they do create one for mating purposes. The male creates a small network of web material in which he deposits his sperm. He picks up the little bundle and puts it into two sacs in the female's abdomen. Apparently this is not a gesture that she appreciates, because she can viciously turn on her new suitor at any time during this process, possibly killing him.

Being a single mom doesn't seem to phase a female tarantula. She stores the little bundles of sperm for a number of weeks, then spins a silk sheet on which she lays up to 1,000 eggs. This may seem like a lot, but on average only two of the eggs will become mature spiders. Predation by small mammals like skunks as well as birds, snakes, lizards and frogs takes its toll.

In six weeks tiny white spiders hatch, staying with the mother tarantula for up to a week, when they leave home (but stay in the neighborhood) to build burrows of their own. Tarantulas don't generally stray far from their original burrow, so if you see one, chances are that others are close by.

As with most wildlife, a naturally timid tarantula tries to run away if threatened. If cornered, it will try to frighten away the interloper with a display of its fangs, which are located quite far back in its throat. If it does bite, its venom has about the same effect as a bee sting or mosquito bite on humans. An unusual defense mechanism can be the hairs on its abdomen, which can cause irritation and a rash in humans. If you've handled a tarantula, don't rub your eyes or touch your face until you wash your hands, because the tiny hairs attack mucous membranes and possibly could cause blindness. This theory is refuted by those who regularly handle tarantulas. They say that such an allergic reaction is unlikely. So you'll have to hold one yourself to see who's right.

Hot Spots

Tarantulas live in the **lower elevations and desert regions** of Southern California. Any backcountry desert roads during warm months can produce sightings, especially in the Sonoran Desert. If you walk an area at dusk and spot large half-dollar size holes in the ground, they probably belong to tarantulas. Hang around. They'll eventually come out to feed.

For a close-up view of a tarantula under glass, you can visit the **Living Desert.** In the area called Eagle Canyon, the hairy spider lives happily in a simulated habitat just inches in front of your face. The Living Desert is 2 miles from Palm Desert, 1.5 miles south of Hwy 111 on Portola Avenue.

35

June Shorttakes

California Gnatcatcher and Coastal Sage Scrub

Although they are here the year around, June is an amiable month in which to take a look at two disappearing species and appreciate how critical habitat can be in sustaining biodiversity. The federally threatened California gnatcatcher (family Sylviidae), a small gray songbird that is most active in spring and early summer, depends on coastal sage scrub along the southern coast. This habitat is diminishing daily as development eats up open space. **The Irvine Company Open Space Reserve** has asked the Nature Conservancy to develop and implement a stewardship plan for 17,000 acres of wilderness that have been set aside from the communities that The Irvine Company will build. Present are chaparral, oak woodlands, riparian woodlands and the coastal sage scrub on which the California gnatcatcher depends. The Northern Reserve is near Santiago Canyon and the City of Orange. The Southern Reserve is near the city of Laguna Beach and Crystal Cove State Park. Both are accessible only by Nature Conservancy guided tours that do a great deal to increase your chances of spotting an elusive gnatcatcher. Call (714) 832-7478 for tour information.

California gnatcatchers also favor the coastal sage scrub in **Blue Sky Ecological Reserve,** a relatively untouched woodland, where they are actively nesting. Near the town of Poway in San Diego County, take Rancho Bernardo Road off I-15 and go east (the road name changes to Espola) for about 3 miles to the reserve.

A Rose by any Other Name ...

This month hundreds of species of roses are abloom in the 5-acre **Descanso Gardens International Rosarium** in La Canada-Flintridge near Los Angeles. The unique garden is planted with 5,000 rose bushes representing 1,700 antique and modern varieties. Twenty theme garden vignettes include the Children's Secret Garden, a Victorian garden

Descanso Gardens

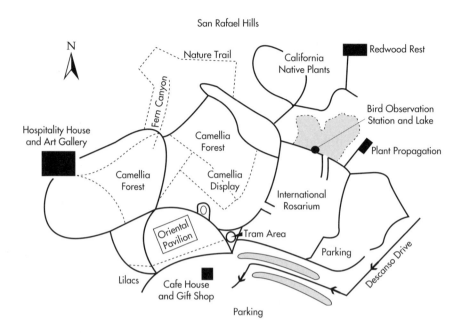

San Rafael Hills

N

Nature Trail

California Native Plants

Redwood Rest

Fern Canyon

Bird Observation Station and Lake

Hospitality House and Art Gallery

Camellia Forest

Plant Propagation

Camellia Forest

Camellia Display

International Rosarium

Oriental Pavilion

Tram Area

Parking

Descanso Drive

Lilacs

Cafe House and Gift Shop

Parking

and Nanny's Park. Detailed signs explain rose varieties and growing information. Groupings include China and tea roses, old European varieties, climbers and ramblers, shrub roses and modern roses. If the profusion of color and abundance were not enough to dazzle, the fragrances certainly will do it. Guided tram tours are offered daily, docent walks are held on Sunday and the San Fernando Audubon Society conducts bird study walks at 8 A.M. on the second and fourth Sunday of the month. The gardens are located at 1418 Descanso Drive. Exit the 210 Freeway at Foothill Boulevard or Angeles Crest Highway and follow signs to the garden. Call (818) 952-4400 for more information.

Cuckoo! Cuckoo!

The yellow-billed cuckoo, listed as endangered at the state level, has set up housekeeping at the Nature Conservancy **Kern River Preserve** at the southern tip of the Sierra Nevada where the South Fork River flows into a broad valley floodplain. The bird's population diminished from an estimated 150,000 nesting pairs in the mid-1800s to fewer than 50 pairs, largely because their riparian habitat is about 10 percent of what it once was. California has the dubious distinction of leading the nation in the loss of streamside vegetation. It has diminished to just 2 percent of the original 2 million acres. But at the preserve, volunteers have planted willows, the cuckoo's favorite nesting foliage, and cottonwoods, where the birds forage for sphinx moth larvae, large green caterpillars and katydids. Other birds to watch for in the preserve in late June are yellow warblers, blue grosbeaks and lazuli buntings. The preserve is northeast of Bakersfield in Kern County, 1.5 miles east of Sierra Way on Hwy 178. Call (619) 378-2531 for more details.

Jacaranda Trees

In June many Los Angeles streets turn into fantasy thoroughfares lined with great billowy poufs of powdery lavender blue. The blossoms belong to the jacaranda tree *(Jacaranda mimosafolia),* an import from Brazil. The trees burst into bloom for just three to four weeks, strewing their spent blossoms like a delicate Oriental rug to soften, at least for awhile, the city's asphalt and concrete.

36

A Closer Look:
Fire!

At one time the roar of a forest ablaze, swaths of flames cutting across a dry grass prairie, a sweep of fire through habitat teeming with life, were events looked on sadly. Tongues clucked at the perceived destruction. But in the last few decades, as environmental studies have tracked new growth, the attitude has changed. One of the most important resource management programs currently used by wildlife managers is prescribed burning.

In many areas a fire company was mandated by law to immediately squelch any fire that was seen as uncontrolled. This included forest fires and all fires in nature such as those caused by lightning strikes. Total fire suppression has caused an overaccumulation of dry brush and debris, turning some open forests into tinderboxes. Small, controlled burns in state parks and forests now are helping to prevent larger, more destructive wildfires that use the excessive dry underbrush as fodder for devastation.

These hotter-burning fires, the kind that linger, have the power to devastate a strong, mature tree. A large, healthy tree can withstand a fast-moving fire that blackens its bark, leaving its core untouched. But when fire lags to burn accrued underbrush, the flames have an opportunity to burrow into trees, weakening and possibly killing them.

Controlled fires burn off built-up duff, dead brush and smaller trees, releasing nutrients back into the soil. In some areas drought has weakened large trees, making them susceptible to infestations of bark beetles, so they are being removed before they become a fire hazard.

On the East Coast, a pale purple flower called the mountain mallow was all but wiped out through lack of fire. For centuries the mallow had flourished in areas swept by periodic wildfires. The fires kept down the low brush that impeded the mallow's growth and heated its seeds to the cracking point so they could scatter and germinate. Recent fires have restored its growth.

Another problem is that an area devastated by fire because of clear-cutting or suppression may be replanted with species that are less fire-retardant. Faster-growing trees that don't have the resistance of the original growth are destined to upset the forest's ecological balance.

Fires in the desert, feeding on dry creosote and mesquite, scatter the rabbit and coyote population to safer ground. The desert tortoise, however, has no such speedy

Controlled burns help plants such as this fireweed flourish again.

advantage. Yet it survives a fast-burning fire well by simply pulling in his head and legs and waiting for the flames to pass. It's not unusual after a desert fire to see an unburned oval patch where a tortoise has weathered the fire, then moved away. Had the fire lingered to feed on built-up brush, the tortoise might not have survived.

Fire plays an important role in the ecosystem of The Irvine Company Open Space Reserve, a 17,000-acre wilderness area in Orange County managed by the Nature Conservancy. Many of the plant communities here rely on fire for survival. Dead plants and leaves are removed by fire, which allows the new growth to accept sun, water and nutrients. If an area is not allowed to burn, plant communities such as coastal sage scrub and chaparral soon exhaust the very resources they need for survival.

In October 1993 a wildfire swept through the preserve's canyons and up its hills, blackening more than 5,000 acres. Many expensive homes were lost in nearby Laguna Beach. But after years without a burn, the reserve bounced back quickly. Indian paintbrush, deerweed, California sunflower, star lily, mariposa lily and wild hyacinths now can find a clear path to the sun. The bird population is thriving as well, feeding on the reserve's seeds and insects.

Once used by the Chumash Indians to ensure that the island would consistently revegetate, fire was suppressed on Santa Cruz Island off the coast of Ventura for more than a century. Along with overgrazing by feral sheep, nonnative plants were completely taking over native species. The Nature Conservancy, which manages the island, began prescribed burns in 1993 and is tracking encouraging results. Four hundred acres of bishop pine forest and 1,600 acres of grassland were carefully burned in 1994. Already pine seedlings are beginning to grow. Native plants in the grasslands responded vigorously, and nongrass herbs, snapdragon, snakeroot, buttercup and bunchgrasses such as purple needlegrass also benefited.

Naturalists point out that a successful burn and its effect on plant communities depends on a number of factors, including the amount of rainfall in the burn area following the fire. Santa Cruz Island was fortunate. In the six months after the burn it received two and one-half times the average amount of rainfall. It is credited with a doubling of native species in the grasslands area. More prescribed burns are planned for the island, with results to be carefully monitored and tabulated so as to track the responses of various plant communities. The Conservancy will use the data to develop fire management programs at other preserves throughout California.

Prescribed burns are also part of the preservation program at Cuyamaca Rancho State Park on Hwy 79 near Descanso in San Diego County. In the Peninsular Range of mountains, the park encompasses a rich forest of pine and oak with patches of broad meadows, flowing streams and riparian areas. Of the park's total of 25,000 acres, 13,000 acres are kept as wilderness in which all vehicles, even bicycles, are prohibited.

Because settlers first did their best to extinguish lightning-caused fires, and subsequent fire abatement measures have been very successful, an unnatural amount of dead plant material accumulated. As a result, in 1970 about half the park's acreage was burned, resulting in significant damage. Now portions of the park are burned systematically when environmental conditions are right. In this way natural landscapes will be restored and the amount of fuel available to cause permanent damage will be reduced. This also will lessen the probability of catastrophic fires.

Wildfires have swept across the slopes of the Nature Conservancy's Sand Ridge Preserve many times, and probably will again in the future, but not to the detriment of its plant life, say preserve managers. Vegetation remains much as it always has been because it is fire-adapted and to some extent depends for survival on the nutrient-rich ashes and reduced competition that follow a fire. Two prime examples are the rare Bakersfield cactus (see chapter 20) and Mormon tea that may appear devastated after a fire but will sprout new growth the following spring.

In remote Hondo Canyon near Topanga Canyon north of Los Angeles, a 1994 natural fire swept over the slopes, apparently wiping out most vegetation. Two years later the slopes were covered with bright yellow bushy poppies. A local naturalist and long-time area resident said that in 50 years he hadn't known the poppies to grow there but that their long-dormant seeds were brought to life by the fire.

Once again it would seem that people have realized that when left to its own devices, nature knows best how to keep things under control.

July

July Hotspots

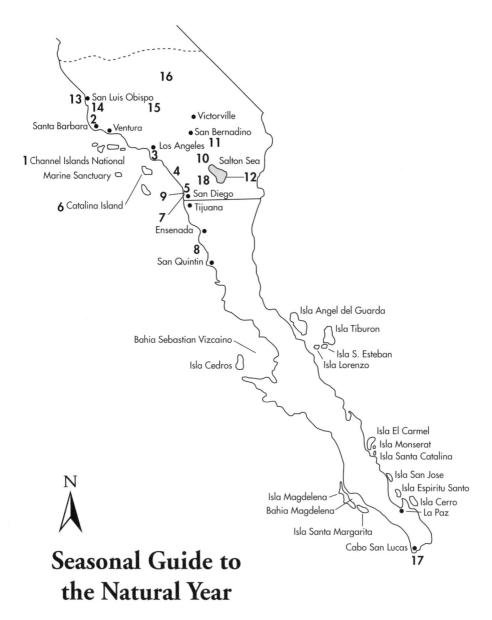

16

13 • San Luis Obispo
14 **15**

Santa Barbara • **2**
• Ventura

1 Channel Islands National
Marine Sanctuary ▢

6 Catalina Island

• Victorville

• San Bernadino
11

• Los Angeles
3

10 Salton Sea

4

18 **12**

5 • San Diego
9 • Tijuana

7
Ensenada •

8
San Quintin •

Isla Angel del Guarda

Isla Tiburon

Isla S. Esteban
Bahia Sebastian Vizcaino
Isla Lorenzo

Isla Cedros

Isla El Carmel
Isla Monserat
Isla Santa Catalina

Isla San Jose
Isla Espiritu Santo
Isla Magdelena
Bahia Magdelena
Isla Cerro
La Paz

Isla Santa Margarita
Cabo San Lucas •
17

N

Seasonal Guide to
the Natural Year

Site Locator Map

LIST OF SITES
July

1. Channel Islands National Marine Sanctuary
2. Santa Barbara
3. Palos Verdes Peninsula
4. Laguna Beach
5. La Jolla Underwater Park
6. Catalina Island
7. Point Loma
8. Pacific coast of Baja
9. Stephen Birch Aquarium-Museum
10. Mount San Jacinto State Park
11. Big Morongo Canyon Preserve
12. Salton Sea National Wildlife Refuge
13. Morro Bay
14. Carrizo Plain Natural Area
15. Lokern Preserve
16. Sand Ridge Wildflower Preserve
17. Los Cabos, Cabo San Lucas
18. Anza Borrego Desert State Park

Notes

37

A "Walk" Through a Kelp Forest

Magnificent forests of giant seaweed called kelp, gently undulating with ocean tides and currents, are the basis of an unusually diverse marine ecosystem that supports an amazing amount of sea life. It is common in the chilly waters off the coastline of California and Baja, choosing the rocky, uneven bed of the sea to fasten its holdfast, which would be called a root structure in land plants. Haptera, intertwining root-like appendages, emit a strong adhesive that securely glues the kelp plant to the stony bottom.

This lovely plant can become more than 200 feet long, its holdfast more than 100 feet below the surface, anchoring the trailing fronds. With the proper sunlight it can grow up to 1 foot a day. Almost 20 kelp species flourish in North America's Pacific coastal waters, the biggest of which is *Macrocystis pyrifera,* giant kelp, the largest aquatic plant in the world.

Kelp depends on seawater and sunlight for its nourishment. Long, flexible stalks or fronds branch into leaflike blades. Bulbous floats filled with carbon dioxide emitted by the kelp form where the blade attaches to the stalk. They encourage the plant upward, toward the sunlight. The sun is essential for the process of photosynthesis that allows the kelp to convert solar energy and carbon dioxide from the seawater into food. This process, which releases oxygen, makes kelp one of the major sources of oxygen for our planet.

There is little indication of the kelp's riches when it is viewed from the surface. Called the canopy, the reddish-brown leaves and gas-filled bulbs seem nothing more than a tangled mass to be bypassed as quickly as possible. Yet sea otters and sea lions swim playfully through this living raft, using its buoyant surface for a sunny nap. Golden garibaldi (see chapter 24) are a brilliant orange flash as they swim through shafts of sunlight. Schooling fish use it as a safe haven from hungry foes who would rather patrol the perimeter of the forest than become involved in its undulating confines. The kelp fish, however, uses its resemblance to the kelp blades as camouflage while it waits in ambush for suitable prey.

Kelp beds are a nursery for fish and invertebrates. Fry can hide among its leaves and shadows, while crabs and mollusks attach themselves to the broad leaves, feeding on other invertebrates as well as the kelp itself. At the kelp's holdfast on the rocky bottom another layer of life exists. Anemones, nudibranchs, spiny lobsters and others use the kelp for shelter and protection.

Beachcombers often find strands of the huge seaweed washed up on shore, perhaps torn loose from its anchoring roots by a storm, or the propeller of a passing boat. Its gas-filled bulbs keep it afloat for great distances. More than likely, however, the beachcombers are seeing kelp that has broken off naturally as part of the sloughing process that creates room for new growth. Some fronds sink to the bottom to become food for a variety of invertebrates such as the abalone.

As with a forest on land that has clearings, the kelp forest is dotted with sandy planes. These areas are home to angel sharks, halibut, turbot, flounder and other bottom fish. The red octopus uses the sand for concealment. On the kelp's sandy periphery, enormous schools of male and female squid meet each spring to mate, then return to the bottom where the female anchors the egg case in place above the sand adjacent to the kelp forest. In summer, schools of graceful bat rays assemble in forest clearings to mate.

Despite its strength and size, giant kelp has enemies. Although its flexibility allows it to withstand strong currents, high surge and heavy weather, fierce winter storms can be deadly to the forests. Vicious winds can rip plants from the ocean's floor to wash up on beaches in huge, odoriferous tangles of fronds, bladders and stalks. But the kelp soon regenerates, sometimes becoming thick and luxuriant once again within a year.

A warm current called El Niño, a phenomenon that is peculiar to the Pacific Coast, can cause water temperatures to rise, banishing the cold flows that are rich in the nutrients the kelp requires. Human tinkering with the universe has caused the greenhouse effect (atmospheric warming), which some scientists think will allow for stronger and more frequent El Niños. Another kelp threat caused by people is the overabundance of purple sea urchins that can munch down an entire kelp forest in a short time. The urchins' natural predators, sea otters, were hunted to the point of endangerment long ago. Another predator, the sheepshead, has been almost fished out. A fishery market in Asian countries is developing for the eggs of red urchins, but the smaller roe of purple urchins is less in demand. These lavender marauders can gobble up holdfasts and set whole kelp forests adrift to die.

Fortunately kelp is far from in trouble, and in fact has been harvested for almost a century. About 100,000 tons of kelp are gathered statewide each year, almost 75 percent of it in Southern California. It has been reaped for commercial use by at least one Southern California firm since 1929. Kelco Company of San Diego, controlled and regulated by the California Fish and Game Commission, markets the kelp for its algin, a gelling and stabilizing agent used in canned and frozen foods, ice cream, salad dressing, gunpowder and some medicines and to put a head on beer. It is used as fertilizer and becomes food for commercially farmed abalone. The harvesting process involves clipping off just the top 3 feet of the kelp canopy, leaving the remaining plant intact to continue its growth. Although scuba divers and some environmental groups have expressed concern that overharvesting may be harming the kelp and the creatures that depend on it for existence, marine biologists say there is little cause for alarm. Because kelp grows so quickly, at worst it simply looks, for a short period, like it is having a bad hair day.

Other kelp forms along the Southern California coast, smaller and less spectacular than the giant kelp, are often seen in intertidal areas. Southern sea palm rarely grows taller than 2 feet in shallow waters, 4 feet in deeper waters. It stands erect on a sturdy stalk that has two leafy fronds branching from the top. Feather boa kelp, unmistakable and aptly named, has thin, brown blades interspersed with flat, broader blades. It appears to be freshly plucked from the tail plumage of a passing winged creature. It can grow to several feet in low intertidal zones and in deeper waters has reached 30-foot lengths.

Hot Spots

Getting Wet

Any certified diver with scuba gear and a wet suit (California coastal waters rarely rise above the low seventies even in mid-summer) can swim among the kelp forests from dive boats out of Los Angeles, Santa Barbara and San Diego. Many divers consider the kelp a bigger underwater attraction than fish. One diver reports that watching a kelp bed "wake up" on an early morning dive off San Clemente island was the experience of a lifetime. Spiny lobsters, yellowfin tuna and a sea turtle were among the highlights. Experienced divers say that the best kelp-diving days are sunny, with minimum current running.

The **Channel Islands National Marine Sanctuary** in Ventura offers superb underwater views of the magnificent forests. **Santa Barbara, the Palos Verdes Peninsula, Laguna Beach, La Jolla Underwater Park, Point Loma** and the Pacific coast of **Baja California** as far south as San Ignacio Lagoon all are prime dive sites for a slither through the kelp forests. See the Appendix for a listing of dive operators in these areas.

Not Getting Wet

There are a number of ways to view kelp and remain warm and dry. On Anacapa Island, part of **Channel Islands National Park** in Ventura, an underwater video program operates within the National Marine Sanctuary in the Anacapa Island Landing Cove. A park diver is equipped with an underwater camera and full face mask with built-in two-way communications. He is accompanied by two additional divers and is linked to the surface with 125 feet of cable. Thus outfitted, he is able to provide video and audio feed to dockside monitors from the 25-foot-deep waters of the cove. Visitors on the dock watch video screens to see and hear about what the divers are finding. On any given day the diver's "stroll" through the forest might include a look at sea cucumber, abalone, garibaldi, spiny sea urchins, sea lions, bat rays, surf perch and sea hares. The camera is equipped with a light to peer under rock ledges and pierce the shadows. The 20-minute program is presented at 2 P.M. Tuesdays and Thursdays from Memorial Day

Kelp floating on the ocean's surface. Inflated "bladders" help keep kelp afloat.

to Labor Day and is free. See the Appendix for transportation to Anacapa.

At the **Stephen Birch Aquarium-Museum** in La Jolla, part of the University of California and the interpretive center for Scripps Institution of Oceanography, a specially designed viewing gallery provides a comfortable place to pause and study the giant kelp forest. The 70,000 gallons of water, reassuringly restrained by inch-thick panels of clear plexiglass, are kept in constant movement by a wave-making machine. The forest sways gracefully as if respond-ing to a silent symphony. A helpful placard explains that the move-ment is necessary to enable the kelp, and the animals that depend on it for food and shelter, to thrive. Natural light entering through the tank's open top allows the energetic plant to flourish. Patient observers say they've actually been able to see the kelp grow. Call the Stephen Birch Aquarium-Museum at (619) 534-3474.

Great clumps of floating kelp are often visible from beach areas. Tidepoolers often come across Southern sea palm kelp and feather boa kelp, both of which grow in intertidal areas.

38

Industrious Ants

Go to the ant, thou sluggard; consider her ways, and be wise:
Which having no guide, overseer, or ruler,
Provideth her meat in the summer
and gathereth her food in the harvest.

Proverbs 6:6–8

Ants and insects usually aren't something you want to have around. But since 98 percent of the creatures in California's Sonoran Desert are insects, a book of this sort wouldn't be complete without pointing readers in the direction of some of the arid area's most obvious many-legged creatures.

You can tell that seed harvester ants are in the vicinity when you come across an area about 3 feet wide that has been cleared of vegetation. In the center will be a hole, sometimes with a little rise of gravel or sand, in and out of which ants are hustling and bustling. These ants (genus *Pogonomyrmex*), which may appear black but actually are a dark red, are particularly adapted to desert life. Their name means "bearded ant," obviously given for the set of long hairs that extend out from below their lower mandible, in which they carry sand.

Much of their activity is carried out underground in elaborate subterranean nests that reach depths of 6 feet or more. Some of the chambers are used just for the storage of seed. It is interesting to watch as an ant enters the nest carrying seeds that sometimes seem to be as big as the insect itself. Sometimes a rim of seed husks surround the nest, as ants tend to "shell" their seeds before storing them.

"Pogos," as these ants are called by entomologists, have dramatic mating flights inappropriately called nuptial flights. Those who study ants point out that there is nothing nuptial about them as nuptials are strictly a human activity. Ants go through a winged stage somewhere between the third and fifth year in a colony's development. Up until then all ants have been sterile worker ants, but now they are able to reproduce winged males and females. Around the middle of July they are adult and mature. Warm rains are the environmental trigger that releases them from the nest. Mating flights cause the ants to fly to a central place. In neighborhoods it is often the same house or the same block each year. In the desert it is often the same shrub or tree. Males converge on the area, releasing pheromones that will attract females, who arrive and mate before returning to cooperative nests to begin the cycle once again. So if you see a cloud of winged creatures once a summer storm has passed through, they could be harvester ants.

Homeowners that find a congregation of pogos copulating on the roof of their house are advised to just wait it out. Within a day or two the situation will be resolved. Calling an exterminator to spray pesticide gives the appearance that the treatment has worked. However, by the time the exterminator arrives the females have left, and the males are dying anyway as part of the natural process. Clever exterminators then offer a one-year warranty, knowing full well that it will be a year before rains once again precipitate the ants' mating flight.

A second genus of seed harvester ants abundant in the Sonoran Desert are the *Messor* ants, the ant of the Bible as quoted above. This genus is jet black. Both ants are easily observable through California and into northern Baja.

Insects in general tend to be ephemeral, but once you know where to look, their fascination is endless.

Hot Spots Ants are just about everywhere. In addition to roofs of houses during mating time, you can see them in gardens, parks, yards and almost all parts of the Sonoran and Mojave Deserts.

39

Flipper and Friends

In the 1960s the country became enamored of dolphins, as the precocious Flipper dipped and dived his way across motion picture and television screens, wiggling his way into the hearts of a young TV audience. Flipper (actually, there were a half-dozen Flippers who played the role) was a bottlenose dolphin. His on-screen antics not only provided good, clean entertainment but also created public awareness of the high intelligence and capabilities of the cetacean nation in general.

I never gave much thought to dolphins after I grew up, mainly because I lived in landlocked Minnesota where marine mammals are largely unknown and the biggest thing in the water is likely to be a northern pike. Then I moved to California with the ocean in my backyard, and marine life became something other than fillets on ice in a market's refrigerated showcase.

On a bright shiny morning in Oxnard, a small city about an hour north of Los Angeles, along with about two dozen other visitors, I boarded a 55-foot power boat called the *Sun Fish*. We had signed on for a day trip to the Channel Islands run by Island Packers (see Appendix), scheduled to circle Anacapa, then Santa Cruz, and return home.

Morning sun had burned off lingering coastal fog and now glinted on a shimmery sea. Among the crew was tall, blond Paul, a marine biologist who had graduated from the University of Southern California. He was spending his summer working on island-bound boats because he could use his background to enhance others' oceangoing experiences. He explained that we'd be going through an area where offshore winds and a mixing of warm and cold currents can cause rough waters. But we were lucky. The ocean's blue-gray surface was dimpled with an occasional whitecap, but the boat's movement told us that we were in waters unlikely to initiate mal de mer.

We had barely reached open water in the Santa Barbara Channel when Paul announced that a pod of bottlenose dolphins were surfing

Dolphins in Santa Barbara Channel.

the boat's bow wake. What appeared to be a dozen or so sleek, gray creatures used the boat's forward thrust as a surfer uses a wave, to ride with seemingly no effort as they kept pace with the boat. This frolicking apparently is play behavior, indulged in for the simple joy of having fun. Bottlenose are the friendliest of all dolphins, and have been known to approach humans voluntarily, apparently out of curiosity. Paul explained that they often follow fishing boats to feed on the castoffs and the organisms disturbed by the nets.

The bottlenose had hardly disappeared when we spotted a group of what Paul said were common dolphin 100 yards from the boat, easily identifiable because of an hourglass or crisscross pattern on their sides. They leaped and dived, having discovered a school of fish that meant it was mealtime. The sky above the roiling water was thick with birds. We watched large swirls of cormorants—pelagic, double-crested and Brandt's all in the same group—along with California brown pelicans (see chapter 64), feeding on the same schools of small fish that attracted the dolphin.

As we settled in to reload our cameras and exchange impressions of what we'd watched, we were treated to a most unusual sighting. A group of Risso's dolphins, distinguished by unusual white patches along their body, were cavorting with other dolphins in the boat's aft wake. Paul explained that even before their white patches are visible, Risso's dolphins often can be identified by their behavior, which is slower and more deliberate than that of the bottlenose and common dolphin. They also are larger than other dolphins typically seen in these waters. Their light patches are scratchlike scars that are thought to occur during courtship and mating activity. As a final treat, a group of Pacific white-sided dolphin favored us with a display of jumps and bounds. They are much like the common dolphin but have gray flippers and a stripe from eye to flipper. Paul said that although seeing two types of dolphins on this trip is not unusual, glimpsing four such members of the dolphin family was especially lucky.

Dolphins are small-toothed whales of the order Cetacea, which encompasses about 50 species and also includes larger whales and porpoises. Don't confuse them with the dolphin fish, also called mahi mahi or dorado, that is common in warm waters. True dolphins are marine mammals with beaklike snouts and wedge-shaped teeth. Porpoises sometimes are confused with dolphins, but they differ because they are blunt-snouted and are members of a different family.

Dolphins always seem to be smiling. Rather than amusement at some inside marine mammal joke, the "smile" is created by a lower jawbone that flares outward and serves as an extremely sensitive ear that aids them in communicating with other dolphins.

The largest dolphin, the bottlenose, is also one of the most common. It's the one usually seen in marine life shows and usually is about 6 feet long. They feed on live mackerel, herring and sardines, except when in captivity, where they learn to eat the fresh dead fish offered by trainers.

Their smooth, sleek skin has been described as feeling like a cross between an inner tube and a cocktail olive. Although they are mammals with blowholes through which they breathe, their lack of rear appendages and torpedolike shape lead many onlookers to think of them as fish. But they must breathe air and usually stay submerged for about 2 minutes. In that short time they have been known to execute quick, deep dives of more than 1,000 feet. Like other whales, they have a thick layer of blubber that helps keep their body temperature very close to that of humans.

Dolphin research centers and study facilities have sprung up all over the world. While some are thinly disguised amusement parks charging admission to see trained dolphins, others are engaged in studies that genuinely further the cause of understanding these fascinating mammals. Most widely studied are dolphin vocalizations, which range from short, rhythmic clicks to shrill squeals and whistles. Some researchers swear there is a dolphin "language" and that humans must just find the key. It has been verified that their clicking sounds are sonar, used to locate other dolphins, obstacles in the water and possibly fish for food in the same way that bats use their sonar to locate insects and to fly at night without hitting things. The whistle is thought to be more of an emotional vocalization, used to indicate fear. Sounds are emitted through the dolphin's rounded forehead, called a melon.

Part of dolphins' fascination is that they are highly vocal and "chat" among themselves as humans do. This has led to the belief that they have a very high level of intelligence comparable to that of some primates. They are readily trainable and in places like Sea World can be seen doing spectacular jumps and turns.

Dolphins are not hunted commercially, although many still are inadvertently snagged and killed in nets used to fish highly profitable tuna and squid. Most U.S. tuna canneries abide by a 1990 agreement to buy tuna only from fishing companies known to frequent waters where tuna and dolphin swim separately, but enforcement of the agreement is chancy at best. Worldwide fisheries are as yet unregulated and an estimated one million dolphins and porpoises die this way each year, catching teeth, beaks and fins in the mesh and quickly drowning when they cannot return to the surface to breathe. With the exception of a few freshwater Asian dolphins, the mammals are so far neither threatened nor endangered. Marine biologists say dolphins are one of the most accurate gauges of the ecological health of the entire world.

Hot Spots

Simply because it is a warm, pleasant month, July is a good time to look for dolphins. All the world's oceans are home to dolphins, with common and bottlenose dolphins quite easy to spot off the California coast. Bottlenose usually are found in pods of about 10 to 100, which makes sighting them a treat. Just as one disappears beneath the surface in a graceful arcing dive, another appears nearby.

The best sightings are from a boat. If dolphins decide to play with you, you quite literally can look down at them from just feet away as they swim alongside. Waters anywhere from San Diego to Santa Barbara are likely to produce sightings.

40

Nocturnal Mammals

When the sun goes down and the cool stillness of night takes over, some of nature's most interesting creatures are at their active best. Pleasant Southern California summer months are ideal times to set aside an evening for a nighttime prowl in search of wily critters of the dark. Some are as elusive as a shooting star. Others, adapting to urbanization as successive generations learn that depending on humans is far easier than foraging for themselves, will actually pose for photos.

Everyone's favorite, and among the easiest to spot, is the raccoon. I remember one quiet evening in Pine Mountain, a small community near Mount Pinos in the Los Padres National Forest, sitting on the deck of a friend's cabin enjoying the scent of pine and listening to night sounds. As we watched the stars appear among the branches we heard a scuffling noise, snapped on the light and discovered five pair of glowing eyes blinking down at us from a Jeffrey pine. A mother raccoon apparently was giving her offspring a climbing lesson, hoping for a handout as part of the bargain. The family stared at us with interest for some time. When they realized they weren't going to be fed, they backed down the tree and shuffled off toward a neighbor's garbage can whose lid was wisely secured with a heavy rock.

Part of the raccoon's appeal is its "masked" face, which gives it the appearance of at least dressing properly for its midnight thievery. They forage happily in garbage that isn't tightly contained, quickly polish off leftovers in dog and cat dishes and help themselves to food snacks left anywhere that they can access. In some areas they have no fear of humans, having cadged handouts for so long that they're almost another family pet. One rural couple who had installed a doggie door for their pair of springer spaniels tells of the chilly night that the dogs jumped into bed with them. In the morning they discovered they had shared the bed not only with the springers but with a pair of enterprising raccoons. Raccoons don't hibernate, but if the temperature drops several degrees below freezing they will seek out a warm place or fall into a deep sleep and become dormant.

The North American raccoon *(Procyon lotor)* is one of seven species that are divided into about 25 subspecies. They usually weigh 14 to 16 pounds, but a clever, well-fed raccoon that has convinced neighborhood humans that all it needs is a meal and it will love them forever can be as big as 40 pounds. Raccoons' long, coarse fur is gray to grayish brown. They have five or six dark rings on the tail. Living in rotted-out trees, they like woodsy areas near water where their omnivorous tastes can be satisfied. They're also quite at home in suburban neighborhoods.

It is a myth that raccoons wash their food before eating it, as is the tale that they have no salivary glands and must wet their food before eating. This washing behavior is seen only in captivity and is thought to simulate searching for small prey in water. Another theory is that by immersing food the animal is able to feel for concealed objects that it shouldn't eat.

"Playing 'possum" is a phrase that's been around for generations. It refers to the unusual creature correctly called the opossum and its apparent ability to "die" in order to fool predators. I've seen it happen. A friend and I pulled a possum by the tail from a hole in a hollow tree. Long before we had it out it had become a gray, inert mass. No amount of prodding or poking would wake that possum. We carried it by the tail for almost a mile before we sat down for a rest. As we chatted and ate our backpack lunch, the "dead" possum began to move. We sat quietly as it opened its eyes, stretched, then waddled off, confident that it was no longer in danger. Naturalists think that "playing 'possum" is not something that the animal does consciously. Rather, they surmise that fright stimulates the release of a chemical into the creature's bloodstream and temporarily paralyzes it.

Opossums, like kangaroos, are marsupials, the only marsupials found outside of Australia. The common opossum in North America *(Didelphis marsupialis)* is about 20 inches long with an unattractive, rat-like tail that may be ugly but is prehensile, which means it is amazingly adept at grasping. It can hang upside down from tree limbs, swinging to and fro as it plucks succulent plums or figs from nearby branches. The story about raising its young in a pouch is true, except that the pouch is more like a second womb, in which a tiny newborn opossum attaches itself to its mother's teat by swallowing it. They remain in this state for about two months. When they are about the size of a field mouse they may venture out to ride on their mother's back, wrapping their tails around her tail as she curves it over her back.

Although it was originally a forest animal, the opossum, like the raccoon, coyote and other displaced wild creatures, has learned admirably the lessons of urban survival. In the mid-1980s, residents of the San Fernando Valley north of Los Angeles swamped animal regulation phone lines with complaints that opossums were taking over their yards. The clever animals had discovered that fruit trees abound in these quiet residential suburbs and simply moved in to feast, after dark, on their favorite citrus fruits, figs, grapes, berries and other crops that once had grown commercially in this fertile valley.

Some residents, opting to befriend the interlopers, reported that the opossums made good pets, showing up on schedule to be fed along with the family dog and cat. When challenged, the opossum would first try a fierce display of all 50 teeth, lapsing into corpselike torpor if confronted violently. Californians, however, never did seem to learn the lesson that southerners were aware of for generations— opossums taste good, especially when stewed with onions and peppers, with a side of cornbread and sweet potatoes.

A close relative of the raccoon and about the size of a gray squirrel, the ringtail cat has a long, bushy tail that, at about 15 inches, is the same length as its body. It also is called civet cat, coon cat, bandtail cat and miner's cat because frontier miners would take them to work to get rid of rodents. Its face is foxlike with large, dark eyes that look even larger because they are ringed in white. It eats chickens and other birds, lizards, frogs, rats, mice, spiders and eggs. Ringtails, in turn, are preyed upon by great horned owls and bobcats. They prefer to live along rocky cliffs, in caves, crevices or hollow trees and also have been spotted in abandoned buildings and attics.

Although there are plenty of them around, chances of seeing a ringtail are pretty slim. They are elusive and secretive. But you'll know if one has been in the area because of the vile-smelling fluid, much like skunk musk, that it emits when threatened or frightened. Although they have claws that they can partially retract, their tracks show no claw marks and are similar to a house cat's.

The presence of skunks is most often sensed after the fact, so to speak. Two glands at the base of its tail emit a powerful, repelling smell that is its chief form of protection. More than one dog owner has spent several hours bathing the pooch in tomato juice, one of the simplest ways to get rid of skunk smell. But if unthreatened, skunks can be fascinating to watch. The striped, or common skunk *(Mephitis mephitis)* ranges from 11 to 15 inches long but can appear much larger because of its foot-long bushy tail. Their preferred foods are plants or small animals, but many urbanized skunks have developed a taste for dog and cat food. Seen less frequently is the Western spotted skunk, quite common along the Colorado River and differing little except that it has spots rather than stripes.

Skunks breed from February to early March, and about 63 days later produce a litter with one to seven young. By July the little ones are able to scramble around on their own. Some skunk lovers report that if you take a baby skunk from its mother when it is just a few months old, it can be treated just like a cat and will rarely spray because it does not feel threatened in its domesticated situation. Another, more surefire alternative is to have its anal glands removed. Those who have tried it, however, point out that a skunk's sharp claws and digging behavior sometimes make it a less than ideal pet.

Skunks inhabit all of California, preferring forests and wooded areas for their burrows. It's not unusual to catch one of the black-and-white striped creatures in the headlights of your car as it waddles across a little-traveled road. Especially in spring, when breeding season is in full swing, skunks become hazards to motorists as they throw caution to the winds in pursuit of mates. Once widely hunted for their coarse but attractive pelts, they now are simply interesting parts of nature.

See chapter 42 on rats, and chapter 56 on owls, which also are nocturnal.

Hot
Spots

For a good look at nocturnal mammals, find a wooded riparian area and settle in around dusk with a strong flashlight. When you hear scurrying and scratching noises, flick on the light and you'll almost certainly have a night creature in your beam. Although most of them will turn tail and scoot into the bushes immediately, remember that skunks have a very strong defense mechanism. You might want to do your flashlight shining from 10 yards or so.

During warm summer months, raccoons and ringtails like to hang around the tram building in **Mount San Jacinto State Park** near Palm Springs. Raccoons are so common, in fact, that signs plead with visitors not to feed them. Shyer ringtails are more likely to be spotted near dusk along the wooded trails. From the north edge of Palm Springs take Tramway Road off CA Hwy 111 and follow it 3.5 miles up the hill to the Palm Springs Aerial Tramway.

Big Morongo Canyon Preserve in the San Bernardino Mountains near Yucca Valley has a narrow canyon oasis with one of the Mojave Desert's largest cottonwood and willow woodlands. The creek there is a favorite spot for ringtails and raccoons. Take I-10 to its junction with Hwy 62, then go north about 10.5 miles. At the northeast end of the business district of Morongo Valley, turn right on East Drive. The preserve entrance is about 200 yards ahead on the left.

41

July Shorttakes

Wood Storks

A decided rarity anywhere except its tropical homeland in Central and South America, the wood stork is a species that apparently decided to wander. The only nesting colonies in the United States are in Florida.

But during July and August a group of the great birds heads for the **Salton Sea National Wildlife Refuge,** where they are seemingly oblivious to summer's 115-degree temperatures. They are easy to spot in the sea's shallows as they feed on snakes, fish and frogs. Almost 4 feet long with a wingspan of $5^1/_2$ feet, the elegant white bird is a dignified airborne spectacle. It flies with neck and legs extended, slow wingbeats creating its graceful, soaring flights. Formerly called the wood ibis, it is distinguishable from the whooping crane by its dark head. To get to the Salton Sea National Wildlife Refuge, from Hwy 86/78 take Forrster (Gentry Road) north to Sinclair and the refuge entrance.

Sharks

July and August are the months when California's coastal waters are the warmest and are the best time for certified divers to crawl into a wet suit, don scuba gear and head for the **Channel Islands National Marine Sanctuary** for a possible glimpse of sharks. More than 25 shark species live in the sanctuary. Contrary to the bad rap they've gotten in movies like *Jaws,* by nature the animals are shy and reclusive. You are most likely to see the blue shark, usually about 6 feet long, as it travels closer to the islands to feed. The smaller horn shark is happiest around rocky reefs. Huge basking sharks, which can be up to 45 feet long and feed on plankton, are sometimes spotted on the surface as their large dorsal fin breaks the water. If you're over a sandy bottom, look for a leopard shark whose spotted skin helps it blend in with the ocean's floor. To get information on the Channel Islands, call (805) 658-5730.

The feared great white shark is common along the California coast and in the sanctuary, where it cruises in search of the seals and sea lions that are among its favorite foods. The great white shark attacks on humans that create sensational headlines are rare and almost always a case of mistaken identity. The silhouette of a wet-suited surfer, arms and legs dangling over the sides of his board, looks amazingly like that of a sea lion.

At the very tip of Baja California around **Los Cabos** and **Cabo San Lucas,** fishermen regularly pull hammerhead sharks from the warm waters. These odd creatures have a flat, rectangular appendage on their heads that gives them their name. Eyes on the ends of the "hammer" allow them to see in all directions. The smaller young hammerheads often seen by divers near the sandfalls and caves are not considered dangerous to humans. But the pelagics can be voracious predators when hungry. Daily commercial flights from Los Angeles and San Diego go to Los Cabos airport. You can also drive down the Baja Peninsula on Mexico Hwy 1 to Los Cabos and Cabo San Lucas.

Mites

Not usually the sort of thing you'd go in search of, but if heavy summer rains have triggered their appearance this month, you can't help but see giant red velvet mites walking on the ground everywhere in the Sonoran Desert. They're almost a half-inch across and are a brilliant velvety red. They are parasitic and are out to mate and find a new host.

42

A Closer Look: Desert Rats

Rats. Yuk! That's what most people think of these scampering, bustling little mammals. But in the Sonoran Desert, the busy creatures have a much better reputation than their city-dwelling house, roof and sewer counterparts. They are not only clean, they're industrious, intelligent and smart ... by their own standards, of course.

One of the most interesting desert rat dwellers is the pack rat, also called a woodrat or trade rat. More than 20 species range across North and South America. It looks a lot like the unwelcome guest that sometimes shows up in barns, garages and even homes but has larger ears, softer fur and a tail covered with hair. It is also much more particular about where it lives, eschewing garbage-strewn alleys and sludge-filled sewers for homes with a view, such as mountain vistas and desert dunes. In the mountains they often build nests on isolated ledges. In the Sonoran Desert they may inhabit shallow caves or nests in living cactus, because the spines discourage large predators and the clever rat can use the plant as a food source.

Pack rats also may build a home of "litter" that includes sticks, cholla joints, rocks and animal dung, usually at the base of clumps of cactus and low-growing bushes. They don't really burrow but sometimes dig a trench or tunnel under their houses that leads to a soft, grass-lined nest inside. This home is called a "midden."

In Baja California a particularly enterprising pack rat on Espiritu Santo Island constructed his midden from the skeleton of a fallen cardon. He appropriated the long-dead cactus, then dragged pieces of cholla skeleton and twigs to it to create a little den.

A pack rat's midden may serve as home for generations. Anecdotal evidence says that some middens, left undisturbed, can be thousands of years old. To examine one is to prowl through layers of history. They're recognizable as a pile of desert brush, sticks and leaves in a gently rounded mound that can be 6 feet or more across. Somewhere near the ground is an entrance. By urinating on the outside, the rat creates an exterior surface that hardens into an armor-like shell that protects the tunnels inside for hundreds of years.

Because the pack rat's midden offers protection from the elements, particularly in the desert where it provides shade, it becomes habitat for other creatures as well. Lizards, snakes, scorpions, black widow spiders and a strange creature called a kissing bug all may become tenants. The kissing bug not only resides in the nest but sucks blood from the rodent as its main source of nutrition.

Pack rats' middens sometimes help to solve crimes and provide valuable scientific information. Human bones thousands of years old discovered in a midden allowed archaeologists to place a culture in a particular area at a certain time. A pack rat in England helped convict a lying husband of murdering his wife. The wife's wedding ring, lost when the husband dragged her corpse through a deserted thicket, was discovered in the midden. This led police to search the area for the woman's body. When it was discovered the husband confessed.

Pack rats live all over the **Sonoran Desert.** They are nocturnal, emerging at night to search for seeds, fruit and tender new growth. When you spot a midden you may be rewarded with a glimpse of its resident rat if you wait quietly at a distance near dusk.

One of the first sure signs that you're being visited by a pack rat is that small, shiny objects mysteriously disappear overnight. The ever-curious creature will pick up and hide, or carry home, anything that strikes its fancy, which usually is something sparkly and bright. Forks, jewelry, marbles, shiny coins, eyeglasses, keys, even pens and small perfume vials have been found in pack rat middens. On one of its foraging missions it may pick up an object, only to discard it when he finds another that he considers more worthy of attention. This has given it the nickname "trade rat," because the person who misses the eyeglasses may well find a teaspoon in its place.

Perhaps the quintessential example of a creature that has adapted to life in the desert is the kangaroo rat. It is not a true rat and is not related to the kangaroo, but rather is a rodent, dubbed a rat because of its physical similarities to its brother species. Of the 15 different species of kangaroo rat (*Dipodomys* spp.)—among them the giant, Fresno, Tipton, Stephen's and Morro Bay kangaroo rat—all are endangered.

The kangaroo rat also is a nocturnal mammal and is quite difficult to see. It can be distinguished from other small, scurrying desert dwellers by its extremely long hind legs, long tail, and hopping, bounding gait. This is one of the characteristics that enables it to survive the desert's heat. It can move across the sands with a great deal of speed, thus cutting down the time it must spend outside of its cool burrow.

During the heat of the day it lives in an extensive burrow system that it hollows out with its powerful front legs. Its pouchy cheeks are used to carry seeds back to the burrow, where it lolls in comfort, many degrees cooler than the temperatures at the surface. Kangaroo rats often choose patches of natural shade to locate their burrows, such as under stands of grass or desert bushes. Besides keeping the burrow cool, the plants' root structures help hold shifting, sandy soil in place and help prevent the burrow from collapsing.

Other unique adaptations that allow it to be a happy desert dweller include a constant humidity maintained in its burrow from the moisture content of its exhaled breath. And, like all rodents, it doesn't lose moisture through perspiration because it has no sweat glands.

Its most unusual characteristic, however, and the one that allows it to endure the desert so well, is its ability to survive without ever having to drink water. Because its kidneys are four times more efficient than human kidneys, it can excrete urine twice as salty as seawater. It has been known to drink seawater and safely excrete the salt, something that would kill other mammals. But if it never drinks, how does it ingest anything to produce urine in the first place? For one thing, its feces are very dry because their moisture content is reabsorbed through the large intestine before the creature excretes them. Then, it can break down metabolically the plants and seeds that form its diet to provide essential fluids. Although other mammals have this ability, the kangaroo rat is the only one known to survive without additional fluids.

When a mother kangaroo rat is nursing its young in the spring, however, it does need additional fluids in its diet to produce milk.

Fortunately, nature cooperates, and in its seasonal cycle produces moisture-rich grasses, succulents and cacti that have benefited from earlier rains.

The natural enemies of all rats are the keen-eyed swooping, diving predators whose acute vision and hearing allow them to spot their prey from great distances. But the kangaroo rat is prepared. Its nighttime nemesis, the owl, descends with a whoosh of wings that the rodent can hear with sensitive auditory capabilities four times greater than that of humans. It can detect the sounds of a snake as it slithers through the sand, and the soft padding of a coyote as it sniffs out its prey. In a display of nature's irony, the kangaroo rat is preyed upon by another endangered species, the San Joaquin kit fox. Once warned, its great speed allows it to sprint to safety before its predator can figure out what happened.

Some rat species are endangered. Other species, including those that live in the Nature Conservancy's Big Morongo Canyon Preserve in San Bernardo County south of Yucca Valley, where the vegetation zones of the Mojave and the Sonoran deserts come together, are doing fine. Pack rats are quite numerous in the preserve.

The endangered Morro Bay kangaroo rat has the distinction of being found only on 320 acres of land near **Morro Bay,** part of which is Montana de Oro State Park, 6 miles southwest of Morro Bay. From Los Angeles take Hwy 101 north to Hwy 1 and follow it to Morro Bay.

The 180,000-acre **Carrizo Plain Natural Area** in eastern San Luis Obispo County is home to the giant kangaroo rat. Its characteristic tracks belie the fact that it has five toes. Only four are usually visible in its tracks because when it runs the whole foot doesn't make contact with the earth. In Carrizo, the vegetation mix of valley saltbush scrub and valley sink scrub makes a high-quality habitat for the rodents. The giant and Tipton kangaroo rats also live in the **Lokern Preserve** 33 miles west of Bakersfield in the San Joaquin Valley. The Carrizo Plain Natural Area may be reached by going south on Soda Lake Road from Hwy 58 or north on Soda Lake Road from Hwy 166.

In the **Sand Ridge Wildflower Preserve** on the southeast edge of the San Joaquin Valley in Kern County, the kangaroo rat shares a

Mediterranean climate with spectacular wildflower displays. To reach the Wildflower Preserve, travel north from Los Angeles on I-5 about 90 miles to its intersection with Hwy 99. Take Hwy 99 north 23 miles to the turnoff for Hwy 58 at Bakersfield. Go east on Hwy 58 for 13.5 miles and turn right onto Tower Line Road. Go south on Tower Line Road for 1.2 miles to a large road barrier and turn left. Park near the large red-and-white water tank.

The desert sands of **Anza Borrego Desert State Park** often bear the dainty tracks of nocturnal Merriam's kangaroo rats. You'll see their tracks more likely than the rats themselves. Evidence of their night-time activity will be two small footprints (front) flanked by two larger ones (back) and a squiggly line where they dragged their tail. To get to the park, follow Hwy 22 through the town of Borrego Springs (Hwy 22 changes names to Palm Canyon Drive) and follow it 0.5 mile to the visitors' center.

August

AUGUST HOTSPOTS

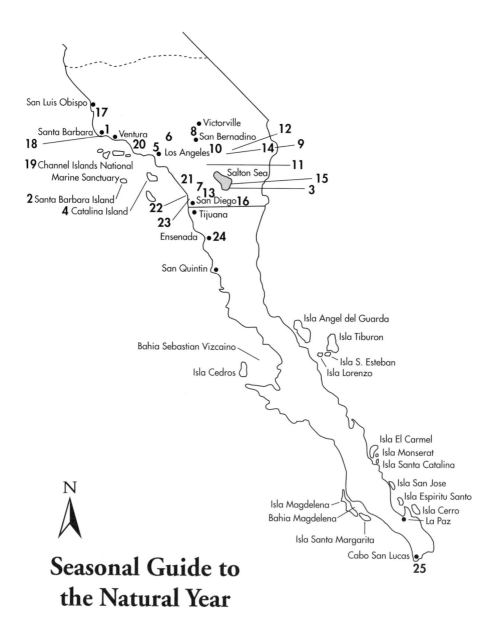

San Luis Obispo
17

Santa Barbara **1** Ventura
18
20 **6**
8 Victorville
San Bernadino **12**
10 **14** **9**
5 Los Angeles
19 Channel Islands National
Marine Sanctuary
Salton Sea **11**
21 **15**
7 **3**
2 Santa Barbara Island
4 Catalina Island
13
San Diego **16**
22
Tijuana
23
Ensenada **24**

San Quintin

Isla Angel del Guarda

Isla Tiburon

Bahia Sebastian Vizcaino
Isla S. Esteban
Isla Lorenzo
Isla Cedros

Isla El Carmel
Isla Monserat
Isla Santa Catalina

Isla San Jose
Isla Espiritu Santo
Isla Magdelena
Bahia Magdelena
Isla Cerro
La Paz

Isla Santa Margarita

Cabo San Lucas
25

N

Seasonal Guide to the Natural Year

SITE LOCATOR MAP

LIST OF SITES
August

1. Andree Clark Bird Refuge
2. Santa Barbara Island
3. Salton Sea National Wildlife Refuge
4. Catalina Island and Avalon
5. Griffith Park Observatory and Planetarium
6. Mount Wilson Observatory
7. Mount Palomar Observatory
8. Mountain Skies Astronomical Society Observatory and Science Center
9. Joshua Tree National Park
10. Big Morongo Canyon Preserve
11. Mount San Jacinto State Park
12. Living Desert
13. Anza Borrego Desert State Park
14. Havasu National Wildlife Refuge
15. Dos Palmas Oasis Preserve
16. Imperial Sand Dunes Recreation Area
17. Pismo State Beach
18. Gaviota State Park and Refugio State Beach
19. Channel Islands National Marine Sanctuary
20. Leo Carillo State Beach
21. Crystal Cove State Park
22. San Elijo State Beach
23. San Diego–La Jolla Underwater Park
24. Ensenada
25. Cabo San Lucas

Notes

43

Gulls

Some people consider them the rats of the ocean, leaving unwelcome calling cards on docks and boat decks. To others, they are as romantic as Jonathan Livingston Seagull from Richard Bach's book, swooping and soaring and performing aerobatics as though they feel they must show off before accepting a handout.

Gulls are abundant, obvious coastal and pelagic dwellers that have not only adapted to human intrusion into their habitat, but have welcomed them. Many abandon their customary sea-based diet of fish, plants and other sea forms scavenged from shorelines in favor of the more easily cadged picnic leftovers and fast-food remnants that humans reliably toss their way. These easy food sources have helped gulls become so numerous that in some areas they may take over the breeding grounds of other birds, to the detriment of the less aggressive species. And almost everyone has read the periodic newspaper accounts of jetliners being disabled when flocks of the creatures have struck planes and been literally inhaled by jet intakes.

Along the West Coast there are more than 20 gull species, plus a few accidentals that stray from the north and south. They breed inland, building shallow nests of debris and seaweed or simply laying eggs in a small depression, but spend most of their lives along the shore. Gulls belong to the subfamily Larinae, with the Western gull the most common species along the coast of California and Baja. It can be as long as 27 inches and is identified by a very dark slate-colored back, white underparts and pinkish feet. Its range extends from Washington State to Baja California and throughout the Gulf of California. It probably descended from the glaucous-winged gull, which can be distinguished from the Western because it is lighter in color.

Also very abundant along the coast, and similar to the Western gull, is the California gull. It's a couple of inches shorter and its legs

A seagull, common along the California coast, soars on coastal thermals.

are yellow-green. Unlike the Western gull that breeds on offshore islands and coastal headlands in colonies, the California gull prefers inland marshes and lakes and even has been known to breed on western prairies as far east as North Dakota.

Heermann's gull is easy to spot because of its red bill tipped in black. In winter its white head becomes gray. Common in Baja, it breeds on islands in the Gulf of California and on islands off Baja's west coast. It is medium sized, with black legs and a slate-colored back. This gull, a highly accomplished scavenger, often is seen following Mexican fishing boats and is not above snagging fish directly from the beaks of brown pelicans.

Gull species are not always easy to differentiate because they go through a succession of colorations as they mature. The Western gull isn't mature until its fourth year. As a youngster it is a sort of overall brown, which changes year by year until the gull develops the characteristic dark back and white head. You can be pretty sure you're looking at a young gull if it is brownish and doesn't yet have a white head. Seasonal variations also change the way a gull looks. Even if you have a detailed, well-illustrated bird book you won't be able to identify every gull you see. Just chalk it up to Mother Nature's whimsy, and enjoy the birds for what they are.

Hot Spots

You'll find gulls anywhere along California's coast. Just stake out a table at any waterfront cafe and you're guaranteed sightings of as many gulls as you wish. Don't feed them. Once you do, you'll be deluged with flocks of hungry gulls, all with an eye on your hamburger.

In Santa Barbara, the freshwater lagoon of the **Andree Clark Bird Refuge** is the place to see gulls galore. Among the clouds of common California gulls, observers report spotting Thayer's and the pink-footed glaucous-winged gull mixed in with the common species. The refuge consists of a peaceful lagoon, gardens and pleasant footpaths. From Hwy 101, take the Hot Springs off-ramp and turn left under the underpass to 1400 Cabrillo Boulevard.

There is a large breeding colony of Western gulls on **Santa Barbara Island** in the Channel Islands National Park. See chapter 60 or call the park's visitors' center at (805) 658-5730 for more information. At the **Salton Sea National Wildlife Refuge** in summer you'll find the yellow-footed gull, which some birders consider a separate species and others think of as a variation of the Western gull. It looks like a Western gull, but is identifiable by its bright yellow rather than pink feet. To get to the refuge, from Hwy 86/78 take Forrster (Gentry Road) north to Sinclair and the refuge entrance.

44

Fish That Fly

They don't really fly and their pectoral fin doesn't flap, but they do soar, sometimes for hundreds of feet at a time. The surface-dwelling flying fish belongs to the family Exocoetidae. They have the same number of fins as other fish, but two sets of very large pectoral and pelvic fins are modified as wings to allow them to fly. The lower portion of their tail is elongated, which helps them perform the aerobatics just above the ocean's surface that delight onlookers. Although it is not considered true flight, they achieve airborne status by racing to the surface, holding their pelvic and pectoral fins outspread and rigid, then gliding in an action that is similar to that of flying squirrels.

The California flying fish *(Cypselurus californicus)* is one of 23 species of flying fish. Mostly open-ocean dwellers, they come to the warm waters around Catalina Island to lay their eggs just below the surface in the thick kelp forests (see chapter 37) from late June into September. They are in residence from May to October. They retreat to deeper waters during the day, roaming close to shore at night to feed on plankton and to hide from larger game fish, returning to the deep as the sun comes up.

Slim, silvery Catalina flying fish can be as long as 20 inches and weigh just over a pound, which puts them among the largest fish in the world that fly. Females are larger than males. They can hit speeds in the air up to 20 miles per hour and soar for 1 to 10 seconds. A series of glides can keep a fish aloft for up to 30 seconds. Glides can extend from 50 to 200 feet. The principles of aerodynamics kick in on windy days, on which the most spectacular flights have been recorded.

It is believed that fish fly as an escape or evasion technique, probably to get away from other fish or something that startles them, like a boat wake. They will often jump a wake as it passes. Many a Sunday afternoon sailor, en route to Catalina from the mainland, has been startled by a flying fish crossing his bow like a winged torpedo. Vessels anchored at night with deck lights ablaze find that the curious fish, attracted by the light, will fly up and land on deck. If they can't flop themselves back into the water, or if someone's not at hand to help them, they'll shortly perish. Even Jacques Cousteau has commented that on the Calypso the frenzied fish will seemingly attack on-deck lights.

Several decades ago the number of flying fish around Catalina dwindled significantly when they were commercially harvested as bait fish. Sport fishermen in pursuit of marlin and swordfish found that the little flying fish, too oily to be palatable to humans, were considered delectable by the larger pelagics. In 1965, the peak year for harvesting flying fish, the catch totaled 171,000 pounds. But as artificial lures became more popular and more effective, their desirability as bait diminished and flying fish numbers rebounded.

The fish never have been endangered or even threatened, a comforting thought when considering the spectacular shows of aerobatics that they perform for countless awestruck observers.

Hot Spots During summer months flying fish stick close to shore where the kelp beds are, so they're readily observable from boats as small as dinghies and as large as ocean liners. Discovery Tours on **Catalina Island** does 55-minute Flying Fish Boat Tours from May through mid-October during which a guide shines a brilliant 4-million-candlepower searchlight from the boat toward shore. The aquatic aviators leap from the sea into the light's powerful beam, putting on a virtuoso performance. Call (310) 510-2500 for more information.

45

Starry, Starry Nights

Romances flourish, legends linger, navigators find safe harbors and new worlds are explored because of the enticement of the heavens. Stars are the subject of love ballads and romance novels. The more you know about them, the more you want to know. Their fascination is endless.

How well you can observe the stars depends on seeing conditions, which in turn are influenced by many things. Especially in August in Southern California and Baja, stargazing is excellent because viewing factors combine auspiciously and the heavens schedule some of their most spectacular displays.

"Seeing conditions," defined by light pollution and clarity, refer to the stability of the air. Thermals from city heat rising in a field of view are called scintillation, a condition that distorts and affects clarity. Inversion and thermal and marine layers, common along California's coast, add additional distortion factors. Local lights such as street and porch lights also can create a cumulative light problem.

Because higher altitudes in general combat a number of these factors, mountains and hillsides almost always offer better star-watching conditions than sea-level spots. First, the skies are cleaner and there is less atmosphere between the earth and the stars. Second, cloud layers at lower levels can block out city lights. At some times of year a marine layer that floats in from California's coast can produce a cloud level at about 3,000 feet. It blocks off star-gazing opportunities for those trying to view from below but forms a protective shield between city lights and the lights of the heavens for those viewing from higher altitudes.

In Southern California at 6,000 feet and above, there is little sky glow to interfere with starlight. At altitudes below 3,000 feet, sky glow lights up man-made as well as natural pollutants such as moisture, air turbulence and haze and can make viewing almost impossible.

Stars in the desert sky, although subject to many light pollutants, have a particular brilliance unlike those in any other place. Water lovers may swear by the radiance of the night sky as seen from a small boat many miles out to sea, but the dry, crisp air of the desert seems to act as a clarifying glass when it comes to observing the heavenly bodies. Scintillation creates distortion but also can act as a magnifier. Once the city and its glow are left behind, desert viewing conditions can be excellent.

When the moon is full (check the current *Information Please Almanac* or your local newspaper for phases of the moon) its brilliance may interfere with stargazing. You can schedule watching times before or after moonset for optimum viewing. Because the moon, Earth and other planets are constantly in motion, specific sightings change from year to year. Consult a current sky chart for the most accurate information.

August, with its Perseids meteor showers and the particularly brilliant Milky Way, is an excellent month to become acquainted with the Southern California skies. Connect-the-dot constellations of mighty warriors, lovely ladies, rampaging animals and insects and birds decorate the night sky, each with a tale that has endured for centuries.

A Navajo legend credits Coyote with giving birth to the stars. When Black God began carefully setting crystals in the sky, Coyote wanted to be involved in ordering the universe. Coyote snatched the pouch of crystals and scattered them to the heavens, creating the many stars that twinkle in the skies, naming some of them for his friends, including Bear and Lynx. Coyote achieved celestial immortality with his own star, Canopus, the most visible star in the Carina constellation. It is listed, along with Vega and Altair, among the 30 brightest stars in the universe.

Although constellations occur as an accident of line of sight and rarely consists of stars that "belong" together, it's still fun to believe in the romanticism of their tales when studying their jewel-like patterns.

Most constellations, like Orion and the Seven Sisters, have stories that stem from the myths of Western Europe. Others have their origins in the cultures of Asia and the South Seas. Observers in the southern United States and Mexico usually get a good look this month at

Tagai's Canoe, a constellation seen by the natives of the Torres Strait, the narrow ribbon of water that flows between New Guinea and Australia. Its legend says that a dozen greedy men, part of the crew of an enormous war canoe, selfishly devoured the provisions that were intended for a succeeding voyage. When Tagai, the leader, found out, he strung the dozen men together and threw them overboard. It is said that a star cluster near the stinger of Scorpius represents the greedy men, while the canoe and its crew appear low in the sky just below Sagittarius.

Residents of the southern United States and Mexico get the best views of the constellation Sagittarius, the archer, low in the southern sky late in summer. If you scan the skies for a group of stars that look like a teapot floating through the Milky Way, you'll spot the archer and his bow. With binoculars you'll be able to see many of the star clusters and gas clouds, such as the Lagoon Nebula that appears near Sagittarius's northern border. Another helpful identifier is the Milky Way, which flows through the constellation.

The heavens' most famous light show, the Perseids meteor showers, usually happens during August. Sometimes the light of the moon can make the showers difficult to see, but with patience you'll unquestionably catch glimpses of what appear to be handsful of jewels flung among the stationary stars. For years it was thought that meteors got their light from friction created as they rocketed through earth's atmosphere, becoming visible about 60 miles above the ground. It is now known that compression creates their light. Unconfined air cannot move faster than the speed of sound, and since meteors move at 30 to 60 times the speed of sound the air cannot get out of the way. Its compression creates heat that is transferred to the moving meteor.

In very simple terms, the Perseids meteor showers are caused by hundreds of tiny bodies that travel in swarms that are traversed by the earth as it orbits. These little pieces of space debris actually vaporize as they hit Earth's atmosphere, creating brief streaks of light. In 1992 the comet Swift-Tuttle passed through our part of the solar system, creating fresh debris that we now see as meteor showers. Under optimum conditions, as many as 60 meteors per hour light up the sky. Take a look at the phases of the moon that appear in the weather section of most newspapers, and you'll be able to tell just how well the meteor showers will show up.

A bright, blue-white star that often appears high in the northwestern sky this month is Vega, part of the constellation Lyra, the harp. It represents the harp of Orpheus, a mortal son of the god Apollo, who created music that made the gods sing. When his wife Eurydice died, Orpheus traveled to the underworld to find her. He played his harp for Pluto, ruler of the netherworld, who was so touched that he agreed to release Eurydice. The only condition was that she would follow Orpheus from the underworld and Orpheus could not look back until they had reached the upper world. But Orpheus could not resist turning to look at his adored wife, whom he saw vanish into the mists as their glances locked. In his grief he wandered the earth until he died, when the gods honored him by placing his harp in the heavens in the constellation Lyra.

The Milky Way flows particularly brightly through the heavens in August. It is a galaxy, a sort of glowing ribbon with the heart of the galaxy inside the constellation Sagittarius, that contains our solar system. One hundred thousand light-years across, from Earth we see its outer edge as the Milky Way proper, a broad band of innumerable stars. Our own sun rests on one of the galaxy's spiral arms, about 32,000 light-years from the center of the galaxy. You can see the Milky Way low on the horizon in the southern sky as a liquid flow of subtle light that becomes more visible as your eyes adjust to its irregular borders.

To see the planet Mars you'll have to be watchful just at twilight, as the so-called red planet sets just a couple of hours after sunset. Don't look for anything particularly red. It looks like any bright star, identifiable as it orbits just north of Spica, the most luminous star in the Virgo constellation. You'll be able to see Mars into the first few weeks of September as it moves away from Virgo, sometimes identifiable because it has brightness, but less "twinkle" than stars in surrounding constellations.

Usually in late August the moon, Mars and the star Spica in the constellation Virgo form a triangle low in the southwestern sky just after sunset. Look for the reddish reflected sunlight from the Martian surface, the blue-white of the super-hot surface of Spica, and easily identifiable moon. Find the moon first, then look to the left for Spica and just above the moon should be Mars.

The planet Mercury usually makes an appearance this month, although it is one of the most difficult planets to spot because it is the closest planet to the sun, whose bright light obscures its glow. If you can leave city lights behind and find a vantage point with true twilight, the elusive planet should be easy to see.

The *Information Please Almanac* carries a diagram of the visibility of planets as well as their positions throughout the year.

Looking for Meteors and Other Summer Sky Jewels

When star-gazing, choose places where there are no lights beside you, above you or close to you. Get as far away from city lights as possible. Sometimes a park, remote golf course or stretch of back road between cities offers a good vantage point.

Spread a blanket or bring a couple of lawn chairs, lie back and let your eyes adjust. Avoid looking at the moon, a flashlight or any other light source. As you become tuned into the darkness, constellations will reveal themselves. Try to picture these imaginary figures as appearing on the inner surface of a huge sphere surrounding the earth.

Some shops, such as The Nature Company, sell glow-in-the-dark star maps that are helpful. But your best bet is to do your homework beforehand, so the sky is like an old friend once you settle into some serious observing. A mounted telescope is a great help, and even a pair of binoculars will reveal stars not visible to the naked eye. *Sky Calendar,* a monthly map of the heavens, is available from Abrams Planetarium, Michigan State University, East Lansing, MI 48824 for about $8 yearly.

Hot Spots

Griffith Park Observatory and Planetarium ([213] 664-1191 for recorded information, [213] 664-1181 to speak to a person), on the south side of Mount Hollywood in Los Angeles, at one time was a wonderful place for visitors to gaze in awe at the heavens through one of the largest telescopes in the world. Unfortunately, urban pollution has obscured the stars to a great extent.

However, on every clear night the telescope is open to the public for free viewing and still offers some spectacular close-up starscapes. What is lost in actuality is made up in simulation in the planetarium, where daily shows duplicate the night sky, accurately mimicking what is going on in the heavens just beyond the starry dome. Frequently, special astronomy programs are offered, and a nightly Laserium show rivals the special effects of *Star Wars*. Enter Griffith Park from Los Feliz Boulevard and Vermont Avenue.

It is worth mentioning because of its fame, but the **Mount Wilson Observatory** just off the Angeles Crest Highway in the San Gabriel Mountains is closed to the public. Its 100-inch reflecting telescope is the one through which it was discovered that our universe is made up of more than one galaxy.

Near San Diego on top of 6,100-foot Mount Palomar, **Mount Palomar Observatory** is home to the 200-inch Hale telescope, the second-largest reflecting telescope in use. In the late 1940s a special road, nicknamed the "Highway to the Stars," was built so that trucks could haul the fragile 200-inch, $14^1/_2$-ton mirror to the observatory site without breaking it. But because it is a research facility of the California Institute of Technology, visitors can only look at the telescope, not through it. Inside the gleaming dome, a small museum has photos taken through the telescope and a video presentation. The silver-domed observatory is in Palomar Mountain State Park. Take I-15 14 miles north of Escondido to Hwy 76, then go east 21 miles to County Road 56. Turn north for 7 miles to a mountaintop intersection. Turn left, then left again onto State Park Road and the observatory. Signs are posted.

The **Mountain Skies Astronomical Society Observatory and Science Center** in Lake Arrowhead is a functioning research observatory and learning science center for public education and youth career development. Located off Rim of the World CA Hwy 18 at an elevation of 5,818 feet, it is surrounded by National Forest, so light pollution is minimal. The site benefits from a "sea of clouds" that keeps lower-elevation light at bay. The planetarium, beneath a fiberglass dome, receives images from a star projector. The observatory has a telescope that the public may use. A larger telescope also is available. Smaller telescopes are scattered around the 6-acre property for the public to use. This nonprofit center is in the process of expanding, so call (909) 336-1699 first to see exactly what facilities are up and running.

46

Bighorn Sheep

One of the most thrilling encounters that nature has to offer is a sighting of a bighorn sheep. Silhouetted against a distant ridgeline, the majestic creatures epitomize a natural nobility that has survived for centuries. More than 50 mountain ranges in the state have bighorns as residents.

The ones seen in California are descendants of wild sheep of Asia that came across the Bering Land Bridge half a million years ago. Glaciers drove them further and further south. As the massive ice sheets retreated, many of the sheep moved with them, but others remained behind to develop into two distinct varieties. Rocky Mountain bighorn are found further north, and desert bighorn remain in the Southwest and Mexico. Some sheep populations in southern California are referred to as peninsular bighorns, but they are no different from desert bighorns. Naturalists say the term is used simply to identify the geographical range that the sheep inhabit.

At one time many more desert bighorns roamed the state. Some succumbed to poaching, but the greatest devastation to their numbers came because of the introduction of domestic sheep that carry strains of respiratory bacteria that kill bighorns. One contact can wipe out entire populations in three weeks. At the end of the 1800s and at the beginning of this century, domestic sheep were grazed in the state's Central Valley. In the spring they were run south across transverse mountain ranges into the desert where their great numbers dictated that they graze wherever they could. They then worked their way north up into the Sierra Nevada. At many points they came in contact with wild bighorns. Domestic sheep grazing has greatly diminished in recent years, which has helped the bighorn population stay healthy.

California's desert bighorns now are confined to small pockets of wilderness, constricted by the intrusion of people and compelled by

The desert bighorn sheep population is increasing in Southern California.

the crucial search for water and feed. They unerringly know every spring and seep in their area, and oftentimes will choose a roaming range that includes wildflowers such as evening primrose and desert trumpet that observers say are among their favorite snacks. When rations are scarce they'll even eat cactus, using their horns to smash the woody outer parts in order to eat the moist, pulpy centers.

At one time they were freely hunted for their trophy horns, but their highly developed evasion tactics helped them endure. Their keen vision enables them to spot a predator, or human, more than 5 miles away so they can disappear long before they've been spotted. One of their few natural predators is the mountain lion (see chapter 32). Although bighorns are not on the federal list of endangered species, in California they are listed as a sensitive species. In the past 20 years their population in the Southwest has increased from 9,000 to more than 15,000.

Desert bighorns are relatively small. Rams weigh about 160 pounds and ewes around 100 pounds. Rams are crowned with characteristic curled horns that can weigh up to 20 pounds. They are part of the animal's skull and have a covering of epidermal tissue similar to human hair and nails. They continue to grow throughout the animals' life. Annual growth rings, identifiable as indentations and dark lines, help determine an animals' age. A large ram's horns can reach a full curl length greater than 40 inches. They can make a complete circle around his face, sometimes obscuring vision to the point at which the ram breaks or wears the tips off by rubbing them against a rock. Together, the head and horns of a mature ram may weigh more than 30 pounds. The horns of bighorn ewes are slender, seeming to sprout out of their heads like commas, never making more than half a circle.

Bighorns are uniquely equipped to adapt to desert climates. They have light buff-colored coats that help reflect light and heat to keep the animals cool in temperatures that can exceed 120 degrees Fahrenheit. Heat dissipates from a well-developed group of blood vessels in the underside of their bodies, which is always shaded. They can lose up to one-third of their body weight through dehydration, then gulp down as many as four gallons of water at one time to replenish. Nature has given them hard, sharp hooves that can withstand the rockiest of surfaces. The center of the hoof is filled with a spongelike pad that extends out to provide secure traction on the sheerest rock. This contributes to their remarkable ability to leap from one cliff face to another, landing securely on ledges sometimes no more than four inches wide.

Rams breed in late November and early December, the only time when they pay any attention at all to the ewes. After engaging in a sort of "arm wrestling" with their horns locked, and a number of crushing horn-to-horn impacts, the dominant rams mate with several ewes. Ram skulls develop a thickness of more than an inch to accommodate these tremendous collisions. They then promptly forget why they cared about the ewes in the first place and go happily back to their bachelor social groups.

Lambs are born in late May and early June. The ewe looks for the most remote, inaccessible place she can find to give birth to a single 8- or 9-pound lamb. Within a week the new arrival begins to feed on tender grasses and plants and is then ready to join the herd with its mother.

Bighorns are reclusive by nature, seeking out areas that are remote and inaccessible, so sightings require a great deal of patience. They are easier to spot in the summer because heat reduces the moisture-rich

Mount San Jacinto State Park

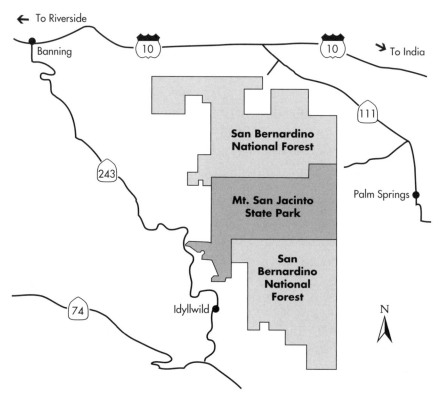

vegetation they feed on, so they are forced to come down from the cliffs to a water source at least once a day. If you quietly hang around an oasis or riparian area during early morning hours, it's possible that the sheep eventually will come to you. Other sightings can be made from a greater distance, when the sheep are prowling the ridges and cliffs in search of the vegetation that is their food. With binoculars a group may be sighted and their movements tracked for a possible closer encounter. Sometimes a glimpse of white rump patch is all you'll see, as a bighorn retreats into brush or around a rocky outcropping.

Feral burros, leftovers from prospecting days, thrive in the desert climate and often compete with bighorns for water. Attempts have been made to remove the burros and to lessen their numbers, but they are assertive and smart and so far have resisted attempts to thin their ranks. Some that are trapped are offered for pets. Contact the Department of Fish and Game for information on how to adopt a burro.

Hot
Spots

A herd of more than a dozen sheep moves between **Joshua Tree National Park** and **Big Morongo Canyon Preserve** in Riverside County. To get to Joshua Tree, take I-10 north to Hwy 62 to the town of Joshua Tree. Turn south on Park Boulevard to the Oasis Visitors' Center. By taking I-10 south, you can reach the Cottonwood Visitors' Center for access to the park. Big Morongo is blessed with two major canyons that extend into the San Gorgonio wilderness area. An average snow and rainfall of 50 inches assures a year-round water supply. The sheep live high up in the San Bernardino Mountains at altitudes up to 11,000 feet, coming down during predawn summer hours to drink and returning to their secret places before the sun is up. The preserve is off Hwy 62 at the northeast end of the business district of the town of Morongo Valley. Turn right on East Drive, then left after 200 yards to go into the preserve.

In Joshua Tree, the Los Palmas area provides good sheep habitat because of its remoteness. Certain areas are restricted to day use only so as not to hamper the sheep from reaching critical water supplies. Heed posted signs that list permitted hours, usually just after dawn and just before sunset.

Mount San Jacinto State Park has a sheep population deep in its remote canyons. This profoundly wild and lovely area, bounded on two sides by the San Bernardino National Forest, is accessible only by rugged hiking trails or via the Palm Springs Aerial Tramway. The tram whisks passengers on a 14-minute glide from the Valley Station at an elevation of 2,643 feet to the Mountain Station at the edge of the wilderness at 8,516 feet. From the north edge of Palm Springs take Tramway Road off CA Hwy 111 and follow it 3.5 miles up the hill. In recent years, residents on the outskirts of nearby Palm Springs report that an occasional emboldened bighorn has refreshed itself at a backyard swimming pool and enjoyed a meal of tender garden greenery before retreating to its mountain aerie.

There have been reports of desert bighorn sightings along Hwy 74 as it descends from the San Jacinto Mountains into the town of Palm Desert. Steep, sheer-sided cliffs are ideal habitat for the sure-footed creatures who apparently roam to the area from other parts of the San Jacintos. And if you miss them there, continue on to the **Living Desert Botanical Garden and Wildlife Park,** where the bighorns are at home on a fenced rocky outcropping. From Hwy 111 east of Palm Springs, turn right onto Hwy 74 and go 2 miles to Haystack Road. Turn left for 1.5 miles, then right on to Portola Road to the parking area.

Anza Borrego Desert State Park actually was named for the bighorn sheep, as borrego means yearling lamb in Spanish. The Palm Canyon Trail as well as Tamarisk Grove Campground are good places to get out your binoculars for sheep sightings along the crests of the surrounding rocky cliffs. Here they are referred to as peninsular bighorns. This population has increased its numbers significantly in recent years since cattle, which competed for vegetation, were removed. The park is just west of the city of Borrego Springs. Follow Hwy 22 (the name changes to Palm Canyon Drive) through town 0.5 mile to the visitors' center.

At California's easternmost edge, along the Colorado River that forms its border with Arizona, **Havasu National Wildlife Refuge** is home to approximately 20 to 30 bighorns on the California side, with an estimated 40 to 45 on the Arizona side. The two populations do not mingle, most likely because the heavy recreational traffic along the Colorado keeps them secluded at high elevations. Occasionally an adventuresome ram has been seen drinking at a lesser-traveled backwater area, but their main water sources are the seeps along canyons. They sometimes are visible from the water, high on the cliffs of Needles Peaks near a bend in the river called Devil's Elbow in 16-mile-long Topock Gorge, part of the Chemehuevi Mountains. Another possibility is seeing the sheep drinking at Bill Williams Delta. You'll never get very close, but their silhouettes against a seamless blue sky are unforgettable.

A small population of bighorns come down from the Orocopia Mountains near the **Dos Palmas Oasis Preserve** to drink at the springs there. The preserve is northeast of the Salton Sea at the base of the Orocopia Mountains off CA Hwy 111 on the Riverside/Imperial County line. The groundwater that gushes to the surface eventually flows into the Salton Sea.

47

August Shorttakes

Spadefoot Toads

During summer monsoons, usually in August, a fascinating phenomenon occurs along the eastern part of the Algodones Dunes in the **Imperial Sand Dunes** Recreation Area. Within hours of a heavy rainfall, thousands of spadefoot toads emerge from their burrows, croaking a welcoming chorus, to begin a complicated mating process. As rain collects in the dunes' low pockets, forming shallow pools, male and female toads migrate to the pools, meet there, breed and lay their eggs. Tadpoles are raised in the pools and become adults, then go off to dig burrows of their own. The whole cycle takes just two or three weeks. No one knows how the spadefoot toads (so-called because their shovel-shaped hind feet help them dig their burrows) perceive when precisely the right amount of rain has fallen to form pools that will last long enough for their offspring to reach maturity, but they do. During drought years the toads don't emerge at all, remaining in a state of estivation, a torpid condition similar to hibernation. The toads' emergence can be unfortunately triggered by man-made stimuli as well as the environmental occurrence of rain. Storms often are accompanied by thunder, a sound familiar to the toads, but which they can confuse with the sound of tires of off-road vehicles rumbling above their burrows. The vibration can cause them to surface at the wrong time, which leads to their death without the support of rain.

The eastern Algodones Dunes is not the desolate, windblown section. It is covered with vegetation including paloverde trees and grasses and has an unusual, wild beauty. To see if the toads are up and croaking, call the Bureau of Land Management at (619) 337-4427. To get there, from the town of Brawley take Hwy 78 east to the dunes.

You Otter Try Clamming

For years Pismo clams have been legendary for their size, sweetness and easy harvesting. Native Americans and sea otters feasted on them until the 1700s, when arriving Europeans scattered the Native Americans, and otters were found to have pelts ideal for winter coats. The clams have been the traditional drawing card to **Pismo Beach,** a small town on the California coast just south of San Luis Obispo. Clams may be taken any time of the year, but it's much more fun to hunt them on a warm and sunny August afternoon than a chilly January one. To be a clammer you need a saltwater fishing license (sold at many area shops), a clam fork and a measuring device called a caliper, normally attached to the clam fork. You need the caliper to be sure you take no clams smaller than $4^1/_2$ inches in diameter, the legal size. When you unearth a clam too small to take, by law you must rebury it.

Try to pick a day with a good low tide (see Appendix for information on tides) and head for the beach south of Grand Avenue any time from a half hour before sunrise to a half hour after sunset. Your limit is 10 clams per day, per person. Bring a bucket and fill it with seawater so that your clams will purge themselves and open slightly, allowing you to remove them from their shells. If you don't, you're guaranteed to find out first hand what "clamming up" truly means.

Your biggest competition in clamming will be from playful sea otters, who consider Pismo clams among life's great treats. For years the otter population was so low as to have almost no effect on clams, which grew larger and more plentiful by the year. Two-footed clammers were the only harvesters. Management and regulation began in 1911 and has continued, to assure a plentiful supply. No one told the sea otters, however, whose numbers have increased to the point where even they have turned to crabs and other food items because the larger clams have become so scarce. But the Department of Fish and Game does report larger numbers of small clams currently being spawned on Pismo Beach. If you time it right, and if enough of the hard-shelled little delicacies survive the four to five years it takes them to become legal size, there could be some mighty good clamming ahead. For more information contact the Pismo Beach Chamber of Commerce, 581 Dolliver Street, Pismo Beach, CA 93449; (805) 773-4382.

48

A Closer Look:
Diving Coastal Waters

With 1,234 miles of shoreline, at least a third of which is in Southern California, and with summer water temperatures in the chilly but manageable low 70s, it's not unusual that a fourth of the state's coastline is managed by California State Parks. Add the shores and temperate waters of Baja California and you have a rich underwater habitat that is readily explorable. From vast kelp forests (see chapter 37) to schools of jacks and mackerels, there is much for the snorkeler and scuba diver to explore.

Among the interesting reef dwellers is the octopus, the many-armed mollusk with an ink-jet system for protection. When in danger from an eel or large fish, it tries to confuse its predator by emitting a black cloud that has the double effect of blunting the interloper's sense of smell and obscuring its vision. The octopus eats crayfish and crab. A pile of their shells is often the first sign that you're near its lair. It simply sweeps the litter of previous meals outside the entrance to its home, usually a hole or crevice among rocks. If an octopus loses an arm it has the ability to grow another, but divers are cautioned to be gentle with them as their population is diminishing along the California coast, mainly because of fishing.

If you're very, very patient, you might be treated to one of the aquatic world's most fascinating relationships—symbiosis. Small shrimp, usually considered a meal for larger creatures, become "dental hygienists" for moray eels. Somehow the eel tells the shrimp that it won't get eaten if it will just do the eel the favor of cleaning the small parasites from the eel's mouth and around its eyes. The "cleaner shrimp" obliges and gets a meal, and the eel gets clean. Other helpful fish include a yellow-orange torpedo-shaped fish called a "señorita," a member of the Wrasse family, the most common parasite cleaner off Southern California's coast.

Divers suited up for a beach entry at Laguna Beach.

In Santa Barbara County at **Gaviota State Park** there is a pier with a 3-ton boat hoist, where you can launch your own boat and zip off to the dive sites between Gaviota and Point Conception. Offshore from **Refugio State Beach** about 18 miles north of Santa Barbara, kelp bass glide through the thriving kelp forest, hunting for the crustaceans and small octopi they love. Kelp perch search for the ectoparasites that it nibbles from fellow fish. Parallel reefs rise from the sand, providing a home for halibut and urchins, gorgonians and nudibranchs (brightly colored shell-less snails) on the rocks. The sandy beach provides an easy entry. Because Refugio is a south-facing beach, one of three along with Gaviota and El Capitan that are nestled under Point Conception, it is shielded from harsh northwest winds and swell, and usually has a warmer water temperature. For more information on Gaviota State Park and Refugio State Beach, call (805) 968-3294.

More than 1,600 square miles extending from the beach to 6 nautical miles offshore from the Channel Islands (see chapter 60) have been designated the **Channel Islands National Marine Sanctuary**. Surrounding the islands of Anacapa, Santa Cruz, Santa Rosa, San Miguel and Santa Barbara, the sanctuary is an underwater continuation of the Channel Islands National Park. In 1969 a spill from one of the many offshore oil platforms galvanized concerned environmentalists into action, and 11 years later the park was designated. The islands are great dive destinations because each has a personality all its own. A mix of warm and cold water masses in the Southern California Bight creates unusual living conditions for sea life. Around San Miguel the cool, nutrient-rich waters harbor fish and invertebrates that are more common off the coast of Northern California. Santa Barbara Island, however, is good for sighting warmer-water fish. Garibaldi, bat rays, skates, starfish and sea lions are attracted by this confluence of warm and cold currents and kelp beds. In addition, more than two dozen species of whales and dolphins, five species of sea lions and seals, and endangered marine mammals including the sei, blue and humpback whales are possible sightings. Besides bottom dwellers, the sea floor is scattered with artifacts from the Chumash Indian civilization as well as more than 100 shipwrecks. Because the area is so popular, overfishing and water pollution are constant dangers. Be sure you know the rules before diving in the sanctuary. Call the sanctuary at (805) 966-7107.

For a look at octopi and nudibranchs, cave divers can head for **Leo Carillo State Beach** on the Ventura/Los Angeles County line. The sand and rock beach has offshore reefs. Look for shallow caves in the underwater rock formations. Call (805) 488-5223 for information.

At **Crystal Cove State Park** great underwater reefs are alive with small opaleye. A marked underwater trail is in the development stage and is expected to be in place by 1997. Call the park at (714) 494-3539 to verify its status before setting out.

San Elijo State Beach in San Diego County between Encinitas and Cardiff-by-the-Sea has a beach entry from the Seaside day use area. During winter months when surf is high the cobble and rock can be a bit hard to negotiate, but once you get in the water the offshore reefs are worth it. The beach is much sandier in summer. Expect to see kelp forests, sea bass, little sand sharks, leopard sharks and blue sharks. You can park in the lot for a short walk to the beach. Call (619) 753-5355 to find out more about conditions at the beach.

The Cove at La Jolla is home to the 6,000-acre **San Diego–La Jolla Underwater Park,** a popular place for divers and snorkelers to explore. In 1971 an ecological reserve was created within the park. It is illegal to remove any plant, animal or geological formation within the 533-acre "look but don't touch" reserve. Fish commonly seen within the park include the jack mackerel, bonito, sardine, anchovy and flat, bottom-scudding California halibut.

There are many good beach-accessible dive sites at **Laguna Beach,** which is often used by scuba instructors for check-out dives. Sheephead, sanddab and opaleye are reliably seen. Small, harmless horn sharks are quite friendly with divers, often remaining motionless for minutes, which makes them good photographic subjects.

The **City of Avalon Underwater Park** at Casino Point just off the coast of Catalina Island about 22 miles from Los Angeles is a protected environment that attracts divers from all over the world. Wrecks, reefs and kelp forests teem with bright orange garibaldi (see chapter 24), kelp perch, California moray, grouper, red snapper, sculpin, sea urchins and other denizens of the deep. Visibility is usually 30 to 50 feet. Signs direct divers to a sandy area to look for halibut and bat rays, the 1980 wreck of a 65-foot barge called the Sujac, octopus hiding among shallow rocks and other creatures. It is one of the state's most popular dive areas, so the parking lot behind the casino is sometimes jammed with cars and scuba shop vans. But once you're in the water there is a feeling of seclusion. The water temperature is usually 54 to 71 degrees Fahrenheit, with September the warmest, so a full wet suit is a necessity. A number of island dive shops rent gear, have air fills and will tell you about current diving conditions (see Appendix).

Also off Catalina Island, a large pinnacle called **Ship Rock** at the entrance to Isthmus Cove is brushed by fairly stiff currents that feed gorgonian fans and octocorals. Yellowtail, small tuna and barracuda are usually hanging around. Directly west of Ship Rock, **Eagle Reef** has a profuse kelp forest as well as nudibranchs and showy Spanish shawls. Rich brown chestnut cowries cover the bottom.

In **Ensenada**, 67 miles south of the Mexican border, is one of nature's anomalies that draws the curious to view it from above and below. Powerful waves force water up through La Bufadora, the Blowhole, causing huge geysers to squirt into the air. Currents bring in colder water that is rich in nutrients. Ling cod are common sights and are much sought after by divers with spear guns. It's possible to swim through a large arch that's encrusted with barnacles. Entry into the water is over rugged, slippery rocks with lots of surge.

A diver's paradise since it was discovered by visitors with interests other than sport fishing, **Cabo San Lucas** at the very tip of the Baja peninsula offers spectacular warm-water diving. You must watch for boat traffic and other divers and snorkelers, especially around Pelican Rocks, but your reward is a look at the brilliant fish that congregate at a coral reef. A number of angelfish including king and Cortez, butterfly fish, silver-striped chromis, longnose butterfly, long skinny cornetfish, damselfish, Moorish idol and many varieties of wrasse are all sighting possibilities during a single dive or snorkel. Sandfalls, like waterfalls, often are observed cascading from ledges. A number of dive shops rent reliable equipment and have air fills.

Getting Certified

In order to scuba dive, you must be certified. This means completing a course offered by a nationally recognized certifying agency. To find a course near you, call the National Association of Underwater Instructors (NAUI) at (800) 553-6284, or the Professional Association of Dive Instructors (PADI), Training Department at (800) 729-7234.

September

September Hotspots

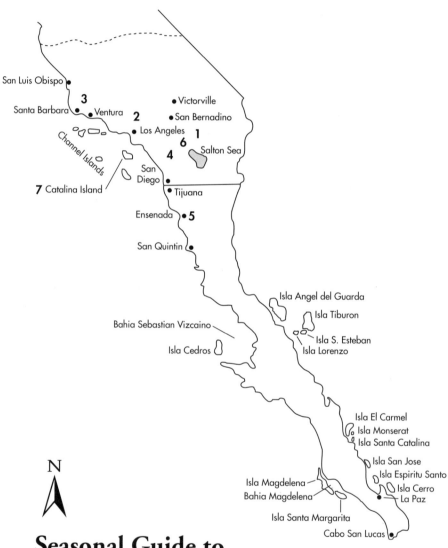

San Luis Obispo •

3

Santa Barbara •
• Ventura

2

• Victorville

• San Bernadino

• Los Angeles

1

6

Salton Sea

4

Channel Islands

San
Diego •

• Tijuana

7 Catalina Island

Ensenada • **5**

San Quintin •

Isla Angel del Guarda

Isla Tiburon

Bahia Sebastian Vizcaino

Isla S. Esteban
Isla Lorenzo

Isla Cedros

Isla El Carmel

Isla Monserat
Isla Santa Catalina

Isla San Jose

Isla Espiritu Santo

Isla Magdelena
Bahia Magdelena

Isla Cerro
La Paz

Isla Santa Margarita

Cabo San Lucas

N

Seasonal Guide to
the Natural Year

Site Locator Map

LIST OF SITES
September

Notes

49

How About a Date?

Ninety-five percent of the dates grown in the United States come from the southern part of California's vast Coachella Valley. Orchards covering more than 5,000 acres line Hwy 111 between Thermal and Indian Wells, with more than a hundred different kinds of dates flourishing on gracefully swaying palms as tall as 25 feet. Medjool, Deglet Noor, the principal commercial variety, and other strains developed here total more than 40,000 pounds of dates a year that are shipped all over the country.

This is the month that the new crop is ready for market. The sweet, sticky fruit ranges from blond to black, depending on type and age of the tree, with most varieties a rich honey or light brown color.

Trees produce a crop every year, up to 300 pounds per tree for real overachievers. Growers say that their trees produce twice the dates that Middle Eastern trees produce because of the encouraging growing weather. Date trees love the dry sunshine and thrive on lands irrigated by the waters of the Colorado River.

Date palms are not native to the Coachella Valley. They were imported by the U.S. Department of Agriculture (USDA) during the 1890s from Algeria, Tunisia, Morocco, Saudi Arabia and other Persian Gulf states, Palestine and Egypt. Dates are the world's oldest known cultivated tree crop. In recent years the valley has had to return trees to their countries of origin to replace the native trees there that have been wiped out by various viruses and diseases.

Date growers say that the only way to propagate the trees and get the same type of date with the same quality is to take offshoots from trees in their first seven to eight years of life. Date seeds, when planted, may grow into a variety different from the tree that produced it. A Medjool seed will produce a Medjool tree, but chances are the tree will not be of as high a quality as a tree that grows from a shoot. The successful varieties of the Old World have developed over several thousand years of selection and propagation of offshoots that were selected from the best possible seedlings.

All of the Medjool date palms now growing in the Coachella, Imperial and Bard Valleys have come from nine offshoots that were brought from southern Morocco in 1927. The shoots were cut from the base of a Medjool palm, packed at an army post, and shipped to the United States where they arrived about five weeks later. The USDA, fearful that the shoots could be infected with a date disease called *baioudh,* insisted that the shoots be planted in an isolated area quarantined from other palm trees. So the fledgling trees were given a new home in southern Nevada, carefully tended and kept in isolation until 1935 when the USDA acknowledged that the shoots were not diseased. They were brought to Indio where their offspring flourish today.

Although you probably won't be allowed in the date groves, many of the neatly planted orchards are easily seen from nearby roads. And most growers keep a fruited tree or two near their retail stands so people can see how dates look when still on the tree.

Hot Spots The following growers have shops and stands that offer everything from stuffed and candied dates to date shakes. Most are open the year around in the **Coachella Valley** except for July and August, when desert heat cuts down on their retail traffic.

- Shields Date Gardens, 80-225 Hwy 111, Indio; (619) 347-0996
- Covalda Date Co., 83-636 Indio Boulevard, Indio; (619) 347-3056
- Indio Orchards, 80-521 Hwy 11, Indio; (619) 347-7534
- Jensen's Date & Citrus Gardens, 80-653 Hwy 111, Indio; (619) 347-3897
- Oasis Date Gardens, 59-111 Hwy 111, Thermal; (619) 399-5665
- Indian Wells Date Garden, 74-744 Hwy 111, Indian Wells; (619) 346-2914

50

Coyotes: Experts at Survival

As the human population increases and sheer numbers demand that more and more land be given over to housing and businesses, decreasing natural habitat means that the creatures that called it home must look elsewhere to sustain themselves.

Coyotes, those sleek, gray-brown, friendly-faced, bushy-tailed creatures that have become a romanticized symbol of the Southwest, are an example of an animal that has cunningly adapted to a changing habitat. And in many cases people aren't particularly happy about it.

Adults weigh from 20 to 50 pounds, similar to a medium-sized dog. Originally they were native only to western North America, but in recent years they've moved into many eastern areas including New England, into habitat that formerly supported wolves. Their diet consists mainly of rodents, rabbits, the eggs of ground-nesting birds and occasionally carrion. They've been spotted at the side of the tarmac munching on roadkills, and when survival dictates they will prey on domestic creatures. Swift and sure runners, they are extremely vocal. Throughout still nights their barks, howls, yelps and yowls are both mournful and fascinating.

Coyotes now roam from Alaska to Mexico, from California to Cape Cod. An early-morning jogger in suburban Los Angeles reported seeing a coyote stalk a cocker spaniel that had been allowed into a yard for his morning constitutional. A homeowner near Canyon Lake watched helplessly from her balcony as a coyote disappeared into the woods with her small dachshund clasped firmly in its jaws. Domestic cats, fat with overfeeding and pampering, are special delicacies. Coyotes even will tip over garbage cans in search of a meal.

They have to be "dealt with," say urban dwellers. They don't belong on our turf. Environmentalists point out that coyotes are not encroaching on our neighborhoods, but rather that our neighborhoods were once their habitat, and they've elected to stay.

A coyote, sleek and well-fed, at a nature reserve.

Coyotes are bold, cautious, pragmatic opportunists. They always know where to find food. Humans have helped to shape this stealthy, sly and tricky character. Two generations ago its voice in the night, raised in communication as it raided a nearby dump, was considered wild and romantic. Today it has become a nuisance.

It is accused of killing defenseless young livestock. Large healthy animals have little to fear, because at an average of 30 pounds the coyote is too small to be much of a threat. However, hungry coyotes quickly learn to bring down slower-moving sheep, easy prey because domestication has bred out defensive instincts.

The coyote's innate cleverness allows it to play dead in order to trick birds into pouncing range. It is equipped with a keen sense of hearing and quick reflexes that allow its catlike attack to dispatch mice and other small rodents quickly and efficiently. Where the coyote population has been controlled, the rodent population often explodes, bearing out the coyote's importance as a predator in reining in rat and mouse populations.

Coyotes are loving parents, behaving in a much more civilized manner with their young than domestic dogs, which immediately rely on humans to aid in the puppy-rearing process. Once a female coyote chooses a suitor to become a pair, gestation takes two months. Denning sites are reused, sometimes for as long as 20 years. A litter, usually consisting of five or six pups but occasionally as many as 10, are born in the mild spring, with parents raising them as a team. The mother coyote nurses her pups standing up so she can watch for danger. At two weeks, when their eyes open, the parents encourage them to view their world from the safety of the den. One parent watches while one stays with the pups.

At three weeks, the father coyote brings home small animals. Ground squirrels, stunned but alive, are presented to the pups as a learning experience and a food source. As the pups acquire eating skills, they must learn to be predators. At this stage they themselves are prey for bobcats, owls and other large birds. Soon they venture out as a family, behavior that gave rise to the erroneous theory that they hunt in packs.

By June, pups are strong, chasing and chewing as they practice to be adult coyotes. Mice, melons, grass and shoe leather all are on their menu. They are about to become an "urban menace."

When they move to town, the vegetation of suburban yards provides cover and food. A trio of coyotes fitted with radio collars revealed an amazing ability to adapt to human activities, with a prey base of rats, cats and small dogs within a small neighborhood. Drainage ditches become coyote highways, with animal remains frequently found in areas of the cement-bound Los Angeles river and in culverts under roadways.

Those who make a study of nature observe that coyotes are victims of their own success. Humans have allowed the coyote population to expand because they have upset the balance of predator and prey. So now they try to manage the coyote's existence.

The legends of Native Americans of the Southwest are filled with coyotes. One says, if a coyote crosses your path, it is calling attention to your obligations and responsibilities in the natural world. The coyote, says another, brings rain, prevents death, places the North Star and guides humans into being.

Tracking Tips

Good places to look for coyote tracks are in riparian areas where the soil may be soft, along roadsides and in sandy areas. Look for breaks in bushes and vegetation that may indicate an access point to water or a coyote trail. Early morning and late evening hours, when the wily coyote is in search of food or water, are the best times. Take a look at the tracks of your dog before setting out so you know what you're looking for. You can tell a coyote's tracks from that of a domestic canine because coyotes walk in a straight line. Their slow, loping gait will leave sets of four aligned prints. Dogs leave side-by-side tracks like humans. Your local zoo also may offer a look at the coyote you're seeking in the wild. Walk softly, pausing often to listen to the sounds around you before moving on. If you should see a coyote, don't approach it. Most likely you will frighten it away. But if it is sick or injured, it may not be able to run and it could inflict a painful bite.

Hot Spots

Urban coyotes are easily observable in newly developed areas where they once lived and where they still can sustain themselves. Suburban dumps, picnic areas, wooded patches near homes and developed areas that back up to forested land all can sustain a coyote population. Or, it's possible you may see one drinking from your swimming pool as you glance out your kitchen window.

Coyotes are most likely to be seen as the weather cools and food sources may be in shorter supply. They become bolder, often wandering presumptuously into backyards in search of a luckless household pet.

Coyotes in Baja California have quite a different attitude, surviving as they do not on urban handouts but on the rabbits, rodents and other small mammals that are their natural prey. In unpopulated areas they may be elusive, not having learned that humans also mean food sources. Sometimes the only indication of their presence is a set of tracks tracing a path from the beach to high-tide scrub.

Sometimes a regional Fish and Wildlife Department knows where coyotes have been spotted because hunters want to know.

Even the local Humane Society may have a fix on coyote where-abouts, especially if one has been shot or captured recently.

One assured way to see coyotes is to visit the **Wildlife Waystation,** a sort of halfway house for injured birds and animals. Those that can't be returned to the wilds are kept and cared for at the Waystation. At any given time, at least a half-dozen coyotes are permanent residents there. The Waystation is at 14831 Little Tujunga Canyon Road, Angeles National Forest, CA 91342; (818) 899-5201.

51

Fruit of the Vine

Whisper the word "wine" in the state of California and the rows of Napa's vineyards, as neat as nuns' embroidery stitches, come to mind. The southern part of the state, however, also produces grapes with character that rivals that of its northern counterparts. Although admittedly lesser known, these vineyards are rapidly forging a reputation and a demand that extends nationwide.

Best known and established of the non-Napa vineyards are those in the south central coast areas of Santa Barbara, Santa Ynez and San Luis Obispo Counties, where the wide flat valleys and rolling hills, cool coastal breezes and temperatures make it an exceedingly versatile grape-growing region. Beginning with vineyards surrounding the Santa Barbara Mission, the area has a history of grape growing that dates back 200 years. You'll probably have to look at a map to see how this works, but the Santa Ynez Mountains actually run east and west close to the coast, forming the longest stretch of transverse mountains in North America. This creates valleys open to the inland flow of cooling ocean air and fog that keeps the climate temperate. The soil contains a good deal of limestone, rock and diatomaceous earth that make it well draining and low in nutrients. Vintners say this inhospitable situation makes the plants struggle to be hardy and sturdy, ultimately producing more and better grapes. More than two dozen vineyards occupy 10,000-plus acres that grow all the classic wine grapes from which come chardonnay, chenin blanc, pinot blanc, muscat, pinot noir, cabernet sauvignon, zinfandel and many others. The four coastal valleys—the Edna, Arroyo Grande, Santa Maria and Santa Ynez—are noted for their pinot noirs and chardonnays, Rhone varietals and sauvignon blanc. Further from the Pacific Ocean, cabernets and zinfandels flourish. The grape harvest can begin as early as the end of August if temperatures are cool and generally extends through November. Most wineries have tastings.

Grapes from California's wine country.

It may not have the trendy reputation of Northern California, or even the upscale image of the wine-producing regions along the central coast, but the small grape-growing area in Temecula can be justly proud of its vintages. A unique microclimate on a high plateau 23 miles inland from the Pacific Ocean and well-drained decomposed granite soils make it much like California's north coast winelands. Even the white riesling of Germany's Rhine flourishes here. An elevation of 1,500 feet means that summer nights are cool, and ocean breezes sweep through a gap in the coastal mountains.

Temecula has 13 wineries, with Callaway perhaps best known and largest, now producing an award-winning chardonnay called Calla-Lees that is aged in large stainless steel vats rather than oak barrels. It has resulted in a fresh, distinct varietal flavor. Maurice Cárrie Winery produces 14 different varietals. Santa Margarita specializes in aged cabernet sauvignons. Little Hart Winery has gained a local reputation for handcrafted, barrel-aged reds and dry, full-bodied whites.

Go in September for the grape harvest, or wait until the third weekend in November for the New & Nouveau Wine and International Food Festival to sample the newest wines of the harvest.

Temecula Vineyards

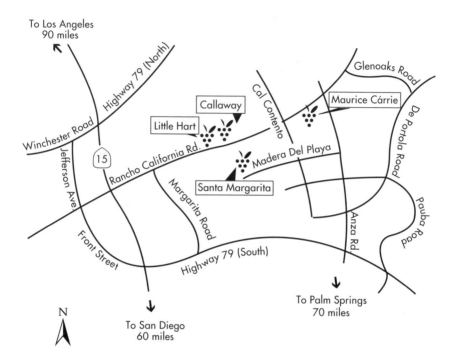

Gaining solid footing in the world of wine are the unexpected newcomers, the vineyards near Ensenada, Baja California's grape country in the Guadeloupe Valley. About an hour and a half south of the California border, this hub of Mexico's wine country thrives on cooling breezes sent inland by cold water upwellings in the bay. They maintain a climate friendly to grape growing and have helped produce an industry that is celebrated in Baja's August Harvest Festival. Cabernets, chenin blanc, merlot and other varietals have won awards and are well worth sampling at half a dozen tasting rooms in Ensenada. Santo Tomas Winery offers good cabernet sauvignon, pinot chardonnay, chenin blanc and blanc de blanc as well as a limited quantity of a lovely sparkling wine. You'll have to pick up a bottle of it at the winery, because it is made in such small quantities that it is not exported.

The **Santa Barbara County** wine area is north of the city of Santa Barbara. Many wineries are just off U.S. Hwy 101, and others are centered around the Danish town of Solvang. Among the largest is the Gainey Vineyard, at (805) 688-0588, where you can sample award-winning varietals, then picnic on the picturesque grounds. Recently, Wild Horse Winery and Vineyard, at (805) 434-2541, has won platinum medals for its chardonnay, pinot noir and merlot. Just off Hwy 101, Leeward Winery is Ventura's local winery, offering tours of its huge barrels and wine presses; then settle into the tasting room for some serious sipping. Call (805) 656-5054. Information on wineries that have tastings, wine touring maps and specific harvesting times is available from the Santa Barbara County Vintners' Association, P. O. Box 1558, Santa Ynez, CA 93460-1558; (805) 688-0881 or (800) 218-0881.

To get to the **Temecula** vineyards, 90 miles southeast of Los Angeles and 60 miles north of San Diego, take the Rancho California exit off I-15 from the Riverside area and head east for about 5 miles and you'll find that you're surrounded by vineyards. For information on tastings and a map for self-guided touring, contact the Temecula Valley Vintners Association, P. O. Box 1601, Temecula, CA 92593-1601; (909) 699-3626.

Ensenada, 67 miles south of the California border on Mexico Hwy 1, has spruced up in the last few years since major cruise ships began using it as a port of call. For information on its wineries, contact the Ensenada State Tourism office at Avenue Lopez Mateos, 1350-B, Baja California, Mexico, or call 011-52-617-23033.

52

Julian's Apple Harvest

Ninety minutes northeast of San Diego, a little mountain town called Julian produces some of the country's best apples. Beginning in mid-September the trees are laden with red, green and golden orbs that look like Christmas ornaments, ready to be harvested at their crunchy best.

Julian wasn't always an apple town. One hundred years ago miners began grubbing gold from the surrounding quartz hills. Remnants of that era are so firmly imprinted on the little burg that much of its dusty history is a charming part of the present.

After its boomtown days, Julian didn't become a ghost town. Today, its population ranges from 2,000 to 3,000, depending on who's home. The town simply traded gold for golden delicious. The first apple trees were introduced in the early 1870s by people who figured that the altitude and cold winters might make good apple habitat. (At an elevation of 4,235 feet, the smell of woodsmoke verifies that even summer mornings require a fire to chase away the chills.) They were right. Apples from the fledgling orchards were taken to the 1893 World's Colombian Exposition in Chicago where they beat out Eastern fruit for first prize. They also garnered honors at the San Francisco World's Fair of 1915.

By the time the gold ran out completely, apples had become a mainstay of the Julian economy. Varieties of the tasty fruit grown in local orchards draw visitors from all over. Baskets of red, green and yellow varieties line shops along Main Street to be purchased by the pound, bushel or simply one at a time to munch as you stroll. Although fresh cider is pressed and available only in the fall, the aroma of apple pie wafts along Main Street all year long.

The large display windows at Mom's Pies showcase the art of apple pie baking at its best. The fragrance of baking pies lures you into the shop, where you can watch white-aproned ladies heap pans with apples

Tasty message on the side of a delivery truck in Julian.

that have been dredged in sugar, cinnamon and butter. You can dig into a fresh, warm slice right there or take a whole pie home.

More than two dozen apple varieties are at the core of Julian's appeal. Beginning in mid-September, for two months the shiny, colorful spheres draw hoards of visitors from San Diego and Los Angeles. The town is the center of apple mania. The circa-1886 Julian Drug Store serves apple pie ice cream at its antique soda fountain, and the local doctor's sign sports a rosy red apple and, you guessed it, the classic homily "An apple a day … ." Shops sell apple potpourri, apple-printed towels and T-shirts, apple Christmas tree ornaments and just about anything you can think of with an apple on it. Since 1949 Apple Day has been one of the town's most cherished holidays.

From the day it's planted, an apple tree takes about eight years to bear fruit, depending on growing conditions and variety. New apple varieties are being added yearly to Julian's repertoire of fruit.

Hot Spots You can visit orchards in **Julian** to watch the process of picking, peeling, coring, slicing and other preparations for market. Most orchards don't allow you to pick your own because of liability problems. Before setting out to see the apples, call the

Julian Chamber of Commerce at (619) 765-1857 for current orchard information. If you call in advance they'll send a list of open orchards with details about the varieties and products you can expect to find.

Apple Lane Orchard, less than 0.5 mile out of town on Apple Lane, has about 1,200 semidwarf trees on 5 acres. The orchard is known for its winesaps and Jona-golds, a combination of Jonathan and golden delicious. It also produces Granny Smith apples. Earligold, akane, hyslop, Jonathan, McIntosh, golden and red delicious, Rome beauty, winesap, Granny Smith, lady and pippins are available at The Apple Store, Julian Orchard, 1255 Julian Orchards Drive, Julian, CA 92036. Manzanita Ranch, located at 4470 Hwy 78/79, about 5 miles west of Julian, grows apples and pears, a fruit that has much the same growing requirements as apples. Julian is located in San Diego County on Hwy 79, about 90 minutes northeast of San Diego.

53

September Shorttakes

Fringe-Toed Lizard

From May to October, your chances are fairly good of spotting a pale, 6- to 8-inch lizard with feet like flippers that lives in the **Coachella Valley Preserve.** It gets the name from elongated scales on its toes.

The torpedo-shaped lizard is uniquely suited to its desert dune habitat. Its neutral color helps keep it anonymous, and it eludes predators by using its snout like a prow and its feet like fins to "swim" through the sand. About the color of the sand itself, the fascinating creature is elusive, seeming to disappear without moving. It combats the hot sands, whose surface sometimes gets as hot as 160 degrees Fahrenheit, by wiggling down into cooler layers where it can lower its body temperature. Double-lidded eyes and a curve in its nasal passage that traps sand are other tools of survival that are part of the lizard's genetic endowment. The fringe-toed lizard *(Uma inornata)* anchors its sand castle on the windswept landscape by building it near a tenacious desert bush.

Listed as endangered at the state level and threatened at the federal level since all but 2 percent of its habitat has been destroyed by encroaching golf courses and home developments, the fringe-toed lizard exists in a unique environment. Eerily lovely, it is created by sands washed from nearby mountains that are sculpted into dunes by prevailing northwesterly winds. There once were nearly 200 square miles of this windswept land for the lizard to enjoy. But development has reduced that space to a fraction of what it was. Once water began to flow into the valley, homes, golf courses and shopping centers flourished. One of the most destructive moves was the planting of salt cedar trees as windbreaks. This prevented prevailing winds from renewing the dunes where the lizards live.

The Coachella Valley Preserve encompasses about 10 square miles of lizard habitat and will grow through fees paid by developers. You'll have a fairly good chance of spotting a fringe-toed lizard there in the early morning hours, before the desert sun becomes too fierce. A lively group of volunteers from nearby Sun City regularly conducts interpretive walks, birdwatching, crafts and school programs. The preserve is about 12 miles east of the city of Palm Springs. Take Ramon Road east to Thousand Palms Canyon Road, which runs through the preserve.

54

A Closer Look:
Catalina Island

"Twenty-six miles across the sea, Santa Catalina is a'waitin' for me," warbled the Four Preps on a 1958 Capitol Records release. But long before then the isolated island had importance in the natural world.

Until the Spanish explorers reached the California coast in the 1500s, **Catalina Island** was a lush, untouched ecosystem. But the cattle they brought with them and additional grazing animals introduced by subsequent settlers, led to devastation of the island's native plants. Before the cattle arrived, the Catalina Island fox, which eats a mixed diet of berries, fruits, lizards and insects, and the Catalina Island ground squirrel, the island's native herbivore, made little impact on native plants. But the large grazing animals quickly devastated many species, upsetting the balance of the island's ecology. And with no large predators to keep the population of grazing animals in check, they soon multiplied out of control.

In 1919 William Wrigley, of chewing gum fame, purchased the island and initiated conservation practices. In 1972 these practices were cemented in place when 42,135 acres of the island were deeded to the Santa Catalina Island Conservancy. With this gift, most of the island's interior and 48 miles of its coastline are now protected in perpetuity.

Today, the island is a tourist destination with hotels, restaurants, shops and entertainment. September is a good time to visit because kids are back in school and the flood of tourists has been reduced to a manageable flow. Hotels have reduced rates, and weather is still warm enough for camping along remote beaches (permits required). Many visitors arrive by private boat to anchor in the crescent harbor of Avalon Bay.

A coastal view of Catalina Island showing boats in Avalon Bay.

The total population of the island is just 2,000, with most of it concentrated in the city of Avalon, but that easily can swell to 10,000 on a sunny summer weekend. Even then there is a laid-back sense about the place. The number of cars brought to the island is strictly limited, and there are none for rent, but you can find a bicycle or golf cart available at an hourly rate.

Many visitors come to the island simply to soak up sun and relax. But those who look further than the sandy beach and hamburger stands can see more than 100 species of birds that include the Catalina quail, a larger subspecies of mainland quail, and the Catalina Island fox, a small subspecies of the Channel Island fox, about the size of a house cat. Other endemic species are the Catalina ground squirrel and the ornate shrew. The bald eagle recently has been reintroduced to the island and is flourishing, although it is reclusive. Sleek ravens catching the thermals above seaside cliffs are more easily seen.

The island has eight endemic plant species that include the Catalina mahogany, the Catalina ironwood (a majestic tree found in groves in shady canyons) and a lovely, delicate plant called St. Catherine's lace. Its dense flower clusters turn from white to a rich russet brown as seeds mature.

A flourish of poppies on Catalina Island near The Isthmus.

An island anomaly and the subject of recent controversy among environmentalists is the herd of buffalo that roams the island's interior. In 1924 fourteen North American bison were brought to the island for the filming of the movie *The Vanishing American.* Rather than spend the money to barge the creatures back to the mainland, they were left to graze on abundant grassland where they seemed quite happy. Ten years later, 11 more buffalo were brought over to keep the herd viable, which today has grown to about 400 of the shaggy beasts. Since they are a nonnative species, many conservationists feel they should be removed. Other, more economic-minded individuals, considering their value as tourist attractions, want them to stay. Some snack stands proudly offer buffalo burgers on their menus, without revealing that the meat is obtained commercially and not from the animals that live on the island.

Inland tours, as well as seasonal whale watching, flying fish and glass-bottomed boat excursions (which provide a good chance to see the bright orange garibaldi discussed in chapter 24) are available. Jeep tours with a botanist can be arranged. For more information on visiting the island, contact the Visitors' Information Center, P. O. Box 737, Avalon, CA 90704; (310) 510-2500.

October

OCTOBER HOTSPOTS

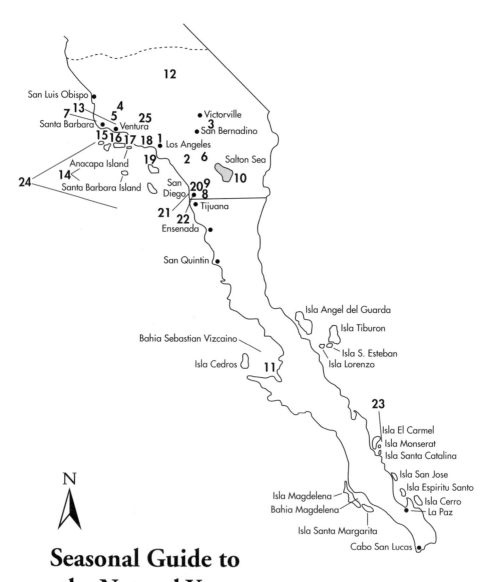

San Luis Obispo

12

Victorville

13
4
7 **5** **25**
Santa Barbara Ventura
3
San Bernadino

15 **16** **17** **18** **1**
Los Angeles

Anacapa Island
19
2 **6**
Salton Sea

14
24
Santa Barbara Island
San Diego **20** **9**
8
Tijuana
10

21
22
Ensenada

San Quintin

Isla Angel del Guarda

Isla Tiburon

Bahia Sebastian Vizcaino
Isla S. Esteban
Isla Lorenzo

Isla Cedros
11

23

Isla El Carmel
Isla Monserat
Isla Santa Catalina

Isla San Jose
Isla Espiritu Santo
Isla Magdelena
Bahia Magdelena
Isla Cerro
La Paz

Isla Santa Margarita

Cabo San Lucas

N

Seasonal Guide to the Natural Year

SITE LOCATOR MAP

LIST OF SITES
October

1. Los Angeles
2. Idyllwild
3. Lake Arrowhead and Big Bear
4. Mount Pinos (Los Padres National Forest)
5. Wheeler Gorge
6. San Jacinto Mountains
7. Nojoqui Falls Park
8. Laguna Mountain Recreation Area
9. Cuyamaca Rancho State Park
10. Salton Sea National Wildlife Refuge
11. Baja California (Viscaino Bay)
12. Kern River Preserve
13. El Capitan State Beach
14. Anacapa and Santa Barbara Islands
15. Mussel Shoals
16. Leo Carillo State Beach
17. Malibu Beach Colony and Point Dume
18. Abalone Cove and White Point
19. Corona Del Mar State Beach
20. Heisler Park and Aliso State Beach
21. La Jolla Cove
22. Point Loma/Cabrillo National Monument
23. Puerto Gato
24. Channel Islands National Marine Sanctuary
25. Guerrero Negro

Notes

55

Autumn: Color It Spectacular

The annual burst of color produced by broad-leafed deciduous trees has been immortalized in songs like "Autumn Leaves" and idolized by throngs of dazzled spectators. At first glance, Southern California's balmy climate may seem to have a lamentable lack of trees that allow fall to oxidize them into the spectacular rusts and golds that prevail in the East and Midwest. In much of the state there are no distinguishable four seasons. But when fall comes to the mountains there is a change in the way the air smells and in how sunlight filters through the trees, creating elongated shadows even at midday. It is definitely fall.

Southern California's deciduous trees may not burst into the exuberant, confetti-like colors that other areas of the country experience, but they do produce rich, subtle shades that satisfy most Californians' desire to spend a day among fall foliage.

When you consider that colder temperatures are required for fall colors to materialize, the logical step is to look to higher altitudes where fall freezes are common and snow is just around the corner. Yellow aspen and an occasional maple are mixed among deep green pine. If you know where to look, you'll find a raft of colorful trees and opportunities to view them.

The imaginative handiwork of Mother Nature begins with the pigment called chlorophyll, a substance in plant cells that uses sunlight to produce food for the tree and makes leaves green. Autumn's shorter days and cooler nights cause the chlorophyll to break down, and photosynthesis ceases as the tree prepares for winter dormancy. The tree withdraws minerals and sugars from its leaves, causing leaf cells to harden and shut off moisture. Without the accustomed sunlight of summer and deprived of water, green coloring fades and other pigments are allowed to show. The hidden colors of the leaves then appear, revealing the brilliant yellow, orange, ocher and red that are the reason the tourist industry thrives on fall foliage tours.

Anthocyanin is the pigment that turns leaves red or red-violet. It also gives red apples their color. After nutrients to the leaf are shut off, the sugars that remain produce anthocyanin, which can vary from year to year depending on sunlight and temperature. So when nights are cool and dry and fall sunlight is blazing, reds will be at their brightest. That's why the same kinds of tree in different locations may show different colors. A south-facing hillside may burst into color a week or more before the northern slope, although both flourish with the same types of trees.

Hot Spots

Right in the heart of **Los Angeles** where temperatures rarely dip below 45 degrees Fahrenheit in fall, there are as many fall colors in nature as there are trees to provide them. A deciduous shade tree called the liquidambar turns a brilliant red-orange every autumn. It's quite plentiful in front and back yards. Walnut and ash trees give Los Angeles a traditional autumn golden hue. Japanese maples that come in many different colors provide spectacular urban displays. Oaks may be yellow or a tawny brown.

In the western suburbs of the San Fernando Valley just north of Los Angeles, many residential streets are lined with Arizona ash, which has bright yellow leaves in fall. Also in the valley, in the Japanese Garden in the Sepulveda Basin near Burbank and Woodley the ridged, fan-shaped leaves of the ginkgo (maidenhair tree) turn the classic autumn gold. They also produce a colorful display in the county arboretum in Arcadia.

Griffith Park in Los Angeles (see chapter 72) burgeons with sycamore, crape myrtle and ginkgo. It is a particularly lovely place to hike slowly, savoring the variety of trees that are indigenous to this vast park. Call (213) 665-5188 for park information.

At 5,400 feet in **Idyllwild County Park** heavy stands of black oak (named for its black, heavily ridged bark) turn a rich golden yellow, while cottonwoods and sycamores become a more subtle, buttery shade. In years that have a longer, milder fall, these trees may develop a beautiful rusty red color. A sharp, sudden deep cold will cause leaves to drop early without fully developing their color potential. Call the park nature center at (909) 659-3850 before setting out. The park is 0.5 mile north of Idyllwild on Hwy 243.

In late October and the first week or two of November, fall color around **Lake Arrowhead** in the San Bernardino Mountains is at its best. Oak, aspen and dogwood are the most colorful specimens. Lake Arrowhead is approximately a 99-mile drive from Los Angeles on I-10 to Hwy 18. Follow Hwy 18 to Lake Arrowhead.

Nearby in **Big Bear,** rust-colored ferns and red and yellow cottonwoods, aspens and creek dogwoods mingle with the evergreens of the pine forest. For a spectacular overview, head for the Snow Summit area where the ski chair lift takes you on a 20-minute ride to the mountaintop restaurant. Attendants will hook your mountain bike on the chair behind you so you have pedal power to explore once you're at the top. The lift operates for cyclists and hikers until there's enough snow for skiers. One of the best things about the San Bernardino Mountains this time of year is that lodging is plentiful and days are clear, crisp and brisk, with very chilly evenings that some call "three-log nights." Big Bear is approximately a 108-mile drive from Los Angeles on I-10 to Hwy 18. Follow Hwy 18 to Big Bear.

Tall, swaying poplars turn a radiant yellow in the **Mount Pinos** area of the Los Padres National Forest west of Frazier Park. Within the community of Pine Mountain, especially along the golf course, there are a number of stands of poplars and aspen that are particularly lovely some years. Take I-5 north of Los Angeles to the Gorman exit and follow signs to Pine Mountain, approximately 17 miles from the I-5 exit.

Also in the Los Padres National Forest, near Ojai, **Wheeler Gorge** is a particularly lovely canyon known for its hot springs. In fall the cottonwoods are decked out in bright ocher, and sycamores turn a dusty yellow. Their fallen leaves carpet the banks of Matilija Creek. Wheeler Gorge is approximately 90 miles northeast of Los Angeles on Hwy 101 to Hwy 33. Follow Hwy 33 for 8.5 miles north of Ojai to Wheeler Gorge.

56

Owls and Other Night Hunters

They glide silently, the night air undisturbed by their soft body feathers, with barely a whoosh of wings to betray their presence and scatter their prey. Their inquisitive "whoo-hoo-hoo who-hoo" is unmistakable. Owls are among the largest and most widely distributed birds of prey. Considered in some cultures to be a bad omen, they may be a nocturnal rat's worst nightmare. But farmers often consider them a boon for helping to control the rodent population in yards and fields (see chapter 42 on rats).

Nature has given them strong legs, hooked beaks and sharp claws to catch the rodents, smaller birds, reptiles, fish and large insects that they seek under cover of darkness. Other unique adaptations essential to their nocturnal prowls are the ability to see well in low light as well as bright sunlight. The owl must turn its head to look up, down and sideways because its forward-directed eyes are immovable. However, some species can turn their heads so far horizontally that it appears they can look behind themselves. Owls have stereoscopic vision that gives them the depth perception vital for spotting small prey.

An owl's ear openings, behind and to the side of the eyes, are not symmetrical in some species. Covered by soft, sound-permeable feathers, these ear openings let the bird compare sound intensity because it is heard differently in each ear, which helps determine the direction from which the sound has come. It also helps them determine the vertical direction of a sound, enabling them to locate prey that may be hiding in grass or bushes.

Owls are of two types, barn owls and typical owls, that together comprise more than 100 living species. The earliest owls lived during the Oligocene epoch, about 38 million years ago. Barn owls have a heart-shaped face and are generally lighter colored on their undersides. The larger typical owls can grow to 28 inches in length and have two tufts of head feathers that look like horns.

Owls hoot as a means of communication. They also communicate with their tufts, laying them flat against their head when frightened or upset and bringing them to attention when alert and comfortable.

Although most are night hunters, the little 7-inch pygmy owl hunts mainly at dawn and dusk. You also may see the short-eared owl, which winters in Southern California, in areas of prairie, marshes and dunes during the day. They are a common winter migrant in the southern deserts. Owls sometimes hunt in groups called parliaments, if an area has abundant prey.

Also a daytime hunter, the lively burrowing owl, common in Southern California and Baja, is considered a desert bird and prefers open grassland and prairies. It nests in burrows that it often appropriates from prairie dogs and ground squirrels and has been known to take over entire prairie dog towns. It even will nest in vacant lots in suburban areas if there are holes for it to move into. Unlike its more dignified cousins that seek high perches from which to swoop gracefully to administer a coup de grace to unsuspecting prey, burrowing owls scurry about on the ground with an occasional spurt into flight to gain the momentum needed to attack their prey. It is recognizable by its long legs, sometimes standing like a front-yard flamingo on a single leg before it scoots off again.

You'll have to venture out at night to glimpse the large, catlike great horned owl, the classic tufted owl that adorns Halloween posters and comes to mind whenever the species is mentioned. It likes forests, streams and open country and sometimes can be seen silhouetted against the moon as it perches on a power pole or winter-nude branch.

This large owl is a fierce and tireless predator and has been known to attack hikers and birdwatchers who ventured too near its nest. It eats almost anything that moves. If you're strolling in the woods and smell skunk, it may really be a great horned owl. They regularly prey on the striped stinkers, ending up covered with the skunk's protective odor.

Much in the news the last few years is the spotted owl, the classic "hoot owl," so-named because of its distinctive call. It is endangered in Southern California and is very different from the great horned. Peaceful and quite trusting of humans, it is a darling of birdwatchers because it is approachable and has an appealing way of winking first one eye and then the other when it is concentrating on something. It needs the thick protection of an old-growth forest to survive. Clear-cutting of this rapidly disappearing habitat has led to its decline. With no cover, it is easily preyed upon by the great horned owl. Spotted owls prefer to live in holes in trees, and in Southern California do quite well in steep canyons with dense conifer forests.

Hot Spots

The barn owl, great horned owl and burrowing owl are abundant, and the western screech owl is fairly common year-round in the lower Colorado River Valley from the Nevada border south to the Mexican border.

The proliferation of small mammals in the spring draws spotted, screech and an occasional flammulated owl to the **Mount Pinos Observation Point** in the Los Padres National Forest. Exit I-5 at Frazier Park and follow signs to Mount Pinos Recreation Area, about 20 miles.

Widely scattered but confirmed as residents, night hunters in the **San Jacinto Mountains** include the screech, great horned, pygmy (identified by its long tail), spotted and barn owls. The mountain town of Idyllwild is a good base for birding this area. From Los Angeles take I-10 east to Hwy 243 and follow it to Idyllwild.

There's a possibility of seeing a spotted owl in the heavily wooded areas of **Nojoqui Falls Park.** Take Hwy 101 north from Gaviota for about 6 miles and turn at the park sign.

Although uncommon, flammulated owls hide in tree cavities in the **Laguna Mountain Recreation Area** about 40 miles east of San Diego. This U.S. Forest Service area in the Cleveland National Forest has an oak woodland and a stand of pines where deadfalls provide homes for the owls. Nearby, in **Cuyamaca Rancho State Park,** nighttime observers are almost sure to spot a great horned owl in the forest, as they are common throughout the year. Both areas are accessible from Hwy 8. For Cuyamaca, turn north on Hwy 79 and go 4 miles to the park entrance. For Laguna, exit on Sunrise Hwy and continue 10 miles to the visitors' center.

The **Salton Sea National Wildlife Refuge** is home to a good population of burrowing owls that have appropriated ground squirrel holes in ditches along and at the end of Vendel Road (see chapter 9).

The deserts of **Baja California** are particularly favored by the little elf owl. Just over 5 inches long, it is most apparent around dusk when it emerges from holes in giant cacti like the cardon.

57

Turkey Vultures

These are the birds that everyone loves to hate. They circled ominously over Humphrey Bogart as he lay parched, disabled and dying in the film *Treasure of the Sierra Madre.* Their favorite meal is something dead. When frightened or challenged they often regurgitate the evil-smelling contents of their stomachs. And if that weren't enough, they are as ugly as warts. They appear to be birds with few endearing features.

Not so, say turkey vulture lovers (and there are quite a few). *Cathartes aura,* relative of the almost-extinct California condor (see chapter 12) is an immense bird that can be up to 3 feet long with a 6-foot wingspan. Its admirers point to its soaring techniques, which enable it to hover on thermals for hours as it searches for the carrion that is its favorite meal. Its head, a muted red in adult birds, is not covered with feathers but rather is bare and wrinkled. Smart design feature, vulture aficionados point out. When the large bird feasts on the carcasses of deer, cattle and other animals, it often gets its entire head inside the dead animal's body cavity. If it were covered with feathers, it would be messy indeed, and the vulture needs clean feathers for proper flight.

The large bird of prey is particularly popular in Kernville, a small city 57 miles northwest of Bakersfield that has an annual holiday celebrating the bird's migration. For perhaps thousands of years the vultures have passed through the South Fork Kern River Valley on their migration along the west side of the Sierra Nevada. Naturalists believe that the vultures use the Kern River site because as they move toward the southern Mojave Desert, suitable nocturnal roost sites are less plentiful. The riparian forest along the Kern River is their last reliable roost before they reach the desert, even though they are nonriparian birds. The next site along their route is Victorville, about 100 miles to the southeast.

Within the past few years, vulture counts have been conducted in and around the Nature Conservancy's Kern River Preserve. An astonishing 27,415 turkey vultures were tallied in a 46-day period, with more than 4,500 vultures recorded on the highest count day. They begin arriving the first week in September and seem to have moved on by the last week of October, with the week that bridges September and October usually yielding the highest concentration.

In late September or early October, the Kern Valley Vulture Festival celebrates the big birds' passage as they take to the sky in great swirling masses. In addition to simply marveling at the sheer numbers of the big birds, the festival includes bird netting and banding demonstrations by the Kern River Research Center and tours of the Kern River Preserve. Call the Kernville Chamber of Commerce at (619) 376-2629 for exact dates.

So what warrants all this fuss about a bird that considers a road kill a gourmet repast? Look at the positives, say buzzard boosters (the term buzzard is really a misnomer, having been hung on the birds as a carry-over from when it referred to buteo hawks). Turkey vultures may be the ultimate environmentalists, the consummate clean-up crew. They go where few other birds choose to venture and scavenge what others shun.

They have adapted to their frailties in a number of ways. Whereas the regal eagle can grasp live prey with its powerful talons, the turkey vulture's talons have little strength, so it has learned to rely on already dead prey that can't wiggle away. Its hooked bill enables it to shred food efficiently. Amazingly, its digestive system and overall physiology enable it to ingest decomposed animal flesh and gain nutrients from it without becoming ill.

Turkey vultures often perch on bare snags, using their extremely sharp eyes to help locate food. It is their sense of smell, however, that is most helpful when in search of a meal. This sense is so sharp that experiments have shown that vultures can find decaying food even when it is hidden under brush or encased in metal, so long as the odor reaches them.

Although sometimes confused with hawks and other raptors, a turkey vulture is relatively easy to identify in flight. Its size tends to

Kern River Preserve

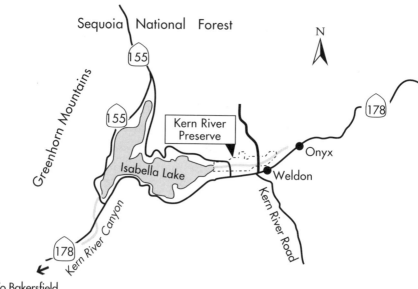

categorize it, as well as its short neck and two-toned underwings. Feathers at the end of its wings appear separated, each individually visible. To differentiate a vulture from a hawk, look for wings held in a shallow V-shape when in flight. Hawks' wings are generally flat. Vulture flight looks tippy and off balance, as though they are constantly correcting. Compared with eagles and hawks, vultures are less graceful.

Vultures don't build nests. Females find a sheltered ledge, cave, hollow in a tree or even rafters in an abandoned building and lay one to three white eggs spotted with brown. Their preferred habitat is dry, open country with roads that have enough traffic to produce the occasional road kill, yet without quantities of speeding cars that will frighten the birds. They are shy and quiet (rarely uttering a sound) and are experts at finding the thermals that let them glide effortlessly.

What about the charge that they routinely defecate on their own legs? Well, it's true. But, vulture aficionados point out, the bird's bad manners are not without purpose. At least one natural scientist thinks that this is a cooling mechanism the birds employ because they have no sweat glands and their natural habitat is dry and hot. Moisture in their offal helps keep them cool as it evaporates.

Hot
Spots

The **Kern River Preserve** hosts the largest migration of turkey vultures north of Mexico in September and October of each year. Access to the preserve is by advance arrangement only; call (619) 378-2531. From Bakersfield take Hwy 99 to Hwy 178, then go east through the Kern River Canyon and Lake Isabella areas. At 1.1 miles past the Kernville Airport turnoff, you'll see the preserve sign.

Vultures also are scattered in trees that border open fields, ungroomed parks and woodland. Just keep your eyes open for circling birds.

58

Exploring Tidepools

Don reef walkers or an old pair of tennis shoes, toss on a windbreaker and a pair of jeans and get set to explore some of the sea's most fascinating habitats. Don't be deterred by chilly spray and ankle-numbing water that can reach the temperature of a well-chilled beer. It's precisely these gray winter months that are the best for exploring California's coastal tidepools because daytime low tides are the lowest and the greatest amount of the pools' rich and abundant life is visible. Head for the lowest exposed tidepools, those that are deepest, where creatures will be feeding. Try to time your tidepool explorations when the tide is going out, so that when you want to return your path isn't blocked by the surging surf of an incoming tide.

To figure optimum times for visiting tidepools (those with the lowest possible tides, generally near a full or new moon), obtain a tide table from the Southern California Fish and Game Department, 330 Golden Shore, Suite 50, Long Beach 90802; (310) 590-5143. As a general rule, Southern California has two high and two low tides per day. You can do your own rough calculations without a tide table if you remember that because the moon makes a complete rotation around the earth every 28 days, a spring (high) tide happens every 14 days, at the new moon and at the full moon. At quarter-moons the low, or neap tides, occur. So, if the tides are low at 8 A.M. on Saturday, they will be high at 8 A.M. the following Saturday, low again the next Saturday, and so on.

Intertidal areas are composed of several sections, the highest of which is the spray zone. This is where droplets from wave action hit the rocks. It is home to creatures that are as well adapted to water as they are to land. Periwinkle snails and shore crabs live here.

Below the spray zone are the high, middle and low intertidal zones, each with its particular group of plants and animals. In the high zone are mussels and barnacles, able to survive because they can close up

Children enjoy a man-made tidepool at the Stephen Birch Aquarium-Museum.

and preserve their natural moisture when the tide retreats and exposes them to air. Middle-zone creatures are less tolerant to air, and those in the low intertidal zone must be kept wet almost continually. This is where five-armed starfish (carnivorous invertebrates also called sea stars), sea hares and sponges live. If they are subjected to air exposure for any length of time, they will die.

Below the low intertidal zone and sharing many of its life forms is the always submerged subtidal zone. Fish often are found in the shallow pools that make up this sector.

Along Southern California's coast are two other important features—embayments and headlands—that dictate the types of sea life that will be found in tidepools. Embayments are inlets or coves; headlands are generally rocky spits of land that jut out into the ocean. The protection provided by an embayment allows more delicate life forms, such as sand castle worms, to flourish. The wave action that headlands experience brings oxygenation and plankton that form the diet of creatures that include sea anemones.

Almost all of Southern California's beaches are publicly owned, which means that people have legal access just about everywhere. The public boundary is the mean high-tide line, better understood as the wet-sand area. While this is a wonderfully democratic attitude, it also means that tidepools are fast becoming depleted. If you don't find appropriate life in one location, try another. If you've come at the end of a busy weekend you'll find fewer creatures than if you look during the middle of the week.

A Word to the Wise

A word of caution before you set out. Tidepools are among the world's most fragile habitats. If you pry a starfish from the rocks, you can easily damage the tube feet that allow it to cling. Without this grip, it can easily be picked up by gulls and terns. Pretty brittle stars can lose an arm just by being touched roughly. Some creatures can die if you move them from zone to zone. A slithery nudibranch won't live long if it is taken from its watery habitat and placed higher up where the rocks are drier. Walking on barnacles will almost surely damage the plates that they rely on for protection. So tread lightly, and observe without touching. Many areas are designated preserves, and souvenir taking of any kind is strictly prohibited.

Cautions are in order for you, as well. Exposed rocks are often slippery with algae, so move with low, shuffling steps. Wear long pants rather than shorts because, if you do take a tumble, you want as much protection as possible. A pair of heavy work gloves can be useful for turning over rocks and for maintaining balance as you work your way along craggy cliffs. If you do your investigating at night, be sure to have a flashlight and a backup light with you. Line up your entry point with something that will remain visible on shore, such as a street light rather than a light in a home that will be extinguished when the occupants go to bed. And day or night, be always vigilant for an errant wave that could knock you off your feet and against sharp rocks. Some of these areas require an entrance fee, and many have picnic and bathroom facilities. Many are just off Hwy 101, which is the main north-south freeway along the southern California coast, and some are off Pacific Coast Hwy 1, but all are readily accessible from public roads.

Tidepooler finds sea urchins and anemones.

Getting Wet

El Capitan State Beach north of Santa Barbara has a parking lot from which you can follow a smooth path to the beach, then head to the southeast to find the anemone-filled tidepools. Lots of algae make the boulders quite slippery, but the rewards are sights of ochre sea stars, giant green anemones, encrustations of California mussels and leaf and acorn barnacles. Bring a picnic lunch to enjoy at a shady table.

Moving south, if you exit Hwy 101 at Casitas Pass Road in Carpinteria, you'll come to **Carpinteria State Beach** where rock bench tidal areas are rich with stalked tunicates, sponges, ochre sea stars, aggregating anemones and brilliantly colored large green anemones. The pleasant beach park here is often quite crowded, but few beach-goers are interested in tidepools so you'll have little competition.

Offshore from Santa Barbara, you'll find some of the best tidepooling on the coast on **Anacapa and Santa Barbara Islands,** which are part of the Channel Islands National Park. Do not collect anything. Because this is part of a California State Ecological Reserve, everything is protected. It also makes for excellent tidepooling, with sea urchins, tidepool sculpin, aggregated anemones, mussels and periwinkles usually plentiful. You'll need your own private boat or a ride with Island Packers (see Appendix) for transportation to the islands, which are about 25 miles from the mainland. The company runs special tidepool exploring trips November through April on days of low tides.

Amid large boulders and cobbles near Ventura, **Mussel Shoals** is aptly named for the carpet of California mussels that lives here. Carefully pick your way among the boulders and you'll see several types of anemones, stalked tunicates, acorn barnacles, purple olives, scaly tube snails and little sand castle worms. This is a good place to find feather boa kelp washed up on shore (see chapter 37). Take the Ocean Avenue exit off Hwy 101 to the Richfield Pier. Mussel Shoals is just south of the pier.

Near busy Los Angeles just off Pacific Coast Highway 1, **Leo Carrillo State Beach** sits just about on the Ventura/Los Angeles County lines and stretches almost a mile from the beach up to Point Fermin. The rocky pockets of shoreline are wiggling with marine life. Pools harbor thousands of chitons burrowing in the soft sandstone of the cobbles, boulders and rock benches here. Hermit crabs scurry within their purloined dwellings. Striped shore crabs, sea slugs, mussels and limpets make up the aquatic population. Purple sea urchins practically carpet the bottom of some pools, growing in unchecked abundance because their natural predator, the sea otter, has been almost wiped out. By gently turning over a rock it is possible to find a small, 1-inch size bat starfish, easily spotted because of its rich, orange-yellow color. Even an occasional little octopus ends up wedged in a crevice. Sargasso weed, sea lettuce and washed up feather boa kelp provide a look at rich vegetation from the sea. An especially good place to look is near the mouth of Arroyo Sequit Stream in the rock intertidal area. Limpets, turban snails, sea anemones, sea slugs, sea urchins, sea stars, mussels, tube worms and octopi may be seen. For low-tide information at this particular site, call (310) 548-7562.

The beach near the **Malibu Beach Colony,** homesite of the rich and famous, is one of the few private stretches of California beach, but it does have a number of access points. At low tide there is plenty of room at the wet-sand line to step along the tidepools. Tidepoolers come here as much for the marine life as for the views of beachfront homes owned by people with faces seen most often on television and the silver screen.

Its rocks and boulders are steep and difficult to climb, and winter's determined surf can splash and even knock you off your feet, but **Point Dume** has a great variety of life clinging tenaciously to its rough outcroppings. From the parking lot at Westward Beach Road, proceed cautiously. You'll see the California mussels that favor these waters, leaf barnacles and large numbers of velvety red sponges and ochre sea stars. If you choose a sunny day, this is a good site to photograph. Even when the weather is cloudy, good moody-broody shots are often possible.

Along the Palos Verdes Peninsula south of Los Angeles are an aggregate of beaches that can offer rich tidepooling experiences. At the southeast end of **Abalone Cove,** don't be discouraged by the long path and stretch of rough beach. The tidepools are worth it. Ochre sea stars abound, as do the chubby, eared California sea hares and red and purple sea urchins. Periwinkles, tegulas, coralline red algae and hermit crabs all are in residence here.

South of Abalone Cove, **White Point** harbors what many consider to be the area's best tidepools. Just park in the lot and you're at the edge of the pools. An interesting feature here is what looks like a "bathtub ring" and a rotten-egg smell at many pools. The white scum is a bacteria that loves the sulfur in hot springs that come from offshore geothermal vents. An old hot springs spa, remnants of which are nearby, once did a thriving business here. Pudgy sea cucumbers prefer the flat rocks further out, as do sea urchins. At the point's southern end, an eroded geological anticline has created pools that are home to thousands of troglodyte chitons. California sea hares, limpets, anemones and sand castle worms also abound.

Just south of Newport Bay Harbor, a small cove shelters **Corona Del Mar State Beach,** south of which slippery rocks dictate a slow pace as you scout the local tidepools. Anemones flourish in the protected waters, and giant owl limpets cling to the rocks. Acorn barnacles, scaly tube snails, red and purple sea urchins, chitons and striped shore crabs make for interesting observing.

Right in the middle of trendy, upscale Laguna Beach, **Heisler Park** overlooks an outstanding tidepooling area, with the best exploring concentrated between Bird Rock and Divers Cove. Park your car, shove a fistful of quarters in one of the metered parking slots and walk just a few minutes to the shore. The rocky surface can be slippery with feather boa kelp, so be careful when angling for a better view of volcano barnacles, spongeweed, leaf barnacles, sea urchins, sea hares and anemone. When you tire of aquatic pursuits, the art galleries and bookstores of Laguna Beach's main street are just up the hill.

One of the most prolific tidepool areas along the coast is a 20-minute walk north of **Aliso State Beach** in South Laguna. The brilliant giant green anemones and purple sea urchins can look like an Impressionist painting, especially on a sunny day. Lesser-seen red sea urchins often are at home here, as are various chitons, giant owl limpets, periwinkles, striped and purple shore crabs and more. The shore here is made up of gently sloping rock benches, so walking is easy and safe.

Near the popular resort town of La Jolla in San Diego County, tidepools are formed among the pounding waves and jagged cliffs. At one time they were overflowing with life forms, but crowds of vacationers with little regard for or understanding of the pools' riches have long ago trampled them and walked off with the best specimens. Still, at **La Jolla Cove Alligator Head,** oval depressions in the sandstone outcroppings shelter thousands of troglodyte chitons. Although it has been years since anyone has reported seeing a spiny lobster, tube worms and California mussels still abound, and a sea anemone will still fasten to a bare toe if you stick it in their pool. At the La Jolla Cove at low tide it's possible to explore the caves where it is said that pirates once stored their ill-gotten gains. If this isn't enough excitement for you, the expensive boutiques and restaurants along nearby Prospect Avenue are just a stroll away, and a grassy picnic area has tables and restrooms.

A favorite with locals at the southern tip of **Point Loma** is **Cabrillo National Monument** in San Diego, whose popularity has caused the tidepool area to be designated a natural preserve within the monument. Interpretive signs provide information

266

about the pools' plants and animals. It can be an excellent introduction to tidepooling. A slide presentation called "Steps to the Sea" is available for viewing for those who want to proceed with solo exploration. Especially on low-tide days, volunteers often are available to identify tidepool creatures and provide information.

Tidepools exist intermittently along the coast of Baja California, and in the Gulf of California. The problem is getting to them. If you're fortunate enough to have access to a small boat or skiff, you can set out for isolated areas, pull ashore and wander to your heart's content. A particularly fertile tidepooling area in the Gulf is **Puerto Gato,** which is a beautiful, uninhabited bay about midway down the length of Baja on the Sea of Cortez side. Among the nooks and crannies of its rocky pools and tidal streams are sculpin, various types of coral, shrimp, tube worms and lots of urchins. Much of its appeal is its feel of pristine isolation.

Not Getting Wet

Cabrillo State Beach in San Pedro is an important tidepooling area, if only because **Cabrillo Marine Museum** is just next door. It enables you to see an explanatory slide show, starfish and sea anemones in a touch tank, then move outdoors to see the creatures in their natural habitat.

The most comfortable tidepooling can be accomplished at the **Stephen Birch Aquarium-Museum,** part of the Scripps Institution of Oceanography in La Jolla. On the patio a large man-made tidepool shelters briny creatures in a no-touch, relatively undisturbed habitat. Man-made waves wash gently over the rocks and crannies that hide spiny sea urchins, starfish, graceful sea anemones, sea cucumbers and more. Helpful docents explain the creatures' place in their particular ecosystem.

The man-made tidepools at the **Orange County Marine Institute** in Dana Point, open to the public on weekends, are true touch tanks. Wall-size posters help visitors identify the creatures they're observing, and museum personnel instruct in safe ways to touch.

In Santa Barbara on Stearns Wharf, the **Santa Barbara Museum of Natural History's Sea Center** has a touch tank filled with live tidepool creatures.

59

October Shorttakes

Salicornia

If you're on the Pacific side of Baja California Sur this month, driving near the town of **Guerrero Negro** on Sebastian Vizcaino Bay, you'll see 30 tidy acres neatly planted with rows of bushy foot-high succulents called salicornia. It's an experimental crop that thrives on salt water and grows on otherwise unproductive desert land. In October, when the bushes have ripened from bright green into fall colors of orange, scarlet and gold, the harvest begins. Salicornia is used commercially for food (there's a recipe for shrimp on a bed of salicornia in the *Silver Palate Good Times Cookbook*), cooking oil, flour, animal feed and cellulose to reinforce particleboard. It's a pretty safe bet you'll be the first on your block to serve the salty-tasting salicornia tips for dinner, joining residents of France and southern Britain in enjoying the plant as a delicacy.

Pumpkins

When it's time for the Great Pumpkin to appear, one of the best places for sighting the orange orbs is near the town of Santa Paula in Ventura County. **Faulkner Farm Pumpkin Patch** is an expanse of golds and oranges, open to the public for picking during October. Take Briggs Road west of Santa Paula to the farm.

Fall Wildflowers

Spring has no monopoly on wildflowers. Many species choose the fall to show off to the fullest. They're often found in rocky areas and places where the soil has been recently disturbed, and alongside little-traveled country roads, although the hardiest among them also proliferate adjacent to busy freeways.

You know it's fall when you see the little yellow flowers of rubber rabbitbrush in piñon-juniper country, such as the Los Padres National Forest. The Navajos once used its twigs and flowers as dyes. It seems to thrive on upheaval, which is one reason it flourishes at roadsides. Although it starts its show in spring, the large, white flowers of the Apache plume are common sights along the roads of southeastern California well into October. Its fruit, attached to pinkish plumes, forms feathery fall decorations. By October the trumpetlike flowers of the buffalo gourd have given way to striped, green orbs the size of tennis balls. The leaves of this lush trailing vine have a vile odor, and the gourds are inedible. Their sole raison d'être seems to be decorative. Late summer and fall are salad days for the goldeneye, part of the sunflower family. With yellow centers and petals, it is as attractive to bees as it is to humans.

60

A Closer Look:
The Channel Islands

Off the Southern California coast, at distances of 25 to 40 miles, lies a chain of five islands (there are a total of eight in the entire group) that form unique ecosystems, have unmatched natural beauty and harbor some of the state's most fascinating species. Their craggy cliffs have been shaped by volcanic activity combined with the plate tectonics that have created so much of this earthquake-prone region. Seen through the foggy mist that often settles over the Santa Barbara Channel, it is sometimes questionable whether they're there at all.

All of the **Channel Islands** bear relics of Indian habitation. Kitchen middens as well as discarded shells, bones and tools tell of the Chumash Indians that once called the islands home. Russian fur traders and U.S. ranchers also left their mark in remnants of dwellings and introduced species.

Five of the eight islands in the archipelago—Anacapa, Santa Cruz, Santa Rosa, San Miguel and tiny Santa Barbara Island—were designated as Channel Islands National Park in 1980. Surrounding each of these islands for 6 nautical miles offshore is a sort of aquatic apron called the **Channel Islands National Marine Sanctuary.** To protect the exceptional biological, historical and cultural resources of the areas, strict rules are enforced. There are few facilities other than vault toilets and tables. There are no freshwater sources so you will have to pack that in as well, remembering that if you bring it in, you also take it out.

A good start for visiting any of the islands in the national park is the Visitors' Center, 1901 Spinnaker Drive, Ventura, CA; (805) 658-5730. Island Packers is the designated concessionaire for excursions and transportation to the islands. They leave from Ventura and from Oxnard harbors; call (805) 642-1393. Channel Islands Aviation (805) 987-1303 can arrange air transportation. For information on visiting Santa Cruz contact the Nature Conservancy at (805) 962-9111.

Santa Catalina is the only one of the Channel Islands that has been developed as a tourist destination, with the largest portion protected by the Catalina Island Conservancy. It has several private yacht harbors, and scheduled transportation is available from San Pedro and Long Beach. Call Catalina Express at (310) 519-1212. (See chapter 54 on Catalina Island).

San Nicolas, an outpost of the Pacific Missile Test Center, and San Clemente Islands are owned by the U.S. Navy, and there is no public access.

The five islands that make up the park have a fascination that begins long before you get there. Blue whales, humpback, minke, killer, gray and other species regularly migrate among the islands. On a spring trip to Anacapa, three companions and I piled into a 12-foot rubber boat to observe gray whales up close and came within touching distance of an enormous, curious cow. She simply rolled on her side to expose her eye as she passed within feet of us, apparently wanting a close-up of the odd craft sharing her waters. Despite her proximity and enormous size, she didn't create so much as a ripple as she leisurely dived to avoid our dinghy, her curiosity apparently satisfied.

Whether your interest is history, birds, marine mammals or other aspects of the natural world, the Channel Islands hold fascination in abundance.

Santa Cruz

The largest of the Channel Islands and the most diverse in terms of terrain, Santa Cruz encompasses grasslands, riparian woodlands and a mountain range that rises to 2,400 feet. Ancient volcanic activity is clear to see along its north ridge. The Nature Conservancy owns and manages the western 90 percent of the island. Once a private sheep and cattle ranch, today the island is largely deserted except for two historic ranches that accept a limited number of overnight guests.

The island supports more than 600 plant types, 43 of which are found only on the Channel Islands. The Santa Cruz Island scrub jay, another island endemic, is larger and more brilliantly blue than its mainland relative. Red-tailed hawks and four pairs of nesting peregrine falcons are part of the resident population.

When circling the island by boat, you will find that its craggy cliffs reveal hundreds of seals and sea lions in its protective coves. Caves at water level, formed when gas bubbles were trapped by the molten lava that formed the island, boom with the echo of crashing waves. Red-beaked oyster catchers, sea gulls, the darker Heermann's gull and even an isolated loon or two bob along the shoreline. Pelican Bay is a favorite calm anchorage for boaters.

Island access is limited because of its isolation from the mainland and cost of transportation. Day-use landing permits are available, and overnight stays at rustic nineteenth-century Scorpion Ranch may be arranged through the Conservancy at (805) 962-9111. The island is rough and rugged with few amenities, so only the hardy should make the trip.

A spectacular way to see Santa Cruz is from a kayak. Exploring its sea caves and rocky shoreline has become a trendy sport. For more information contact Island Packers (see Appendix), who can give advice and help you connect with outfitters.

Anacapa

A string of three small, adjacent islets covering a total of just 1 square mile comprise Anacapa Island. Eleven miles southwest of Oxnard, it is the closest Channel Island to the mainland. An extension of the Santa Monica Mountains, what Anacapa lacks in size it makes up in engrossing content.

Uninhabited except for the resident park ranger, Anacapa is a latticework of volcanic rock that has been eroded over the centuries by dashing waves. The lighthouse, built in 1932, was manned until 1966 when its light and foghorn were automated. At Cat Rock, boaters get a good view of a surge channel and blowhole. Arch Rock at the east end is a natural 40-foot bridge, its base usually littered with a colony of California sea lions. Oyster catchers, endangered brown pelicans, Western gulls, cormorants and other sea birds are easy to spot. West Anacapa is a research natural area closed to the public because it is the primary West Coast nesting site for the brown pelican. Day trips and camping permits for the other two islands are available. Year-round day trips include tidepool exploring from November through April, and swim and snorkel trips from June through October.

Cabrillo Arch, Anacapa Island, covered with cormorants and pelicans.

Santa Rosa

At 150 square miles the second largest of the Channel Islands, Santa Rosa is a beautiful mix of cliffs and canyons, rocky terraces and non-native grasslands that conceal more than 180 archaeological sites. Its sandy beaches are breeding grounds much favored by harbor seals. Because of its extensive grasslands it supports large populations of horned larks, meadowlarks and song sparrows. It also has two groves of Torrey pines (see chapter 62) that are known to grow only here and on the mainland just south of the city of Del Mar. The Santa Rosa Torrey pines have a somewhat easier life than their mainland relatives. More rain makes them healthier and therefore more able to withstand wind, the occasional drought and disease. Some naturalists think that these may be a separate subspecies because their cones are larger and heavier and a few individual trees have grown to a diameter of more than 3 feet.

Chances of seeing the little island fox are better here than on any of the Channel Islands. The spotted skunk, found here and on Santa Cruz, is rarely seen but makes its presence known by its five-toed footprints, often with claw marks visible as well.

Enormous kelp beds surround the entire island, providing a home for the food supply that nourishes larger marine mammals and sea birds. The rusting hulk of the freighter Chickasaw, which ran aground off Santa Rosa in 1962, is a landmark on the island's north coast. A few old ranch buildings from the late 1800s are still standing. Permits are necessary to camp and to go beyond the beach. The island is open for camping April through November.

San Miguel

The westernmost bastion of the Channel Islands, San Miguel has more than 500 almost pristine archaeological sites that date back thousands of years. A monument overlooking Cuyler Harbor commemorates Juan Rodriguez Cabrillo, who fell and broke a limb here and is thought to have died of gangrene on the island, although his grave never has been found.

It is wild and rugged, accessible only by a four- to five- hour crossing that can be extremely rough. But its rewards are worth it. The island's most fascinating feature is its caliche forest, a mineral sandcasting formed by claylike soil and salts that stands in groups like rough-hewn sentries. From the ranger station it is a 3.5-mile hike to the forest. On the other side of the island, at Cardwell Point, thousands of seals and sea lions representing six different subspecies are visible from a high overlook. In spring and early summer, some areas are covered with lovely purple bush lupine, California poppies and locoweed. An incongruous group of swaying palm trees are left over from the filming of a 1935 version of *Mutiny on the Bounty*. Expect strong winds, rain and fog if you decide to make the trek. Permits are required for backcountry visits and camping. It is open for camping May through November.

Santa Barbara

Lying far south of the other national park islands and the least-visited of the group, little Santa Barbara looks a bit bleak because it has no shade trees. But it does have one of the largest flowers along the coast, the giant coreopsis, a huge sunflower than can grow up to 10 feet tall. The island is making a recovery from the 1920s when farming, grazing

The Channel Islands

and the introduction of rabbits severely damaged native vegetation. The rabbits have been removed, and the coreopsis now have a chance, despite remaining stands of nonnative oats, barley and brome.

The island is a birdwatcher's paradise. Western gulls nest in abundance. Barn owls, American kestrels, horned larks and meadowlarks also are in residence. California sea lions and, in winter, elephant seals breed on the island. Because it is just 640 acres, Santa Barbara is easy to explore. At the ranger station you can pick up a booklet that guides you over the island's 5 miles of hiking trails. Overnight camping is allowed April through November with an advance permit.

November

NOVEMBER HOTSPOTS

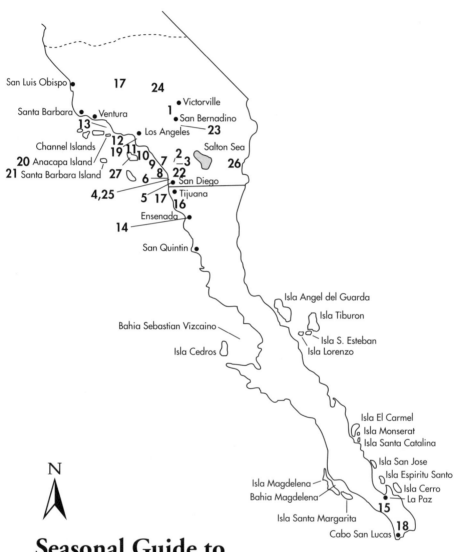

San Luis Obispo •

17   **24**

• Victorville

1

Santa Barbara •

• Ventura

13

• San Bernadino

23

• Los Angeles

Channel Islands

12

Salton Sea

19 **11**

20 Anacapa Island

10 **7** **2** **3**

26

21 Santa Barbara Island

27

9 **8** **22**

6   • San Diego

4,25

5 **17**   • Tijuana

16

Ensenada •

14

San Quintin •

Isla Angel del Guarda

Isla Tiburon

Bahia Sebastian Vizcaino

Isla S. Esteban

Isla Lorenzo

Isla Cedros

Isla El Carmel

Isla Monserat

Isla Santa Catalina

Isla San Jose

Isla Espiritu Santo

Isla Magdalena

Isla Cerro

Bahia Magdalena

La Paz

15

Isla Santa Margarita

18

Cabo San Lucas •

N

Seasonal Guide to
the Natural Year

SITE LOCATOR MAP

LIST OF SITES
November

Notes

61

Gobble! Gobble!

The notion of sallying forth in search of your very own Thanksgiving bird has been around at least as long as the Pilgrims. The only problem with that romantic legend is that it is doubtful that the Pilgrims hunted their turkeys, and are thought to have brought their own domesticated birds with them. Although the wild birds were abundant at that time and remained so until the mid-1800s, the early settlers probably had better things to do than hunt turkeys.

By the 1700s the wild turkey had achieved such gourmet status that Benjamin Franklin wanted to make it the national bird. The eagle, he felt, had "bad moral character." But other forces prevailed and it is not the turkey that we see on the backs of our one dollar bills.

In Southern California it is quite possible that a bird you bagged yourself can end up on the best china in a place of honor between the cranberries and the mashed potatoes. A word that is anathema to environmentalists, "introduced," describes the situation that has made it possible for turkeys to once again claim status as one of California's great game birds.

Although wild turkeys were first introduced into San Diego County in the late 1950s, most of the turkeys that now run wild in Southern California came from the Black Hills area of South Dakota and were set loose in February 1989. Through cooperation among the California Department of Fish and Game and a number of private organizations, birds were trapped for transfer. The clever gobblers, classified by the state legislature as resident game birds, now are nesting and breeding well in parts of San Diego and San Bernardino Counties. In fact, in 1993, 829 people in San Bernardino County were issued wild turkey permits. To the canny birds' credit, the Department of Fish and Game estimates that only 41 hunters reported actually returning home with a tom.

Turkeys are so prolific that a release of a dozen hens and three gobblers can establish a population of 400 birds within five years, according to the National Wild Turkey Federation. An estimated four million wild turkeys now call the United States their home.

In other efforts to revitalize the wild turkey population, birds were pen-raised and then released, which didn't work out at all. The domestically raised birds often transmitted diseases to the existing wild birds, which had no immunity to these alien infections. And the poults never had been taught survival skills such as predator avoidance, communication and foraging.

Despite the fact that they are considered nonnative, turkeys do have a history in California. In the sticky masses of the La Brea Tar Pits in Los Angeles, the number one bird fossils found are those of the wild turkey. There are fossil records of them in other parts of California as well. In Anza Borrego Desert State Park, bone remnants recently found in caves testify that they were a food source for Native Americans.

The transplanted birds probably weren't nearly as traumatized as the turkeys that the Pilgrims prodded onto the Mayflower. Their new environment no doubt seemed very familiar because the Black Hills area of South Dakota in which they were trapped is covered with the very same yellow pine forest (Ponderosa pines are what make the Black Hills appear black) that flourishes in Southern California's San Bernardino Mountains. And lest purists decry the removal of "native" birds from South Dakota to Southern California, the California Department of Fish and Game reports that the founding population of the Black Hills birds came originally from New Mexico. So over the centuries the entire species has become decidedly well-traveled.

From the original 12 birds, the population in South Dakota has mushroomed to the point at which in some areas the birds are a nuisance and the state was delighted to bestow some of its turkeys on Southern California. Pounds of poultry pooh in your backyard are not pleasant to deal with, residents said. And that charming gobble is something to smile about when one or two turkeys are talking. But when several hundred join in a grand gobbler chorus, the noise can be noxious. So the birds are trapped, and many end up in Southern California. A second Southern California turkey release will consist of donor birds from Kansas. So far in California, the feathered immigrants haven't reached numbers where they've become persona non grata, but if they are left uncontrolled, it's a possibility.

The two 1989 releases were made in Miller Canyon near Lake Arrowhead in the San Bernardino National Forest. Those birds have had years to reproduce. In general, a creature introduced into an area at first has few predators and little competition. And given the friendly habitat, an extensive area 30 miles long and 15 miles wide, it is logical that the birds would thrive. They've become so prolific that even the natural barrier of the Cajon Pass hasn't kept them confined. The pass sees more railroad freight traffic than almost anywhere else in the world, so there is lots of disturbance there. And busy Hwy 15 slices through the pass as well. So it might seem difficult for turkeys to get across the pass, but they do. Motorists report roadkills, and turkeys recently have been spotted near the north side of the town of Wrightwood and down into the creek toward the south. Turkeys are now extending into the Angeles National Forest.

What impact do turkeys, a nonnative species, have on creatures who already live there? Almost none, says the California Department of Fish and Game, adding that wild turkeys are a neutral species so far as environmental impact is concerned. Other game birds, such as ring-neck pheasants, also have been introduced without preying upon, displacing or competing for food with native species to the point of causing a detrimental effect.

A turkey's food supply is the seeds of grasses, as well as grasshoppers or arthropods. As adults, turkeys eats more insect life than any other game bird. All types of young game birds must have a very high protein diet in the first 10 days of their feather growth period so that protective feathers develop rapidly. Other favorite foods are acorns and the seeds of yellow pine trees, as well as seeds from other pines. A turkey will eat just about anything it can get its mouth around, but 95 percent of its diet involves those four things just mentioned, wherever it lives.

If turkeys are thriving so mightily, why is it necessary to import more? Because they're so smart, the savvy birds have learned that there is a safe, no-hunting zone in the forest around Big Bear and Arrowhead where they can go to avoid harassment by hunters. So new, uninitiated birds are released to wander open-hunting territory. Bagging them is still not easy, however.

Wild turkeys *(Meleagris galloparvo)* that wander at will through the forests are part of the pheasant family. They are a different subspecies from the frozen Butterball. The supermarket bird is a descendant of turkeys that were introduced to Europe in the sixteenth century when Cortez brought them back from northern Mexico. The bird that graces most American tables at Thanksgiving is the Beltsville white, a domesticated variety developed for its tenderness and large quantities of breast meat. Because a wild turkey has to forage and fly, it is leaner, longer and thinner than its coddled domestic counterparts. When it's on a plate it looks like a stork. A large wild gobbler can weigh up to 28 pounds, and most hens are in the 10- to 12-pound range, respectable weights for serving a number of guests. The difference in taste is about the same as that of fresh pineapple versus canned pineapple. Although there is white and dark meat, wild turkeys are much leaner and more flavorful. Yet they stay juicy during cooking.

The San Bernardino turkeys lay 5 to 17 eggs in a nest on the ground, which hatch in about 28 days. They take their poults into the trees as soon as they can fly. Their mothers protect them from the elements with their wings, often on yellow pine branches 60 or more feet above the ground.

Turkey courtship is loud and ceremonious. The gobbler, not monogamous, goes to his strutting area, known as a lek, and calls, and the hen comes to him. Early in the year when hens are most receptive, a tom can choose from half a dozen female turkeys. He then spreads his tail feathers in behavior called fanning or displaying. Dazzled as the female turkey may be at the time, the next day she will probably visit another gobbler.

A wild tom turkey has metallic greenish, bronze or brownish plumage and a broad fanlike tail and is about 4 feet long. His appearance is something that perhaps only a female turkey could build a dream on. The front of his head has a fleshy growth called a snood. Brightly colored growths called caruncles and a pouchlike wattle hang from his throat. His head, somewhat bare, is normally white, and if he gets excited it turns red. If he becomes very excited it turns blue. Hens are a sedate brown.

Other than hunters with bows and shotguns, turkeys don't have a lot of enemies. Turkey eggs, the most vulnerable state of the bird's development, are delicacies to a number of creatures including big rattlesnakes, weasels, skunks, foxes, coyotes and badgers. The adult turkey, fast and wily, can be taken by golden eagles, goshawks and other large predatory birds. Bobcats and coyotes also can down a turkey. Although some observers report evidence of mountain lions enjoying turkey dinners, others say that the birds are simply too fast for the large cats. Adult turkeys have as their best defense the ability to take flight.

Turkeys do not fly from place to place in a straight line. They tend to remain in an area, although they do move away from snow. They don't like to feed where they can't see the ground.

The normal way to hunt a turkey is to call it. Hunters stake out an area known to have a turkey population, and when the birds fly into the trees to roost for the night, hunters begin calling, pretending they are hens. Toms are cautious, and shun motion and odd sounds. Yet some are so lonesome that they abandon good sense to check out a female's call. This has been the downfall of more than one amorous tom.

A first-year male turkey, called a jake, is among the most fervent turkeys around. When he hears a hen calling from the bushes he wants to get there before the big guys do, so he throws caution to the winds and sets out. The jakes, at about 14 pounds, are young and tender, and are the most sought-after by hunters. As he matures, a jake develops a tuft of hairlike feathers called a beard that protrudes from his breast. When he has one of these, he is considered legal size for hunting. Jakes are the only turkeys that may be taken during the spring hunting season.

There now are turkey seasons in 49 of the 50 states. Alaska has none, Hawaii does. This means that each state's game department has independently determined that there are enough turkeys available so that a hunting program will not damage the sustainability of their population. The season and hours of hunting are strictly regulated.

California's statewide spring turkey season starts the last week of March and ends the first week of May. Fall season begins in November and runs 30 days. In San Diego there is no fall season. For more information on wild turkeys contact the National Wild Turkey Federation, P. O. Box 530, Edgefield, SC 29824-0530; (803) 637-3106.

Hot Spots

Camera buffs and nature observers, much more populous than hunters, say there is little more dramatic show in nature than an adult gobbler fully fanned. This is the traditional Thanksgiving scene that generations have grown up with. To see a wild turkey, use the same techniques as hunters. Watch for tracks, and you'll know the birds are in the area. Turkey calls are available from sporting goods stores that deal in hunting and fishing equipment. With a little practice you may be able to call one out of the trees and into your line of sight.

In San Bernardino County, turkeys love the northern slopes of the San Bernardino Mountains north of the communities of **Crestline, Lake Arrowhead** and **Running Springs.** Since their introduction they have flourished. Take Hwy 18 out of San Bernardino into the mountains and head for small side roads.

In the oak woodland and mixed chaparral of central **San Diego County,** a substantial turkey population exists in the Palomar area and the canyons of the Cleveland National Forest toward Poway, El Cajon east to Pine Valley, north to Julian and in the area surrounding Lake Henshaw. Birds also have been sighted in **Rancho Cuyamaca State Park** north of Julian.

62

The Torrey Pine Hangs On

Among the rugged canyons, colored cliffs and sandstone ridges north of San Diego and south of the city of Del Mar, the exquisitely beautiful Torrey pine makes its last stand. It is the rarest American pine tree and the third-rarest pine in the world. This is the only place that they are found other than a small group on Santa Rosa Island in the Channel Islands chain (see chapter 60). Their home among the steep, jagged cliffs overlooking the surging Pacific is wild and beautiful.

In the Torrey Pines State Reserve the graceful trees have a chance to retreat from extinction. Geological changes in the area have significantly changed the character of the plants and creatures so that the habitat of the Torrey pine is greatly diminished, as are their numbers. Their knotted, gnarled, twisted forms are a response to the constant winds from the sea and to the efforts they must make to maintain themselves in rough, stony soil. Yet the winds help sustain them by bringing cool air from higher elevations.

Dwarfed and bent, the trees cling tenaciously to exposed cliffs. Some seem poised to leap from rocky ledges. It's easy to observe roots that have surfaced above the dry, soft sand-rock in search of moisture and a firmer grasp on the rugged cliffs. Oftentimes they snake down a barren cliff facing in search of moisture and nourishment. Yet the trees' contorted forms have the beauty of works from a sculptor's hand.

Larger trees, some so robust as to seem of a different species, are found in sheltered areas on hillsides and in ravines. Here their trunks can gain a diameter of $2^1/_2$ feet, with the tallest branches reaching 50 and 60 feet into the sky. In these healthier trees, dark patches of witches' broom often appear like a cloud among the branches. It is not a parasite and not a nest, although birds may nest in it. Rather, it is a part of the tree not readily understood. Some naturalists peg it as a fungus that has entered a wound at a growing tip. Others think it may be a virus. A good example of witches' broom is easily observable in the

A Torrey pine clings to a seaside cliff.

reserve across from High Point, and half a dozen others are scattered throughout the area.

The Torrey pine *(Pinus torreyana)* has five long needlelike leaves in a cluster that is surrounded by a sheath. Large, woody cones produce thick-shelled seeds that are prized by nut-gathering animals as well as humans. This maritime pine is a living relic of a time when rainfall along the Southern California coast was frequent and plentiful, nourishing a vast forest of conifers and other plants.

Historically, it is recorded that the little forest was an important landmark for ships battling the dense fog that routinely envelopes this stretch of the California coast. Fortunately, the unique character of the trees was recognized as early as the mid-1800s, so preservation measures were put into place early on. In 1885, a $100 reward, substantial for those days, was posted by the Board of Supervisors of San Diego County for "... the detection and conviction of any person guilty of removing, cutting or otherwise destroying any of the Torrey Pines now growing."

The pines remaining in the reserve today bear the marks of their battles with wind and drought. Downed trees are allowed to remain where they fall, creating a realistic reminder of their mortality.

In 1923 the Torrey Pines Lodge was built on the cliffs overlooking the scenic Painted Gorge. The adobe blocks that make up its walls were crafted on the site, probably by Hopi workmen from Arizona. The one-story structure never housed guests, but meals were served for a number of years. An early menu lists steak, chicken or lobster for

Torrey Pines State Reserve

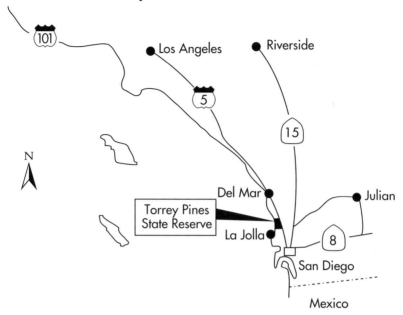

$1 a plate. During the 1920s and 1930s it did a thriving business because the main thoroughfare between San Diego and Los Angeles ran close by. It provided a cool stopping-off point during a journey and was a popular evening supper destination. Most important, it introduced visitors to the beauty of the Torrey pines, thus helping to assure their preservation. The lodge was refurbished and reconstructed in 1988 and today houses the reserve's visitors' center and ranger station.

November is a pleasant month to visit the reserve. Summer's heat has left things a bit dry, but the Torrey pines are lovely any time of year. Ocean breezes keep temperatures ideal for hikes along the half-dozen trails that crisscross the area. Most of the pathways, dotted with interpretive signs and nature markers, are easy to negotiate. Self-guiding maps are available at trailheads.

The 0.66-mile loop that forms the Guy Fleming Trail is the easiest and leads to one of the most interesting examples of eroded sandstone in the reserve. Wildflowers border the path in spring and early summer, and the last half offers see-forever ocean vistas. The steep Parry Grove Trail loops for 0.5 mile from a native plant garden down a hundred or so steps. This grove shows the devastation that drought and the bark beetle can cause. Truly dramatic ocean views characterize 0.66-mile Razor Point Trail, which leads to Yucca Point where benches offer a resting place while enjoying the view. Beach Trail winds 0.75 mile out to flat rock along a not-particularly-scenic route that gets better as it approaches the beach. Little High Point Trail, just off the main road, is simply an access to ocean and lagoon views. Broken Hill Trail affords access to the beach. At 1.2 miles it is the reserve's longest trail, but don't count on walking on the beach. Sometimes beach access is impossible if the tide is in or if waves are breaking high on the cliffs.

Torrey Pines State Beach and Los Penasquitos Marsh also are part of this protected area. The marsh and lagoon, in the northern section of the reserve, are designated a natural preserve. To the uninitiated eye it looks like a large, unattractive mudflat. In reality the lagoon is a rich habitat for creatures including the bay mussel, a 4-inch-long blue-black palate-pleaser that is highly prized by seafood lovers. They are edible, however, only during winter months when the red tide plankton that flourishes during warm weather has subsided. Littleneck clams, jackknife clams, striped shore crabs, fiddler crabs and mudflat crabs also are at home in the lagoon.

One of the most unusual flatfish in the lagoon is the California halibut, which has an eye either on the left or right side of its head. Juveniles often linger in these protected waters before they head off-shore to attain a final growth of up to 5 feet in length. The elusive arrow goby, interesting because it bunks in with worms and ghost shrimps in their burrows, is just 2 inches long and almost impossible to see because of its muddy color. To catch a glimpse of any of these lagoon-dwellers, you must be patient.

Torrey Pines Beach, on the western edge of the lagoon, is the picture-perfect venue for a seaside stroll. Along this windy stretch of sand little clusters of sanderlings, a plump tiny sandpiper, scurry about like teenagers heading for a sale at the mall (see chapter 5). The reddish broad-leafed stalks washed up at the foam line are giant kelp (see chapter 37) ripped from large offshore beds. Bright green surf grass, exposed at low tide, covers flat rocks.

The lagoon and beach, important parts of Torrey Pines State Reserve, are vastly different from the pine-forested cliffs that are less than 0.5 mile away. When viewed together with the pines, they help create a fascinating picture of how divergent ecosystems work together to support a vast array of wildlife.

Hot Spots

Torrey Pines State Reserve is 1 mile south of Carmel Valley Road on North Torrey Pines Road. For an interesting hike, park below the reserve where beachside spaces are available and walk into the reserve, returning to your car along the beach if the tide is out and the waves are behaving.

63

Surf's Up!

Winter months along Southern California's beaches bring the waves that surfers wait for. This is the time of year to snuggle into sweats for a stroll along a misty beach pounded by waves whipped to a froth. Besides the exhilarating tingle of salt spray, the assorted detritus that the waves wash in from parts unknown make beachcombing an ever-changing adventure. Then too, studying a never-ending stream of waves makes many observers wax contemplative, pondering their ceaseless energy.

Waves gently stir the giant kelp forests, create the motion that moves nutrients through the water, and scour the rocks to generate the process of erosion. In ancient times the dramatist Aeschylus thought they laughed, essayist Samuel Eliot Morison said they danced and poet T.S. Eliot was sure they cried. Their romance is unmistakable. Their place in nature is essential.

Surf is the term for the foaming mass of a breaking wave. It's doubtful that the sleek, wet-suited surfers bobbing offshore give much thought to how nature's forces form that perfect wave. But once they catch it, its glorification in the pulsating rhythms of beach songs and the surfers' endless pursuits somehow make sense. At least to them.

Waves breaking on Southern California and Baja beaches were born in nearby storms as well as in disturbances halfway around the globe in areas where the sea is confused. Their motion is produced when air and sea are distorted by a disturbing force such as the wind. A restoring force, in the form of gravity or surface tension, coaxes the water's surface back into its equilibrium position. In the turmoil, waves of many lengths are formed that then travel away from the storm. Each wave moves at its own fixed speed, with waves of like speed sorting themselves into groups so that when they arrive at a distant shore they appear to have a regular sequence.

Waves not under pressure of strong winds are called swells. Waves begin to break on shore when they "feel bottom," which happens

A surfer paddles out into the surf at Laguna Beach in search of the perfect wave.

when they reach a depth shallower than half their length. The famous "curl" that surfers seek occurs when the water depth is 1.33 times the wave height. The wave front becomes so steep that the top falls over and the wave breaks.

Waves can be gentle little ripples caused by an offshore breeze or explosive tsunamis, also called tidal waves, that are created by seismic activity and have the potential to wipe out whole communities. During winter's heavy weather, storm surf can affect beaches that suffer erosion at the hands of choppy, short-period waves. Fortunately, the sand and sediment is often replaced during calm weather when long-period swells surge beachward. More benign waves, such as docile tides, are easily observable almost everywhere along California's coastline.

Predicting the big ones is not only the province of surfers but also of anglers attempting to launch small skiffs through the surf. Various sources swear that every seventh or every ninth wave is the one to catch, but the truth is that a giant wave is formed randomly. When two or more separately sourced crests come together, the swell is high. Statistics have shown that one wave in every 25 will be twice as high as the average wave during that period, while one in every 1,175 will be three times the average.

If you prefer to enjoy the waves as an active participant rather than a passive observer, be careful. Rip currents lurk in areas where incoming waves appear flat and safe. The tip-off is brown, frothy water on the surface. If you are caught in such a current, swim strongly, parallel to the shore, until you get out of the current's clutches.

Hot Spots

South Mission Beach in San Diego has waves of classic proportions that attract the most competent surfers. **Point Loma** also is known for wondrous waves. On the border of Del Mar and La Jolla, **Black's Beach** is the only south-facing beach in the San Diego area. Waves are reliably spectacular. You don't have to crawl all the way down the canyon to enjoy their action. You can stay up on top for a perfectly fine view. Twenty-five years ago it was the nation's only clothes-optional beach. Word of the change still hasn't reached everyone.

At **Windansea Beach** in La Jolla, it is sometimes difficult to see the surf for the surfers. It's an enormously popular spot because waves here are consistent even during summer, and often hit the 6- to 10-foot range. Stay on the bluffs above **Salt Creek Beach** in Laguna Niguel for the best views of breaking waves. A sunset stroll is particularly rewarding. The town of **Carlsbad** has an attractive boardwalk from which to watch the waves roll in. On any given day you can tell how active the surf is by counting the number of exuberant boogie-boarders and surfers.

The Wedge at **Newport Beach** has some of the best surf in the world. Six- to 10-foot waves can be treacherous, dwarfing surfers who disappear for seconds at a time into their deep blue troughs. It's possible to spend hours here, figuring that the last 7-footer was the grandaddy of all waves, only to have it outdone by another crashing breaker. The Huntington Beach Pier that juts out from **Huntington City Beach** in the town of the same name has such great wave-watching even during the summer that two major surf championships are held there. In winter, the waves are totally awesome. During the 1950s an artificial reef was constructed offshore that generates rolling megawaves. That and the currents created by the pier make this a wave-watcher's delight. Stop by the Huntington Beach Surf Museum, right on the sand, for a look at the historical effects of the waves.

At **Seal Beach** just south of Long Beach, you can roll up your sweats and get knee-deep in surf without worrying about being swept out to sea. The break here is very close to the shoreline, putting waves as well as surfers within easy shutter-snapping range.

The waves at **Malibu Surfrider State Beach** have a mesmerizing consistency. A rounded point of land initiates swells of marvelous shapes that seem to roll forever. At least movie moguls thought so, because they used the waves in countless forgettable surfer films including Frankie and Annette's tour de force, *Beach Blanket Bingo*. Other good wave-watching venues in the Malibu area include **Zuma Beach, County Line** and **Topanga Beach.** All are accessible from Pacific Coast Hwy 1.

Off the coast of Ensenada in the Bay of Todos Santos in Baja California, an island called **Isla de Todos Santos** is noted for thrill-a-minute wave-watching. Take a boat out of Ensenada to get there. South of Ensenada about half an hour is a spectacular blowhole called **La Bufadora,** about 13 miles out on the Punta Banda peninsula. Wild waves force water into a tidal cave with a vented top, creating a spurting geyser that shoots more than 100 feet into the air. Although walkways have been created and railings are in place, watch your footing—the constantly spraying water has created slippery walking conditions. About 800 miles south of Ensenada, the town of **Todos Santos** (not related to the island) has surf so high that it's dangerous for casual swimmers but exhilarating to watch. Swells come out of deep water to break with gusto very close to shore. **Calafia,** on the way to Rosarito Beach, has a little restaurant from which it's possible to view the waves. Beyond the Tijuana beach area, **Baja Malibu** is small but noted for spectacular waves. Some of the peninsula's best waves are at its very tip, between **Los Cabos** and **Cabo San Lucas,** where the Pacific meets the Sea of Cortez. Huge combers regularly curl picturesquely shoreward, breaking on sandy beaches, sometimes causing serious riptides.

You can get inside a wave without getting wet at the Stephen Birch Aquarium-Museum, part of the Scripps Institution of

Oceanography in La Jolla. An interactive "wave machine" lets visitors crank a handle to learn the secrets of how waves are formed as they follow a breaker from ripple to exhausted beach foam. Wall charts further explain the interaction of wind and waves.

At **Dockweiler State Beach** just south of the Los Angeles Airport, great waves were subdued and robbed of most of their energy by the construction of an oil jetty in the mid-1980s. Protests by surfers prodded the Coastal Commission into action and, for the first time, a government agency acknowledged that rideable ocean waves are a resource to be protected. By the end of 1997 it is planned that an artificial reef consisting of thirty 300-ton bags of sand will be in place. How effective it will be in re-creating the surging surf is unknown, but the move is being applauded by surfers and environmentalists as well, who see a possibility that the new reef could restore previously destroyed habitat.

64

Pelican Brief

A wonderful bird is the pelican.
His bill will hold more than his belican.
　　　　　　　—Dixon Lanier Merritt

On a crisp, sunny winter day, bouncing across the waves from the Santa Barbara coastline to any of the Channel Islands (see chapter 60) you'll most likely see phalanxes of California brown pelicans skimming the water in linear perfection, like a precisely strung chain of oddly shaped beads. Sometimes hundreds of the birds will converge on a section of ocean to feed frenetically on small fish that swim just beneath the surface.

Seeing so large a number of active, healthy birds seems to verify that the California brown pelican *(Pelecanidae occidentalis)* is well on the way to recovery. Decimated in the 1950s and 1960s by the same pesticides that almost did in the peregrine falcon, it was placed on the federal list of endangered species in 1970. The toxic substances polluted the fish that were the birds' food sources and affected their calcium metabolism, thus weakening their eggshells to the point at which baby pelicans would break through the shells before they were mature enough to hatch.

Now the purse-faced birds appear to have rebounded, coming close to shore during winter months after spending spring and summer breeding on Anacapa and Santa Barbara Islands.

The pelican seems to be one of the most oddly constructed, ungainly creatures to waddle the earth. It has a long neck, broad wings and an expandable skin pouch on the lower half of its beak that it covers with the upper beak like a lid to prevent live catches from jumping out. Yet, as Dixon Lanier Merritt opined, when it trains its eye on fishy prey just under the water's surface and goes into its diving mode from as high as 30 feet, it is a marvel of aerodynamics as it

The California brown pelican is recovering well from pesticide poisoning.

plunges beneath the waves. More times than not it will emerge with a flopping, wriggling fish clasped firmly in its beak that it then maneuvers into its pouch to be enjoyed later. Strong fliers and swimmers, pelicans also can bob on the surface, seining for small crustaceans and passing fry.

Colonies often are comprised of thousands of gregarious pelicans. Females lay three pale eggs, one of which usually makes it through the five- to six-week incubation period. Unless the food supply is especially abundant that year, one or both of the other two chicks will starve or will be crowded to death by stronger siblings. Featherless chicks begin to fluff out in a week or two when they become identifiable as pelicans, but they won't seek out mates until they are three or four years old.

Although their numbers now seem robust, counting pelicans is a difficult job. They can live up to 30 years, so there is little doubt that the same birds return year after year to the Santa Barbara coast. In addition, Mexican pelicans that are migrating through can swell the count artificially. And people are still a major threat. In the Santa Barbara Channel where the birds are most prolific, offshore oil wells pose a constant threat of spills. The area also is an active sport and commercial fishing spot. Pelican bodies, imbedded with fishhooks, tangled with line and washed up on sunny beaches, are not unusual sights.

One of the reasons the pelican thrives in the channel is that the unique confluence of warm- and cold-water currents supports the rich sealife on which they depend for food. In some years El Niño, the warming currents that sometimes invade the channel, conspire to force the sardines, mackerel and anchovies favored by the pelicans to colder waters. A reduced food supply can limit the number of new pelicans that survive. These factors make an accurate pelican count all but impossible. California Department of Fish and Game officials say, however, that up to 6,000 nests on the two islands have been counted in a single year. The number of young produced is another question.

Land birds are most active in the early morning and evening, but sea birds have habits dictated more by the tides, which also can affect the schools of fish on which they feed. You're almost guaranteed to see brown pelicans if you hang around Stearns Wharf in Santa Barbara or the Ventura or Oxnard marinas.

Hot Spots

On **Anacapa Island,** part of the Channel Islands National Park, there is a colony of thousands of pelicans nesting on cliffs and slopes. West Anacapa, the primary breeding site in the western United States for the endangered bird, is a designated research natural area and is closed to the public, although you can view from the water. A spectacular look at the island's rocky face, covered with thousands of pelicans and cormorants, is at Arch Rock on the island's east end. The only way to do this is from the vantage point of a boat, either your own small private craft, or by taking a trip with the park concessionaire, Island Packers (see Appendix).

Tiny, remote **Santa Barbara Island,** 46 miles offshore from Ventura, is home to a smaller pelican breeding population. Because of its inaccessibility, most visitors camp for several nights.

65

November Shorttakes

Snipe

This medium-sized streaked brown bird with long legs has an odd reputation for such an innocuous creature. For generations it has been the object of the tongue-in-cheek "snipe hunt" in which an uninitiated soul is given a gunny sack and pointed in the direction of a dark marsh and told to wait for others to herd the snipe into the bag. The "friends" then disappear, leaving the luckless one to figure out he's been duped, then find the way home.

The snipe also gives its name to the unattractive practice of taking verbal pot shots at others as opportunity offers, or to attack with petulant or snide criticism. To snipe at someone is generally considered bad manners.

In reality the common snipe *(Capella gallinago)* is a lovely bird, handsomely marked, that winters in California marshes and bogs. In some areas it is a favorite game bird because it flushes abruptly, breaking into a zigzag flight pattern that makes it a challenging target.

Snipes look very much like other birds in the sandpiper family, except for their distinctive, white-striped head. The best places for sightings are around mudflats where the bird uses its long, thin bill to probe for small, edible creatures. They remain in Southern California until spring.

During winter months the snipe is fairly common in the **Kern River Valley,** one of its nesting sites. It is a winter resident of **Los Penasquitos Marsh** adjacent to Torrey Pines State Reserve, and also winters along the **Lower Colorado River** and on **Catalina Island.**

66

A Closer Look:
Pronghorn Antelope and Tule Elk

The Carrizo Plain Natural Area has the distinction of being the only place in California, and perhaps the nation, where pronghorn antelope and tule elk, two native species, exist together on native range. Quite often the two groups can be seen within several hours' drive of each other.

A herd of more than 400 graceful pronghorn antelope, a species found naturally only in North America, often graze on the west side of the natural area. The herd roams through a series of valleys that extend north, tending to congregate in the places where their ancestors once grazed.

In the 1800s, pronghorn were common in California's central and southern valleys and deserts. Around 1912 the last of the original animals fell victim to unrestricted hunting and conflicts with sheep, cattle, horses and other domestic grazing animals. In the early 1960s the state's sheep industry declined dramatically, freeing up grazing land. Grazing permits were cut back at about the same time, so the antelopes had a much improved chance of finding the leafy plants, grasses and sagebrush that are staples in their diet.

Reintroduced to their historic habitat in 1987, 1988 and 1990, the new animals now thrive in abundant natural surroundings. Bucks can weigh 80 to 110 pounds. Does are a bit smaller at about 70 to 90 pounds. The reintroduced animals were moved from Modoc County on the California-Oregon border, an area that had such high antelope population levels that the herd was causing agricultural damage and animals were beginning to feel the stress of overcrowding.

The pronghorn, although it is a family of its own, is generally lumped in with antelopes because it has true horns that grow over a bony core like those of bighorn sheep and goats. The horns of mature bucks can be as long as 20 inches. They look like dangerous weapons, but the pronghorn rely on speed and exceptionally keen eyesight for protection. They also have an unusually marked coat, a sort of terra cotta, that gives them protective coloration so they blend almost indiscernibly with natural backgrounds.

The "powder-puff" rump so characteristic of these animals can be fluffed up whenever they wish, usually as a silent alarm to warn others in their herd that danger is nearby.

Pronghorn are born in May and June, with twins often born to older does. They mature quickly, learning to walk almost immediately. Before they are a month old they usually can keep up with the adults in the herd.

In some areas the pronghorns have rebounded to the point at which annual hunts are necessary to preserve a sustainable population. The California Department of Fish and Game has determined that if the optimum ratio of 20 bucks per 100 does is exceeded, a hunt for buck only is held by permit.

Before the mid-1800s tule elk were thought to number nearly 500,000. They are called tule because hunters drove them to seek refuge in the tule marshes of Central California. Their numbers diminished also because the large (bulls up to 900 pounds, cows up to 400 pounds) creatures competed with agriculture, doing extensive damage to the fragile farming environment. But in the 1870s a rancher in the San Joaquin Valley discovered elk on his land. By 1873 the state legislature had put a ban on elk hunting, and with the rancher's added protection, the small herd flourished. The last tule elk, also called dwarf elk because they are some 200 pounds smaller than the more common Roosevelt elk, was believed to have been killed in about 1869 by hunters procuring meat for mining camps in the Sierra Nevada during the state's Gold Rush.

Tule elk, whose native distribution is limited to California, have impressive antlers that are shed in March and are fully grown again by September. A big rack is an elk status symbol and often identifies dominant bulls. As soon as new antlers are in place, the mating season gets into full swing. If you're in elk territory, there is no doubt that mating is in progress because the bulls make a peculiar sound called bugling that calls the cows to them. It sounds like a cross between a whistle and a chorus of sopranos and is eerily beautiful on a crisp, fall day. During the late fall breeding season and winter months the herds stay in larger groups, before females split off from the main herd into individual breeding territories in preparation for having their young. This makes fall a good time to spot elk in large numbers.

As do pronghorn babies, calves mature quickly and are fully independent by fall, but often stay with their mother through winter months.

In 1983 and 1985 tule elk were reintroduced to the Carrizo Plain Natural Area, where today a healthy herd of about 700 animals exists happily, increasing every year. There now are viable herds in more than a dozen California locations with an estimated population of more than 2,000 elk statewide. But because elk are large animals and need vast land areas to provide sufficient food, balancing their requirements with California's increasing population and the need for agricultural and residential lands is a difficult task.

In eastern San Luis Obispo County west of Bakersfield, the best sightings occur in the southern portion of the natural area along **Soda Lake Road** and **Elk Horn Road.** Just be patient, use your binoculars and it is very likely a herd will drift into view.

The Painted Rock Visitor Center for the **Carrizo Plain Natural Area,** which is owned by the Bureau of Land Management, is located on Soda Lake Road. From Buttonwillow and I-5, take Hwy 58 west 45 miles to Soda Lake Road and turn south 14 miles to the visitors' center.

Tule elk also are alive and well at the **Tupman Tule Elk State Reserve** near Bakersfield. This herd of 42 elk is flourishing mightily, to the point that there are now more elk than range conditions at the reserve can sustain and some are relocated to habitats such as the Carrizo Plain, which once supported much greater numbers.

This tule elk population is particularly interesting, because these are the direct descendants of the "surprise" elk that were discovered in the 1870s, long after the species was thought to be extinct. All tule elk that exist today are descendants of this herd.

It's possible to see newborn calves in the spring, usually in the month of May, lovingly tended by their mothers as they lurch and teeter on tentative legs. In the fall huge bulls, with magnificent racks of antlers, vie for the attention of females. This area of natural grasslands is maintained as habitat for the elk, and if you join one of the guided tours you're almost guaranteed to glimpse a number of the noble beasts. From I-5 near Bakersfield, take the Stockdale Exit west 1.5 miles to Morris Road and follow signs to the reserve.

December

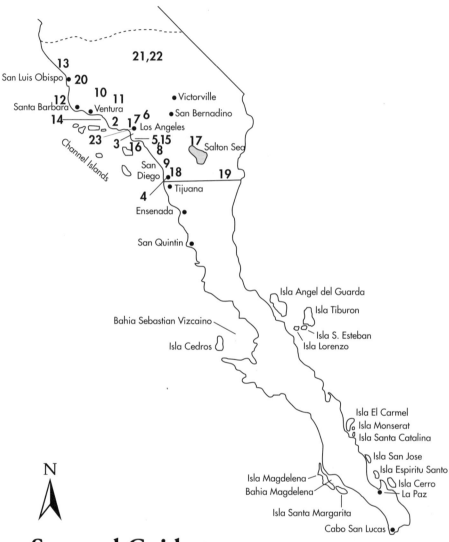

13

San Luis Obispo ● **20**

21,22

12
Santa Barbara ●

10 **11**

14

● Victorville

● San Bernadino

Ventura ●

2 **17** **6**
● Los Angeles

23

3

5,15

16

8

17 Salton Sea

San
Diego

9

18

19

4

● Tijuana

Channel Islands

Ensenada ●

San Quintin ●

Isla Angel del Guarda

Isla Tiburon

Bahia Sebastian Vizcaino

Isla S. Esteban
Isla Lorenzo

Isla Cedros

Isla El Carmel
Isla Monserat
Isla Santa Catalina

Isla San Jose

Isla Espiritu Santo

Isla Magdelena
Bahia Magdelena

Isla Cerro
La Paz

Isla Santa Margarita

Cabo San Lucas

N

Seasonal Guide to
the Natural Year

SITE LOCATOR MAP

LIST OF SITES
December

Notes

67

Christmas Bird Counts

The National Audubon Society tells us that birds are the first group of animals to be affected by various environmental threats such as habitat destruction and pollution.

That is one of the reasons the Audubon Society's Christmas Bird Count is gaining in importance. It is an attempt to gather an accurate bird census, so that when viewed over time the data gathered during these counts can be an indicator of the long-term health of bird populations and of the environment. Birders all over the world participate during a two-and-a-half-week period between mid-December and early January. Recruiting volunteers from an increasing number of birdwatchers is an easy task. According to the American Birding Association, an influx of aging baby boomers has more than doubled the ranks of birders since 1990.

The count's origins date to 1900, when ornithologist Frank Chapman organized a unique protest to the slaughter of birds in the annual holiday "side hunt" during which the team that shot the most birds and other small animals was the winner. Employing his friends as allies, Chapman began counting birds rather than shooting them. Today more than 1,650 counts are held from Canada to the Caribbean, throughout Central and South America and in the Pacific Islands. Central and South America are especially important because many North America's breeding birds spend their winters there.

The National Biological Service makes use of the Audubon data in monitoring all biological inventory in the United States as well as Canada and Mexico. The Christmas Bird Count is an important window on the bird population. The service has more than 30 years of birding information that it uses to analyze changes in winter bird populations, and it can draw on data that goes back as far as 1901. They search for patterns that may indicate unusual changes, with an eye to locating unusual declines. Besides noting declines in specific species, the service looks for larger themes in these changes, such as associations with particular habitats or migration patterns.

Some years ago the Bureau of Biological Survey ran the Bird Banding Lab, a version of which is still active today. Bands back then, similar to those currently in use, were printed with a number plus an abbreviated address indicating that the band was to be returned to the Washington Biological Survey (Wash. Biol. Surv.). Upon finding one of the bands, an Arkansas farmer returned the band to the bureau with the following letter: "Dear Sirs: I shot one of your crows the other day. My wife followed the cooking instructions on the leg tag and I want to tell you that bird tasted just horrible."

Birds are an excellent measure of environmental health in general, whereas humans are not. If human beings run out of food, they go to the market and buy more. They no longer have to plant, hunt and gather. If any component of the environment changes in a way that impacts the birds' health, however, they react right away. They either die or leave the area, becoming a direct and immediate measure of the quality of the environment. Birds were the first accurate indication that DDT was extremely harmful. This discovery led to its removal from the market in time to protect babies and nursing mothers from being poisoned by food that was sprayed with DDT.

Pesticide contamination and oil spills are responsible for poisoning and starving many bird species. The decline of the California condor can, in part, be traced to the big birds eating carrion polluted with lead from hunters' bullets. Along the Southern California coast, agriculture and urbanization have overtaken more than 80 percent of the landscape of sage, buckwheat and succulents called southern coastal scrub between Baja California and Ventura County. It provides habitat for the California gnatcatcher, coastal cactus wren and San Clemente sage sparrow, all of which are now endangered. The California brown pelican is endangered because of commercial and industrial development.

Data show a long-term decline in species that breed and winter in grasslands, such as Eastern and Western meadowlarks, horned larks, bobolinks, rusty blackbirds and others. In addition to the Audubon data, the Breeding Bird Survey also has shown this species decline. As a result, conferences and research programs in government as well as academic agencies are able to focus on solutions to the problem.

Today's counts follow just a few simple rules. Each bird-count area is roughly a circle 15 miles in diameter that covers approximately 177 square miles. Volunteers count every bird and bird species over one calendar day, from midnight to midnight. More than 50 counts are conducted in Southern California each December.

Participating in a bird count is a rewarding experience for beginners as well as experienced birders. An extra pair of eyes is always welcome, and the camaraderie with other birders is fun. To participate in a Southern California Christmas bird count and to locate the bird count nearest you, contact the Audubon Society Western Regional Office, 555 Audubon Place, Sacramento, CA 95025; (916) 481-5332.

68

Urban Birdwatching

As the great white egret came flashing out of the sky, the fourth-grade class stood mesmerized. A few awkwardly raised the binoculars that they'd just been handed, but most simply gazed skyward, following the bird's path of flight until it winged out of sight. "I've never seen a bird as big as me," breathed one awed youngster.

At the Sepulveda Basin Wildlife Refuge in Los Angeles, the nearby freeway provides a dull background roar. The surrounding high-rises glint with reflected midmorning sun. Planes and helicopters drone overhead. It's a tribute to their tenacity that bird species not only survive but actually thrive in such a metropolitan milieu, adding a spot of unexpected beauty to concrete jungles and asphalt deserts.

Birds migrate from Alaska as did their ancestors before there was a Los Angeles. Where once there was a broad range of habitat including a swift-flowing river, there now is a patchwork of places for birds to live. But so long as there is a food supply and habitat, the birds adapt. Peregrine falcons used to nest on cliffs. Now they use the ledges of tall buildings. Cormorants and herons share waters with paddle boats. If other conditions are right, wildlife can adjust to many disturbances.

The experience of the 10-year-olds is becoming more and more typical in the cities of Southern California, as groups such as the National Audubon Society interact with educators to spread the word about the wildlife riches right at their back door. Fortunately, wetland ecosystems are not uncommon even in urban areas.

November through March are best for seeing the greatest number of birds in Southern California's urban wetlands settings. Migratory water birds have arrived for their winter respite, and regular residents are enjoying the cool weather.

The Sepulveda Basin Wildlife Refuge, in the heavily populated San Fernando Valley in Greater Los Angeles, was created by accident when soil was scooped out of the Sepulveda Dam Recreation Area to use in a building project. Today an adjacent water reclamation plant keeps a small lake adequately filled. On winter mornings a translucent fog filters sun rays before they reach the lake, a condition that occurs when warm water from the treatment plant mingles with chilled morning air. Its ethereal beauty attracts observers, grateful that the birds have come to stay.

More than 200 species have been attracted to the area by its diversity of habitat. It provides an important wintering spot for ducks, Canada geese and migrating pelicans.

Egrets are common in the San Fernando Valley.

Permanent residents, easily observable most days, include the snowy egret with its black beak and golden slippers, great egret, great blue heron and countless pairs of mallards. Lesser known are the bufflehead, red duck, white-cheeked ruddy duck, richly colored cinnamon teal and green wing teal.

It's not unusual to see a gathering of double-crested cormorants on shore. They become slim cigars in the air, sleek torpedos in the water. Other sightings include a black phoebe catching flies near a water-egress point, a sharp-shinned hawk in a walnut tree, a pair of yellow-rumped warblers, a stubby-nosed pied-billed grebe cutting through the calm pond like a little tugboat, a caucus of raucous crows and a convention of red-winged blackbirds in a cottonwood tree.

Red-tailed hawks often pause in treetops, scouting out a scurrying field rat or baby rabbit as a possible meal. Little Anna's hummingbirds, the only "bumblebird," as one child called them, in the refuge in winter, flit among the mulefat bushes along with ruby-crowned kinglets, warblers and finches. The little green heron, difficult to spot because of its protective coloration, often prowls the reserve's damp

A female mallard enjoys early morning sun at the Sepulveda Basin Wildlife Refuge.

drainage ditches. On the flat open meadows and in grassy areas, groups of killdeer scurry around, their dull camouflage colors becoming brighter during breeding season.

Great blue herons and great egrets exhibit amazing patience as they stand motionless in the shallows, then quickly dip their heads into the water to skewer a wriggling fish. It is not unusual, during winter months, to see them on dry land stalking mice and voles that have left their rain-flooded burrows. In nearby Balboa Park, along the dirt jogging trail that borders the river, you can look up at the tops of the eucalyptus trees and see the huge, messy blue heron nests, sticks protruding untidily. Herons begin nesting in mid-February, and by April the downy heads of new hatchlings are visible through binoculars as the young peek over the top of the nest.

A few dyed-in-the-wool birders acknowledge that there is a "birders' language" spoken by those with a penchant for feathery creatures that fly. A "granny birder" is someone not terribly serious about birdwatching, who can become excited about seeing the crows in the backyard. An "owl prowl" is a birding expedition at night, and a "gashawk" is an airplane. "Peebeegeebees" are pied-billed grebes, a "TV" is a turkey vulture, and a "TV dinner" is roadkill.

Land birds are most active in early morning and evening, before the sun goes down, tending to sleep and rest at midday. If you plan your birding for these times you'll greatly increase chances of spotting interesting species.

The San Fernando Valley Audubon Society has been leading beginner and advanced bird walks in the basin for many years. Anyone wanting to join in has only to show up at the north end of the refuge around 8 A.M. on a weekend morning.

Hot Spots

The **Sepulveda Basin Wildlife Refuge** in the San Fernando Valley is just off Hwy 405 (San Diego Freeway) at Burbank Boulevard, between Burbank and Victory Boulevards. From Burbank, take Woodley Avenue north 0.25 mile to the entrance to the Donald C. Tillman Water Reclamation Plant. Follow signs to the refuge.

About 5 miles east of the refuge, along Victory Boulevard, the open fields and meadows at **Pierce College** in Woodland Hills welcome flocks of Canada geese for the winter. Nearby, the college's nature preserve is a good place to spot raptors during winter months. Take the DeSoto exit off Hwy 101 (Ventura Freeway) and go north to Victory Boulevard. Turn right onto Victory Boulevard to drive along the fields where the hefty honkers settle in.

The **Santa Monica National Recreation Area**, a 150,000-acre patchwork of public and private lands, ranges from just south of the Ventura Freeway north of Los Angeles south to the ocean, and from the city of Santa Monica north to Point Mugu. Within its boundaries are 369 bird species. Thirteen species of nesting raptors include the red-tailed hawk, red-shouldered hawk, ferruginous hawk, Cooper's hawk and sharp-shinned hawk. The area is accessible from Malibu Canyon as well as Pacific Coast Hwy 1.

Right in the heart of a large cluster of homes and apartment buildings, **Ballona Creek** in Playa Del Rey is an unexpectedly rich marshland. Loons and sea ducks as well as a variety of shorebirds including terns are usually in residence. The breakwater that parallels the creek is a good place to look for the stocky dark sandpiper called a surfbird. The wandering tattler also bobs along the pebbly beach where the creek joins the ocean. From Hwy 405 (San Diego Freeway) take Hwy 90 west and exit on Culver Boulevard. Take Culver to Pacific and follow Pacific to its end.

Balboa Park in San Diego attracts many species to its woodsy setting. The remarkable bird collection of the famous San Diego Zoo attracts the inhabitants' wild brethren to this area of natural canyons. In addition to common species, birds that may winter there include the American redstart and the little yellow-breasted warbler called a northern parula. From I-5, take Park Boulevard north to the center of the park.

Other urban areas almost guaranteed to produce interesting winter urban birding include **King Harbor** in Redondo Beach, where loons and gulls abound. **Descanso Gardens** in La Canada-Flintridge has a pond for nesting wood ducks, and a live oak forest that attracts vireos and flycatchers the year around. Call the gardens at (818) 790-5414. The palms and pines in **Rosedale Cemetery** at the busy corner of Normandie and Washington in Los Angeles appeal to a variety of species.

Although not exactly a recommended hotspot, planes on the runway at **John Wayne/Orange County Airport** have been known to share their taxiing space with great blue herons. The large birds are drawn to the airport by its location less than 5 miles from a protected wildlife area. Passengers frequently glance out their windows, expecting to see ground crew and baggage loaders and instead find they are watching a great blue heron.

69

Monarch Butterflies

Of the two monarch butterfly populations in the United States, California is fortunate to host the one that summers west of the Rocky Mountains and winters along the California coast and in Baja. They travel in groups, decorating branches of trees like brightly colored leaves. They've been clocked at speeds of up to 30 miles per hour, which helps them make the journey in decent time. Some as-yet-undefined monarch radar seems to guide them to the same place year after year, although no single butterfly does a complete round trip.

Some naturalists theorize that the showy creature was named for King George III, an eighteenth century monarch who fancied a royal cloak with orange and black colorations.

Magnificent orange and black monarch butterflies begin their journey south from Wyoming, Montana, southern Canada and other locales west of the Rockies in early autumn, heading for warmer climates in search of life-sustaining nectar and a mate. Arrival and departure times vary from year to year, but generally the first group arrives in October, and the bulk of them leave by the end of February. They are particularly fond of California's mild coastal areas. They hang on trees in lovely, lustrous clumps, waiting for warmer weather and the urge to merge. Don't be alarmed if you see monarchs fluttering on the ground, seemingly breathing their last. It's part of their wake-up-and-mate routine, accomplished on terra firma after hanging from branches for many months.

Monarch females lay their eggs on milkweed plants and the young become caterpillars that bulk up on the plant's juicy leaves for their two-week slumber as a chrysalis. They then emerge as full-blown butterflies. As with many of nature's creatures, the monarch's bright colorations tell other species that they're not good to eat. In fact they are toxic to many birds.

Although it seems hard to believe that anything as fragile as a butterfly wing could support a tag, more than forty thousand monarch butterflies are tagged annually in the United States. Tags are gently glued to the creature's hind wing, or carefully folded over the forewing. Tags bear information on whom to call and where the butterfly should be returned (usually they are found dead). Tags help scientists determine migration patterns, which in turn focuses attention on breeding habitats that must be preserved.

When the temperature rises over 55 degrees Fahrenheit your chances of seeing monarchs aflutter are excellent. If it's colder than that or damp and rainy, they will remain in the trees, seeking other monarchs for warmth. Wherever they alight they are a source of delight, guaranteed to inspire awe and an appreciation for the intricacies of nature.

Hot Spots

A guaranteed place to view monarchs is at the **Butterfly Vivarium,** a 1,200-square-foot structure that houses native butterflies in all stages of life. According to *The Monarch Newsletter,* the netted structure is a model ecosystem for butterflies and serves as an educational environment. Inside, redwood chip pathways wind among ponds, waterfalls, trees and nectar-producing "butterfly-friendly" plants. It is presently the only "monarch laboratory" in the nation where the life cycle of monarchs may be seen every month of the year. The Vivarium is at 450 Ocean View Avenue, Encinitas, CA 92177. Admission is by appointment. Call (619) 944-7113.

In Santa Barbara County, five areas called the **Ellwood Sites** usually play host to wintering monarchs. From Hwy 101 north of Santa Barbara, take Storke Avenue south, turn right on Hollister and left on Coronado to the dead end. There is a clearing that may be full of monarchs just to the right as you enter the gully. The eucalyptus groves of **Lake Los Carneros County Park** in Goleta also host the butterflies.

They also favor the eucalyptus in **Pismo Beach State Park** near the North Park Campground. From the community of Oceano on Hwy 1, turn west on Pier Avenue. Docents and rangers lead weekend butterfly walks. Butterflies also mass at the mouth of **El Capitan Creek** at El Capitan State Beach about 20 miles north of Santa Barbara. The campground at **Morro Bay State Park,** about 12 miles north of San Luis Obispo, is the winter home of a group of monarchs.

You may see monarchs in the wild clustered on trees in Ventura County on Sycamore Canyon Campground in **Point Mugu State Park.** Drive south from Oxnard on Hwy 1 12 miles to the park entrance.

In **Bolsa Chica Ecological Reserve** south of Huntington Beach in Orange County, you may see them hanging from the trees in the eucalyptus grove at the bluff overlook. **Doheney State Beach** often has clusters in the eucalyptus trees in the parking lot west of the visitors' center. Take Hwy 1 south of Huntington Beach to the reserve entrance.

A roost at **Dos Palmas Oasis Preserve** provides a home for hundreds of monarchs. Take CA Hwy 111 about 50 miles southeast from Palm Springs. The preserve is just northeast of the Salton Sea at the base of the Orocopia Mountains on the Riverside-Imperial County line.

Check the southeast side of Canary Island Pines at **Fort Stockton** behind the Serra Museum in San Diego County. On the campus of the **University of California at San Diego** there may be a large aggregation of monarchs in a eucalyptus grove northeast of Mandeville Performing Arts Center.

Remember that what was a major gathering place for monarchs one year may have just a few the next. Before setting out on a long journey, call the area first to see if the monarchs have arrived.

70

Sandhill Cranes

Spectacular 4-foot-tall sandhill cranes, on the state list of threatened species since 1983, begin arriving in the Golden State in November, and by this month their presence is well established.

One of nature's largest birds, the greater sandhill crane can be as tall as 5 feet and weigh up to 12 pounds. Its 5-inch bill is not only a menacing weapon, but also is useful in prodding out the worms, insects, mice and small reptiles that supplement its grain diet. Its stately gray silhouette is one of nature's most impressive sights. Lesser sandhill cranes are almost carbon copies of the greater, except for their size. At 4 feet, the lesser is about 1 foot shorter than the greater and weighs 2 to 4 pounds less. Mature adults of both have a bright red crown.

Once almost doomed to extinction by hunters who wanted their spectacular feathers, the cranes suffered additional losses because the wetlands, marshes and open grasslands that support them were bull-dozed for development and farmland. Crowded into ever-decreasing habitat, the spread of deadly avian cholera further diminished their numbers. Today about 25,000 lesser sandhills and 6,000 greater sandhills spend the winter in California.

Cranes are among the world's oldest living species. For centuries they have fascinated observers with their graceful dances. Usually done as part of courtship, the avian ballets involve dipping and bowing as the cranes spread their massive wings and move in rhythmic patterns. Other occasions for dancing are frustration or excitement. When a curious observer moves a bit too close, an entire group of cranes may stretch their necks, holding their heads high and erect as if at attention. With sharp, high-pitched calls they may rise into the sky, forming a dark cloud as they disappear. It is believed that their cry also is used to keep family members in touch and to strengthen pair bonds.

When they are about two or three years old, cranes take a lifetime mate, constructing untidy nests of grass and reeds on the ground near shallow water. Some are cleverly built so that they will float if the water rises. Both parents incubate the pair of large, spotted, olive-colored eggs, regurgitating food to feed the fledglings. Because the young don't fly until they are nearly the size of adults, they are particularly subject to predation by raccoons, coyotes and ravens. Their chief defense is to run and hide. At night the adults sleep standing in shallow water, which generally deters raccoons and coyotes, their chief natural enemies.

By February the cranes have gained enough weight and gathered their energy to take to the skies in the familiar V formation to return to their breeding grounds. The lesser cranes return to mating grounds in the Arctic, and the greater cranes return to northeast California, Oregon and British Columbia to nest. They'll be back the following year to introduce new offspring to their favorite winter haven.

When setting out to observe cranes, your first indication that they may be on their way in to roost can be their trumpetlike call, audible for great distances. The California Department of Fish and Game offers these tips for successful viewing:

- Limit your movement. While feeding, some cranes will be on the lookout. Your close movement will cause the flock to fly away, using valuable energy reserves.
- Keep your distance to at least 400 yards.
- Be quiet. While there may be only a few watching for you, they will all be listening for you.
- Use blinds. To get a closer look, use vegetation or a car as a blind. Cranes are not spooked as easily by slow-moving or parked cars as by people on foot.
- Be patient. Once you get a good view, sit tight and you're likely to see some interesting crane behaviors.
- Be safe. Don't park or stop on narrow roads because this creates traffic hazards.

Hot Spots Near the town of **Imperial** in Imperial County cranes usually are in residence until about mid-February. They have been sighted just west of Hwy 111 in an open field. From Hwy 86 going south from Brawley, turn left onto Harris Road. You may have to slowly drive the area to find them on any given day. Because they are gray and tend to blend into the landscape, they are often difficult to spot. The optimum time for seeing them is late afternoon when a flock of about 300 returns from their day's feeding to roost. These birds are part of the Lower Colorado River greater sandhill crane population that returns to northern Nevada in the spring to nest.

Each year thousands of lesser sandhill cranes, and a smaller number of greater, winter near Soda Lake in the 180,000-acre **Carrizo Plain Natural Area** in eastern San Luis Obispo County. The lake is dry most of the year, but fall rains come just in time to transform it into a glassy wetland that provides a winter home for the cranes. From Hwy 58 go south on Soda Lake Road, or from Hwy 166 go north on Soda Lake Road.

Also check the **Kern National Wildlife Refuge** in Kern County for cranes. Take the Hwy 46 exit off I-5 east about 4 miles. Refuge headquarters is located at the junction of Garces Hwy and Corcoran Road, 19 miles west of Delano. During winter months the cranes often feed in the field near Corcoran Road and Hwy 46.

71

December Shorttakes

Mistletoe

For decades its purpose has been to allow a stolen kiss when the kissee unsuspectingly stands under it at holiday time. But in nature mistletoe is a parasite with leathery yellow-green leaves and red or white, waxy berries that can be poisonous to humans yet are delicacies to some bird species.

It appears as big green nestlike clumps anchored among branches of winter-bare trees and as glossy, shaggy patches when its host tree has its leaves. It prefers broad-leafed trees such as oak, but any supportive host plant will do. Paloverde trees, common in the desert and along washes, often find themselves unwilling benefactors of mistletoe. Although it can create its own food by photosynthesis, mistletoe attaches itself to the host tree by penetrating its bark with modified roots, then extracting water and nutrients. Most healthy trees can withstand a mistletoe attack, but some varieties, especially the dwarf mistletoes, have been known to kill conifers. Some mistletoe seeds are spread by bird droppings, but others have the power to "shoot" seeds as much as 40 feet from berries that quite literally explode.

Native Americans boiled the berries as food and believe that mistletoe tea had contraceptive qualities. Its origins as the "kissing plant" are uncertain, but some think the plant's mystique dates to the time of the Druids.

You can see and collect mistletoe (the host tree will be delighted) in many coniferous and deciduous forests. Along the River Trail in the **Kern River Preserve** there are large mistletoe clumps in cottonwoods and in a big willow tree that is clearly marked. Because clumps are fairly close together, it is assumed that the parasite used its "shooting" technique to propagate here.

Fishing Urban Lakes

This is the month that the California Department of Fish and Game's Urban Fisheries Program begins stocking trout in 20 urban and sub-urban lakes in and around Los Angeles. Call (310) 590-4835 or the 24-hour Fish Stocking Information Line at (310) 590-5020 for a free brochure on where to pursue the wily trout, known for its wariness. The lakes are stocked with catfish from May through November. Lakes include Balboa Park Lake in the San Fernando Valley, Cerritos Park Lake, John Ford Park Lake in Bell Gardens, and 17 others.

72

A Closer Look:
A Winter Hike in Griffith Park

Right smack dab in one of the most highly urbanized areas of the country is a park so lovely and pristine that in some parts the only indication of civilization is the hum of traffic from the freeways that crisscross below.

Griffith Park, 3,050 acres of wilderness in the middle of Los Angeles, was given to the city in 1896 by Col. Griffith J. Griffith. His largesse was not a completely altruistic move—he chose to donate the land rather than pay taxes on it. His motivation is secondary, however, to the enjoyment the park brings to more than four million visitors per year. Through acquisitions the park has grown to 4,127 acres, making it one of the largest city parks in the world.

Griffith Park is part of the Santa Monica mountain range, which gives it its rugged terrain. Within its boundaries, 52 trails connect ridges, canyons, valleys and scenic viewpoints, beginning at 490 feet and climbing to 1,650 feet at the top of Mount Hollywood. They draw outdoor lovers from all over the world, at all times of year, thanks to the area's agreeable weather. Although the transition of seasons is subtle, winter, with it cooler days and fewer visitors, has special rewards for those who wander the park's piney pathways. Vestiges of autumn remain in the pattern of rust-colored leaves swept by wind to the edge of the trail and in the yellow-leafed sycamore that won't become completely denuded until a new season's buds are ready to appear.

Chumash Indians were among the earliest inhabitants of these lofty peaks and shadowy canyons. Much of the fun of hiking here is learning that many of the plants that the Chumash depended on still exist. The citrusy bark of the eucalyptus was rubbed on chests for colds. Tall, spindly fennel was used for licorice, tea and eyewash. Prickly pear cactus became a survival tool. Its fat juicy leaves render moisture that can quench a thirst, and its cactus "apples" may be cooked and eaten.

Griffith Park

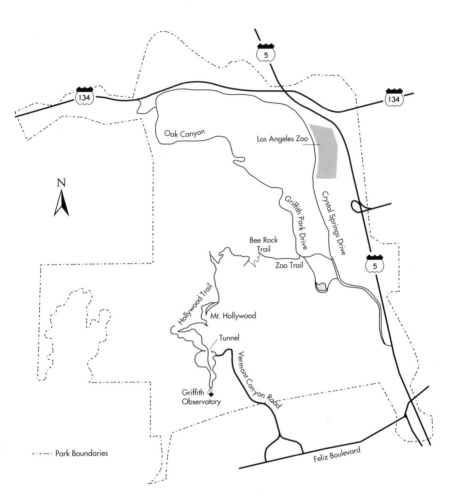

Dried bushes of laurel sumac, which blooms in late summer, have an oil content used to repel gnats and bedbugs—nature's version of Black Flag. Crush the dried berries of the "lemonade" bush to smell a pungent citrus that was used for hot drinks. The sugarbush's pale pink berries also were sought as ingredients for soothing teas. The small whitish flowers of the horehound weed, dried at this time of year to pungent berries, once were popular in penny-a-stick candy. Centuries before it was used by the Chumash for poultices.

Wild lilac blossoms, purple and fragrant in summer, now are dried and shriveled, ready to be rubbed between the palms for a shampoo

Visitors enjoy a cultivated garden at Dante's View, Griffith Park.

or bath soap. A springy saplinglike tree called mountain mahogany produced the wood once used for hunting bows. And the unusually long needles of the Coulter pine were employed as brooms to keep early Chumash dwellings spic and span.

Even green-leafed poison oak, which can produce an irritating itchy rash, obliges the park's December visitors by lying dormant during winter months.

California holly, or toyon berries, are a favorite of noisy blue scrub jays. The plump red berries form a striking visual contrast to the jay's vivid blue feathers. Groups of robinlike Say's phoebes, the rusty-bellied males and all-gray females, take a break in treetops from their insect-catching pursuits. Tiny Anna's hummingbirds, the only hummers commonly found in California in midwinter, dart and chirp among the bushes. Flitty little bushtits hunt for seeds in a sumac thicket, sharing with the brown towhee that skims just above the earth in search of seeds that have fallen to the ground. Overhead, red-tailed hawks, the topside of their characteristic rufous tail catching the sunlight, hover gracefully on canyon thermals in search of prey.

Hikers in the park find that they are walking on bridle trails (motorized vehicles are not allowed) and will almost surely encounter equestrians. The soft dirt treadway records not only the shod hoofprints of the horses but often presents the dainty vee'd prints of mule deer and pawprints of an occasional mountain lion. Raccoon, skunk, gray and red fox and squirrels also are permanent residents.

The park's geological history is evident in coquina along the trails, a soft whitish rock made up of fragments of clam and snail shells and coral, telling of the park's one-time submersion. Griffith Park's many vistas include views of homoclines in the sandstone, uplifted by volcanic action. Basalt cliffs also verify its volcanic origins. A handful of soil contains decomposed granite, quartz, mica and feldspar. Vistas also give clear sightings of the area's many earthquake faults, visible as ridges through the trees.

Many hikers choose the approximately 2.5-hour climb to the windy summit of Mount Hollywood, which can be bitingly cold on a winter day but rewards the intrepid with a 360-degree view of the Los Angeles area. The wind is a double-edged sword. While it can be bone-chilling, it also clears the smog from the Los Angeles basin, providing views that can reach to the coastline.

Hiking trails are marked with numbered signs that correspond to free maps available at the ranger station at 4730 Crystal Springs Drive in the park. Distances and landmarks, such as water tanks, are noted. Sturdy hiking shoes or boots and water are necessities on the trails. The park is open from 5:30 A.M. until 10 P.M. and is accessible via clearly marked exits from I-5 and I-134.

Free, escorted hikes are led by Sierra Club members and include night hikes that offer a sparkling, after-dark view of the city. For information contact the Sierra Club Los Angeles Chapter, 3345 Wilshire Boulevard, no. 508, Los Angeles, CA 90010; (213) 387-4287. For park information call (213) 665-5188 to speak to a ranger.

Appendix

National Parks, Forests and Monuments

Cabrillo National Monument
1800 Cabrillo Dr.
San Diego, CA 92106
(619) 557-5450

Channel Island National Marine Sanctuary
113 Harbor Wy.
Santa Barbara, CA 93109
(805) 966-7107

Channel Islands National Park
1901 Spinnaker Dr.
Ventura, CA 93001
(805) 658-5730

Death Valley National Park
Death Valley, CA 92328
(619) 786-2331

Joshua Tree National Park
Twentynine Palms, CA 92277
(619) 367-7511

Los Padres National Forest
Santa Lucia District
(805) 925-9538

State, County and City Parks, Refuges and Preserves

Antelope Valley California Poppy Reserve
(805) 724-1180

Anza Borrego Desert State Park
200 Palm Canyon Dr.
Borrego Springs, CA 92004
(619) 767-5311
Visitors' Center: (619) 767-4205

Bureau of Land Management
3801 Pegasus Dr.
Bakersfield, CA 93308
(805) 391-6000

Bureau of Land Management
California Desert District (desert tortoise)
6221 Box Springs Blvd.
Riverside, CA 92507-0714
(909) 697-5200

Crystal Cove State Park
(714) 494-3539

Cuyamaca Rancho State Park
12551 Hwy 79
Descanso, CA 92016
(619) 765-0755

Gaviota State Park and Refugio State Beach
(805) 968-3294

Griffith Park
Los Angeles, CA
(213) 665-5188

Idyllwild County Park
Nature Center
Idyllwild, CA 92349
(909) 659-3850

Lake Cachuma Recreation Area
Star Route
Santa Barbara, CA 93150
(805) 568-2460

Leo Carillo State Beach
(805) 488-5223

Mount San Jacinto State Wilderness
P. O. Box 308
Idyllwild, CA 92349
(909) 659-2607

Palm Springs Aerial Tramway
(recorded information)
(619) 325-1391

San Elijo State Beach
(619) 753-5355

Silverwood Lake State Recreation Area
14651 Cedar Circle
Hesperia, CA 92345
(619) 389-2303

Torrey Pines State Reserve
(619) 755-2063

Tucker Wildlife Sanctuary
29322 Modjeska Canyon Rd.
Silverado, CA 92676
(714) 649-2760

Upper Newport Bay Ecological Reserve
600 Shellmaker
Newport Beach, CA 92660
(714) 640-6746

Wildlife Waystation
14831 Little Tujunga Canyon Road
Angeles National Forest, CA 91342
(818) 899-5201

Nature Conservancy and Other Conservancy Preserves

The Nature Conservancy of California (state office)
201 Mission St., Fourth Floor
San Francisco, CA 94105
(415) 777-0487
The Nature Conservancy has a World Wide Web site at
http://www.tnc.org

Big Bear Valley Preserve
P. O. Box 1418
Sugarloaf, CA 92386
(714) 866-4190

Big Morongo Canyon Preserve
P. O. Box 780
Morongo Valley, CA 92256
(619) 363-7190

Carrizo Plain Natural Area
P. O. Box 3098
California Valley, CA 93453
(805) 475-2360

Catalina Island Conservancy
P. O. Box 2739
Avalon, CA 90704
(310) 510-2595

Coachella Valley Preserve
P. O. Box 188

Thousand Palms, CA 92276
(619) 343-2733

Dos Palmas Oasis Preserve
(recently changed to share management with the BLM, managers not always on site)
P. O. Box 2000
North Palm Springs, CA 92258-2000
(619) 251-4800

The Irvine Company Open Space Reserve
(accessible only by guided tour)
(714) 832-7478

Kern River Preserve
P. O. Box 1662
Weldon, CA 93283
(619) 378-2531

Lokern Preserve
P. O. Box 3098
California Valley, CA 93453

Ramsey Canyon Preserve
27 Ramsey Canyon Rd.
Hereford, AZ 85615
(520) 378-2785

Sand Ridge Preserve
San Joaquin Valley Office
5401 Business Park South, no. 206
Bakersfield, CA 93309
(805) 546-8378

Santa Cruz Island Preserve
213 Stearns Wharf
Santa Barbara, CA 93101
(805) 962-9111

Santa Rosa Plateau Preserve
22115 Tenaja Rd.
Murrieta, CA 92562
(909) 677-6951

Organizations and Foundations

American Birding Association
P. O. Box 6599
Colorado Springs, CO 80934-6599
(719) 578-1614

Audubon Society
Western Regional Office
555 Audubon Pl.
Sacramento, CA 95025
(916) 481-5332

Bat Conservation International
P. O. Box 162603
Austin, TX 78716
(512) 327-9721

Butterfly Vivarium
450 Ocean View Ave.
Encinitas, CA 92177
(619) 944-7113

Cahuilla Tribal Council Office
960 E. Tahquitz Canyon Wy.
Palm Springs, CA 92262
(619) 325-5673

Kern River Research Center
P. O. Box 990
Weldon, CA 93283
(619) 376-2629

Los Angeles Audubon Society
7377 Santa Monica Blvd.
West Hollywood, CA 90046-6694
(213) 876-0202

The Monarch Program
P. O. Box 178671
San Diego, CA 92177
(619) 944-7113

Mountain Skies Astronomical Society
Observatory and Science Center
2001 Observatory Wy.
Lake Arrowhead, CA 92352
(909) 336-1699

National Association of Underwater Instructors
(800) 553-6284

National Audubon Society
700 Broadway
New York, NY 10003
(212) 979-3000

National Wild Turkey Federation
P. O. Box 530
Edgefield, SC 29824-0530
(803) 637-3106

North American Butterfly Association
4 Delaware Rd.
Morristown, NJ 07960
(201) 285-0907

Professional Association of Dive Instructors
(800) 729-7234

Rocky Mountain Elk Foundation
P. O. Box 8249
Missoula, MT 59807-8249
(800) CALL-ELK

San Fernando Valley Audubon Society
P. O. Box 2504
Van Nuys, CA 91404
(818) 347-3205

Santa Barbara County Vintners' Association
P. O. Box 1558
Santa Ynez, CA 93460-1558
(800) 218-0881
(805) 688-0881

Sea and Sage Audubon Society
P. O. Box 25
Santa Ana, CA 92702
(714) 261-7963

Sierra Club, Los Angeles Chapter
3345 Wilshire Blvd., no. 508
Los Angeles, CA 90010
(213) 387-4287

Temecula Valley Vintners' Association
P. O. Box 1601
Temecula, CA 92593-1601
(909) 699-3626

Theodore Payne Foundation
10459 Tuxford St.
Sun Valley, CA 91352

State Offices

California Department of Fish and Game
1416 Ninth St.
Sacramento, CA 95814
(916) 653-7664

California Department of Fish and Game
330 Golden Shore, Suite 50
Long Beach, CA 90802
(310) 590-5113

California Department of Fish and Game
Urban Fisheries Program
(310) 590-4835
24-hour Fish Stocking Information: (310) 590-5020

California Department of Parks and Recreation
1416 Ninth St.
P.O. Box 942896
Sacramento, CA 94296-0001
(916) 445-6477

California Department of Parks and Recreation
(in the Los Angeles area)
1925 Las Virgines Rd.
Calabasas, CA 91302
(818) 880-0350

Rare Bird Hotlines

Los Angeles: (213) 874-1318
San Diego: (619) 435-6761, or (619) 479-3400
Orange County: (714) 640-6746

Wildflower Hotline

Los Angeles: (818) 768-3533

Whale Watching and Nature Trip Operators

Baja Expeditions
2625 Garnet Ave.
San Diego, CA 92109
(800) 843-6967

Desert Jeep Tours
67555 E. Palm Canyon Dr.
Cathedral City, CA 92234
(619) 324-5337

Fillmore & Western Railway Company
351 Santa Clara Ave.
Fillmore, CA 93015
(805) 524-2546

Golden Eagle Tours
P. O. Box 356
Twentynine Palms, CA 92277
(800) 428-1833

Heli-Tours, Inc.
302 Moffett Pl.
Goleta, CA 93117
(805) 964-0684

Island Packers (seasonal whale watching, Channel Islands trips)
1867 Spinnaker Dr.
Ventura, CA 93001
(805) 642-1393

Special Expeditions
720 Fifth Ave.
New York, NY 10019
(800) 348-2358

Scuba Dive Operators

Anacapa Dive Center
22 Anacapa St.
Santa Barbara, CA 93101
(805) 963-8917

Atlantis Charters
210 Whalers Walk
San Pedro, CA 90731
(310) 592-1154

Catalina Scuba Luv
126 Catalina Ave.
P. O. Box 1402
Avalon, Catalina, CA 90704
(800) 262-DIVE

Catalina West End Dive Center
Box 5044
Two Harbors, CA 90704
(310) 510-2800

Horizon/Ocean Odyssey
2803 Emerson
San Diego, CA 92106
(619) 277-7823

Pacific Scuba Center, Inc.
3600 S. Harbor Blvd., Suite 215
Channel Islands Harbor
Oxnard, CA 93035
(805) 984-2566

Underwater Sports
The Breakwater
Santa Barbara, CA 93101
(805) 963-DIVE

Transportation

Catalina Express
Schedules and Reservations: (310) 519-1212

Island Express
Schedules and Reservations: (310) 510-2525

Flying Fish and Glass-Bottomed Boat Tours

Discovery Tours/Santa Catalina Island Company
P. O. Box 737
Avalon, CA 90704
(310) 510-2500

Museums and Aquariums

Cabrillo Marine Museum
3720 Stephen White Dr.
San Pedro, CA 90733
(310) 548-7546

Orange County Marine Institute
24200 Dana Point Harbor Dr.
Dana Point, CA 92629-2723
(714) 496-2274

Sea Center
211 Stearns Wharf
Santa Barbara, CA 93101
(805) 962-0885

Stephen Birch Aquarium-Museum
Scripps Institution of Oceanography
8602 La Jolla Shores Dr.
La Jolla, CA
(619) 534-3474

Arboretums and Botanical Gardens

Cactus Ranch
19420 Saticoy Ave.
Reseda, CA 91335-2342
(818) 894-5694

Descanso Gardens
1418 Descanso Dr.
La Canada–Flintridge, CA 91011-3102
(818) 952-4400

Living Desert Reserve
47-900 Portola Ave.
Palm Desert, CA 92260
(619) 346-5694

Los Angeles State and County Arboretum
301 N. Baldwin Ave.
Arcadia, CA 91007-2697
(818) 821-3222

Quail Botanical Gardens
230 Quail Garden Dr.
Encinitas, CA 92024
(619) 436-3036

Rancho Santa Ana Botanical Gardens
1500 N. College Ave.
Claremont, CA 91711-3157
(909) 625-8767

South Coast Botanical Garden
26300 Crenshaw Blvd.
Palos Verdes Peninsula, CA 90274
(310) 544-6815

Beach and Tidal Information

For Orange County beaches: (310) 808-8463, then press *5000
For Los Angeles/Ventura County beaches: (310) 808-8463, then press *5010
For Santa Barbara area: (805) 962-0782
For San Diego County: (619) 221-8884
For Malibu area: (310) 457-9701.

Selected Bibliography

The Audubon Society Field Guide to North American Fishes, Whales &
Dolphins. New York: Alfred A. Knopf, 1983.

Bowditch, Nathaniel. *Waves, Wind and Weather.* New York: David
McKay Company, 1977.

California Wildlife Viewing Guide, A Publication of the California De-
partment of Fish and Game. n.p.: n.d.

Fischer, Pierre C. *70 Common Cacti of the Southwest.* Tucson: Southwest Parks and Monuments Association, n.d.

Iacopi, Robert. *Earthquake Country.* Tucson: Fisher Books, 1995.

National Audubon Society. *A Selection of Familiar Birds of North*
America. New York: Chanticleer Press, 1993.

Shanks, Bernard. *California Wildlife.* Helena, Mont.: Falcon Press
Publishing, 1989.

Udvardy, Miklos D.F. *The Audubon Society Field Guide to North Ameri-*
can Birds, Western Region. New York: Alfred A. Knopf, 1977.

Index

About the Author

Judy Wade is a freelance journalist who contributes to national publications including *Cosmopolitan, Los Angeles Times Syndicate, Cruise Travel, TravelAmerica* and others. She contributed to *Travelers' Tales: A Woman's World,* which won the 1996 Lowell Thomas Award for Best Travel Book, and received the Arizona Press Women 1996 First Place Award for a travel article. She works with her husband/photographer, Bill Baker, who illustrates many of her articles and is also a pretty good traveling companion.

TRAVEL/NATURE $16.95

SEASONAL GUIDE
TO THE NATURAL YEAR
A Month by Month Guide to Natural Events

Southern California and Baja

The Travel Guide for Nature Lovers

Catch 12 months of nature's beauty at its peak! Amateur naturalists of all stripes—bird-watchers, photographers, wildflower buffs and eco-travelers alike—will want to catch all of nature's best shows in the region with well-known travel writer Judy Wade.

- Observe the California gray whale migrating along the coast in January
- Watch roadrunners sprint in the Living Desert in February
- Discover the desert in bloom in April
- View butterflies in the San Gabriel Mountains in June
- Investigate the "walking" kelp forest in July
- Explore the many splendors of the Channel Islands in October
- Hike through Griffith Park in December

This *Seasonal Guide to the Natural Year* is one of a series of guidebooks with a difference: a guide to natural events that takes a *when*-to-go approach with the emphasis on timing according to season. This book will enable nature lovers to view, first-hand, many of the exciting natural events in the region.

Praise for the Seasonal Guide series:

"Must-have books for outdoor enthusiasts!"

—Associated Press

"If you are wise enough to carry this wonderful guide, you will be able to find that 'union of time, place and biological circumstance so delicate it takes one's breath away'."

—National Geographic Traveler

Fulcrum Publishing
350 Indiana Street, Suite 350
Golden, Colorado 80401-5093
(800) 992-2908 • (303) 277-1623

591-271-0

51695>

9 781555 912710